The Work of Gender

GENDERING ASIA
A Series on Gender Intersections

Gendering Asia invites book proposals on gender issues in Asian societies, including Asia in the world. The series is multidisciplinary and concerned with the wide range of understandings, practices and power relations in Asian societies. It explores theoretical, empirical and methodological gender issues in the social sciences and the humanities.

Series Editors: Wil Burghoorn, Monica Lindberg Falk and Pauline Stoltz (contact details at: www.niaspress.dk/series/gendering-asia/).

1. *Working and Mothering in Asia. Images, Ideologies and Identities*, edited by Theresa W. Devasahayam and Brenda S.A. Yeoh
2. *Making Fields of Merit. Buddhist Female Ascetics and Gendered Orders in Thailand*, by Monica Lindberg Falk
3. *Gender Politics in Asia. Women Manoeuvring within Dominant Gender Orders*, edited by Wil Burghoorn, Kazuki Iwanaga, Cecilia Milwertz and Qi Wang
4. *Lost Goddesses. The Denial of Female Power in Cambodian History*, by Trudy Jacobsen
5. *Gendered Inequalities in Asia. Configuring, Contesting and Recognizing Women and Men*, edited by Helle Rydstrøm
6. *Submitting to God. Women and Islam in Urban Malaysia*, by Sylva Frisk
7. *The Authority of Influence. Women and Power in Burmese History*, by Jessica Harriden
8. *Beyond the Singapore Girl. Discourses of Gender and Nation in Singapore*, by Chris Hudson
9. *Vietnam's New Middle Classes: Gender, Career, City* by Catherine Earl
10. *Gendered Entanglements: Revisiting Gender in Rapidly Changing Asia*, edited by Ragnhild Lund, Philippe Doneys and Bernadette P. Resurrección
11. *Queer/Tongzhi China: New Perspectives on Research, Activism and Media Cultures*, edited by Elisabeth L. Engebretsen and William F. Schroeder (with Hongwei Bao)
12. *Cultivating Gender: Meanings of Place and Work in Rural Vietnam*, by Cecilia Bergstedt
13. *Follow the Maid: Domestic Worker Migration in and from Indonesia*, by Olivia Killias
14. *Queer Comrades: Gay Identity and Tongzhi Activism in Postsocialist China*, by Hongwei Bao
15. *Deities and Divas: Queer Ritual Specialists in Myanmar, Thailand and Beyond*, edited by Peter A. Jackson and Benjamin Baumann
16. *The Work of Gender: Service, Performance and Fantasy in Contemporary Japan*, edited by Gitte Marianne Hansen and Fabio Gygi

NIAS Press is the autonomous publishing arm of NIAS – Nordic Institute of Asian Studies, a research institute located at the University of Copenhagen. NIAS is partially funded by the governments of Denmark, Finland, Iceland, Norway and Sweden via the Nordic Council of Ministers, and works to encourage and support Asian studies in the Nordic countries. In so doing, NIAS has been publishing books since 1969, with more than two hundred titles produced in the past few years.

UNIVERSITY OF COPENHAGEN

Nordic Council of Ministers

The Work of Gender

Service, Performance and Fantasy in Contemporary Japan

Edited by
Gitte Marianne Hansen
and
Fabio Gygi

The Work of Gender
Service, Performance and Fantasy in Contemporary Japan
Edited by Gitte Marianne Hansen and Fabio Gygi

Nordic Institute of Asian Studies
Gendering Asia, no. 16

First published in 2022 by NIAS Press
NIAS – Nordic Institute of Asian Studies
Øster Farimagsgade 5, 1353 Copenhagen K, Denmark
Tel: +45 3532 9503 • Fax: +45 3532 9549
E-mail: books@nias.ku.dk • Online: www.niaspress.dk

© Gitte Marianne Hansen and Fabio Gygi 2022

A CIP catalogue record for this book is available from the British Library

ISBN 978-87-7694-311-0 Hbk
ISBN 978-87-7694-729-3 Ebk

Typeset in 11.5 pt Arno Pro by Don Wagner
Printed and bound in the United States by Maple Press, York, PA
Cover design: Marcello Francioni/NIAS Press

Cover illustration by Marcello Francioni

Contents

Contributors	vii
Foreword: Reflections By a Culturally Incompetent Customer *Gitte Marianne Hansen*	xi
Acknowledgements *Gitte Marianne Hansen and Fabio Gygi*	xix
1 Gender as Work *Fabio Gygi and Gitte Marianne Hansen*	1
2 Serving Gender: Performing Gender Roles at a Gay Bar in Tokyo's Shinjuku Ni-chōme *Marcello Francioni*	31
3 (Re)searching (for) Identities: Crossdressed Ethnography in a *Dansō* Escort Company *Marta Fanasca*	60
4 Professional Amateurs: Authenticity and Sex Work in a 'Delivery Health' Shop *Nicola Phillips*	88
5 The Coin-Operated Boyfriend: Recognition and Intimacy as Commodities in a Japanese *Josei-muke* Adult Video Fan Community *Maiko Kodaka*	118
6 Intimacies of Exposure: Public Space, Gendered Presence and Performance at a Tokyo Train Station *R. J. Simpkins*	146
7 I Sing the Body Contingent: Transition as Gender-Work in Contemporary Japan *Lyman R. T. Gamberton*	180
Epilogue: Gender, Substance, Fantasy *Fabio Gygi*	206
Colour figures	217
Index	225

Figures

Bold = Colour

2.1	A view of the building where Zenith bar was in Shinjuku Ni-chōme	33
2.2	An example of what customers get with their 'cover charge'	36
2.3	Katsu behind the counter at Zenith bar	44
3.1	One of crossdressers' shared wardrobe	72, **217**
3.2	Two *dansō* waiting for customers in the office near the lockers	73, **218**
3.3	Marta Fanasca posing as André in a promotional flyer for Dreamland	75, **219**
4.1	A screenshot of Deadball's homepage for the Uguisudani branch, 23 August 2019	91, **219**
4.2	A worker's profile in the style of a baseball card, 23rd August 2019	92, **220**
5.1	Oikawa, Mukai, Uehara and Azuma at SILK Fest November 2018	128, **221**
6.1	On the south side of the station, a passerby mistakes Fuji for a popular musician	155, **221**
6.2	Reina's mask was effective in drawing attention	164, **222**
7.1	Examples of FTM lifestyle magazines, from the 2019 Kansai Queer Film Festival at the Kyoto Seibu Kōdō	197, **223**

List of Contributors

Marta Fanasca obtained her PhD in Japanese Studies from the University of Manchester with a thesis investigating the phenomenon of female-to-male crossdresser (*dansō*) escorts in contemporary Japan. Her research interests include gender studies, queer theory, the commodification of intimacy and contemporary Japanese culture and arts. After completing a Postdoctoral Fellowship at the Centre for Youth Studies, School of Social Sciences and Area Studies of the Higher School of Economics in St. Petersburg, Russian Federation, Fanasca is currently a Research Fellow at KU Leuven, Belgium. Her publications include 'FtM Crossdresser Escorts in Contemporary Japan: An embodied and sensorial ethnography' in *Asian Anthropology* (2019); and 'When girls draw the sword: *dansō*, crossdressing, and gender subversion in Japanese *shōjo manga*' in *Queer Studies in Media and Popular Culture* (2021).

Marcello Francioni is associate lecturer at Oxford Brookes University after obtaining his PhD at the School of Oriental and African Studies, University of London. His research interests include the service industry in Japan and understanding how care, gender, sexuality and race all weave together within this. During his 14-month fieldwork, Francioni worked as a bar help at a Japanese-style gay bar in Japan's largest 'gay city', Shinjuku Ni-chome (Tokyo), learning about 'That Bar Life' (the title of his PhD thesis). More recently, he has been researching systems of production in Japanese fashion, while engaging in ethno/graphic storytelling in order to merge his passions for anthropology and comics.

Fabio Gygi (editor) is lecturer in anthropology with reference to Japan at the School of Oriental and African Studies, University of London. He is interested in the intersection of material culture and medical anthropology, with a particular focus on how gender shapes social and medical categories. Recent publications include 'Things that believe: Talismans, amulets, dolls and how to get rid of them' (Japanese Journal of Religious Studies 45, 2018) and 'Hôtes et otages: Entasser des objets chez soi dans le Japon contemporain' (L'Homme 231–232, 2019). He is currently working on a book on rites of disposal for dolls in Japan.

Lyman Gamberton is a PhD candidate in Social Anthropology at the School of Oriental and African Studies (SOAS), University of London. He received his BA in Litterae Humaniores from Oxford University and an MA in Anthropology from SOAS. His MA thesis was on gendered experiences of A-bomb survivors in postwar Nagasaki; his PhD dissertation, supported by a generous grant from the Sasakawa Foundation, is on transgender lives and communities in the Kansai region of Japan. His research specialism is 'the othered body in Japanese social contexts', encompassing gender, sexuality, and disability.

Gitte Marianne Hansen (editor) is Reader in Japanese studies at Newcastle University in the UK. She is an AHRC Leadership Fellow and PI for the project 'Gendering Murakami Haruki: Characters, Transmedial Productions and Contemporary Japan'. More generally, her work focuses on Japanese culture since 1980, especially issues related to gender and character construction. She is the author of *Femininity, Self-harm and Eating Disorders in Japan: Navigating Contradiction in Narrative and Visual Culture* (2016) and editor of *Murakami Haruki and Our Years of Pilgrimage* (2022, with Michael Tsang).

Maiko Kodaka is a PhD candidate in Social Anthropology at the School of Oriental and African Studies, University of London. Before joining SOAS, she was awarded a BA in Art from Tokyo University of Foreign Studies in 2014. Born and raised in Tokyo, her main academic interests are gender, sexuality, and power dynamics in Japanese mass media. Her doctoral research is an anthropological study of the fan culture of pornography aimed at women in Japan, a project funded by the Sasakawa Studentship Programme and a JRC Fuwaku Scholarship. She also works as a freelance writer for Japanese web magazines.

Nicola Phillips completed her degree in Oriental Studies and Japanese at Oxford in 2015. After some years spent teaching in Hong Kong and Peru, in 2018 she was awarded the Daiwa Japanese Studies scholarship to study for an MA in Social Anthropology at the School of Oriental and African Studies, University of London. Her work is concerned with the intersection between intimacy, sex work and identity, and she is firm supporter of sex workers' rights. Her master's dissertation involved ethnographic interviews with 'delivery health' sex workers in Tokyo.

Robert Simpkins is an anthropologist with research interests in creativity, music, sound, urban space and wellbeing. His doctoral research at SOAS investigated the lives of musicians seeking a career in the music industry after arriving in Tōkyō from prefectures across Japan, the adversities they face and the readjustments they make in order to keep on making music. His work centres on the relationship between creative practices and social issues such as insecurity, isolation and precarity. He is also interested in the social aspects of the creative process, and the methodological boundaries of art and anthropology with respect to both research and presentation. Robert's research has been supported by a MEXT Postgraduate Scholarship, Sasakawa Postgraduate Studentships, and a postdoctoral fellowship at the Sainsbury Institute for the Study of Japanese Arts and Cultures.

FOREWORD

Reflections By a Culturally Incompetent Customer

Making Sense of Gender, Fantasy Spaces and Those Who Perform There

Gitte Marianne Hansen

It was 1995, and I had recently arrived in Japan. I was 21 and this was my first trip outside Europe. I had not begun studying Japanese yet and back then there was of course no internet so my knowledge of Japanese culture was limited to what my Japanese friends told me and what I read in the English language books I could pick up in foreign bookstores in Copenhagen. Leading up to my trip, I had with great interest read a few books about Japanese women, including Anne Allison's *Nightwork: Sexuality, Pleasure, and Corporate Masculinity in a Tokyo Hostess Club*, which had just been published at the time. I recall trying to understand this thing called hostess clubs and the fact that married men would go there to buy the company of women, not in a sexual sense – and that puzzled me the most – if not sex, then what exactly were these men paying for? I remember pondering over this, and I even asked my friend and his family, with whom I was staying, about it. I recall how surprised I was when the father replied – without the slightest shame (and looking back now that was probably what really confused me) – that he regularly went to one with his colleagues. My confusion must have been written all over my face, because *Yokoe*-san, this nice family man, then decided that the best way to explain would be to take me along to the hostess club he frequented with colleagues. So, unsure of what to expect (or maybe I was in fact too sure, due to my naive understanding of how things must work), I set off with Yokoe-san to downtown Osaka.

Time has not tarnished my ability to recall the leather sofa in the dimmed room and that the hostess, probably just slightly older than myself, looked more ordinary than I had imagined. While better than my non-existing Japanese, her English was quite limited, but even if we could have communicated, I felt so out of place that I probably wouldn't have been able to ask her good questions anyway, and I am quite sure that within the specific setting, she would also not have been able to give me that many answers. A true regular, Yokoe-san had his personal whiskey bottle brought out for us, and, as our hostess poured us drinks and lit up Yokoe-san's cigarette, he explained how the lack of customers was a result of the poor economy Japan was facing. Trying to do her job, the hostess complimented me on my beautiful nails and blonde hair, and I immediately felt very conscious of the fact that I was not male (which I assumed her usual customers would be). While Yokoe-san seemed more relaxed than I had seen him at home and clearly felt comfortable with the space and the entire situation (well, I imagine apart from having me – a white European woman – tagged along), to me, the whole thing seemed fake and made-up. I felt uneasy about being served like this and would have preferred either to pour my own drink or at least to have poured hers in return. So, when Yokoe-san finally got up to leave, I was still just as clueless and no closer to understanding the gendered fantasy that Yokoe-san was clearly used to enjoying there. Two months later my stay in Japan was over, and I went back to Copenhagen to begin my undergraduate studies in Japanese studies. Even though a fellow student who had worked as a hostess during the bubble years later enlightened me with her personal experience, I never came any closer to really understanding the concept of men paying to be served by women in this way.

While I have not previously connected the dots, it occurs to me now that it was the exact same issue that again made me uneasy ten years later when I visited a maid café in Tokyo. By then I had been living in Japan a few years, working on my MA degree. My curiosity about women in Japan had persisted all those years since my first visit, and this interest had become more academically informed. Yet even with an improved understanding of Japanese culture and concepts of gender – that is to say, I was now more able to step back and look at situations with a knowledge of gender as performance, based on my readings of first Simone de Beauvoir and later Judith Butler – I still found it hard to grasp the phenomenon of maid cafés or why heterosexual male customers would pay to be served cheap coffee and food by women dressed up as Victorian-era-inspired maids. So, when Miyaji-san, a friend from the gender circle I attended at Waseda university, suggested we visit Mai:lish, a maid café in Akihabara, I was eager to go.

The next day, Miyaji-san, her boyfriend and I set off for Akihabara. After waiting in line for quite some time, we made our way up a steep staircase, at the top of which we were greeted by a young girl dressed, as expected, in a Victorian-inspired maid costume. Bowing, she uttered the appropriate phrase '*Okaerinasaimase, ojō-sama*' ('Welcome back, my princess') to me and Miyaji-san, and to Miyaji-san's boyfriend she said '*Okaerinasaimase, goshujin-sama*' ('Welcome back, my lord'). Miyaji-san had only visited a maid café once before, yet she was clearly more at ease than me with the fact that what we bought was a highly choreographed and gendered experience. Emerging in Tokyo in the early 2000s, maid café culture had already, by the time we visited this one, moved from primarily attracting male fans – of *manga* and *anime*, specifically – to including more mainstream customers such as ourselves. I remember finding this disappointing and being more interested in the lonesome-looking man at an adjacent table (who fitted my stereotypical idea of the male maid café customer) than in the young girl serving us. By then, I had come to understand that these women were dressing up to temporarily perform a gendered character in a fantasy space, and I acknowledged that this could be a job like any other. But once again, I was perplexed about what exactly it was customers – like the single man looking down at his coffee and *omu-raisu* (omelette with fried rice) – received from this temporary experience. With rubber-covered wooden chairs and posters of maids and *manga* characters plastered all over the walls, the space was in no way as sophisticated as the hostess club had been, and the interaction we were offered by the maid serving us was also much more distanced and passive (although it was clearly choreographed) than what I had experienced in the Osaka hostess club. So, when our session was up and we made our way down the staircase to street level, I was again left with a rather flat feeling without finding myself much wiser.

Years later, having completed my PhD and begun work as a lecturer in Newcastle, I was invited by a PhD student who was interested in butler cafés to join him for a visit to one in Tokyo. I had not really thought much about Japanese maid cafés since my visit to Mai:lish more than 10 years earlier, and at that point, I had no clue that butler cafés – which, in terms of gender, seemed to be its 'opposite' – even existed. But I was on research leave and anticipated that it would be great to get away from my literary research for an afternoon. So, a few weeks later, with little background information, I arrived at Ikebukuro station, where we had agreed to meet and to make our way to the café together. Walking east, we soon found ourselves on *Otome* (Maiden) Road. Although the street name explicitly targets fans of *otome* – a genre featuring romantic relationships between female protagonists and male characters – this area of Tokyo is not only known to attract *otome* fans, but also heterosexual women readers of *yaoi* ('boys' love'), a *manga* genre featuring male homoerotic relationships. While only 200 meters long, the atmosphere stood in sharp contrast to that of Ikebukuro's East Gate – here, rather androgynous-looking male characters from *manga* and *anime* decorated large billboards above several boutiques and bookshops selling character goods and *manga* intended for a female readership. Unlike these billboards and shops, Swallowtail, the butler café we were about to enter, was not easy to spot; however, as my guide pointed out, the unremarkable ground entrance functioned to enhance the fantasy experience sold within. This was a space where the relationship between the female protagonists and male characters from *otome* and *yaoi manga* was translated into interactions between the male butlers and the predominantly female guests.

Descending underground, we were met by a young doorman, who greeted us politely, addressing my male guide with '*Okaerinasaimase danna-sama*' ('Welcome back, my lord') and myself with '*Okaerinasaimase ojō-sama*' ('Welcome back, my princess'). Without asking for our reservation, the doorman simply looked at us, with an anticipatory smile. The fantasy had already begun, and, as our servant, it would have been odd for him to ask for such details, my guide explained later. Prompted by this tacit understanding, as any costumer would be expected to have (but which I obviously wasn't), my guide offered the information. The doorman informed the personnel inside of our arrival, and, through the translucent glass, I could see moving shadows. As I wondered what was going on, the doorman said: 'My lords, we are ready to receive you.' The shadow appeared again, and the door opened. A man in his late forties, with a warm smile, greeted us: 'Welcome back, my lords. We are glad to have you back. Please come inside.' A detailed introduction to the butler and to the footman who received us then followed. I was too tense to recall their names or what was said, but I am sure that a more culturally competent customer would have been able to produce some meaning from this. Looking back now, I think my nervous feelings sprang – just as they had the other times, at the hostess club and at the maid café – from the fact that I was unable to immerse myself in the fantasy world presented to me. In contrast to the other times, I was, of course, more aware of gender and fantasy as a commodity; and, distancing myself from the situation, I tried to consider what it might feel like to be a regular in this world. As the footman took us to our seats, my guide explained that he did not have prior knowledge of who would be serving us, since customers cannot request specific butlers, and this made me imagine what it might be like, as a regular, to feel delight or indeed disappointment already at this stage.

The café looked more like a massive theatre stage than an average dining space. Matching the outfits of the men working there, the room was decorated like a country house in Victorian-era Europe as this is represented in Japanese popular culture, with chandeliers, paintings, antique clocks and flowers. Silver plates were neatly arranged and displayed in a showcase. On the right, there were four compartments, which were partially obscured by heavy red velvet curtain, and on the left, a long sofa, divided into sections by pink lace curtains. This was already very different from the ordinary chairs I had sat on at Mai:lish and even the leather sofa at the hostess club in Osaka. The fantasy stage of this space was clearly much more refined and choreographed than either of the other two establishments I previously visited. There was also a stronger sense that, as a customer, I was also supposed to perform a certain role. A very large mirror was mounted on the end wall; this allowed customers to discreetly observe not only what unfolded at their own table, but throughout most of the café. It seemed to both reflect and augment the theatricality of the space and I suspect it also encouraged customers to better experience themselves as characters contributing to the fantasy.

The butler-waiters themselves all wore heavy makeup, including eyeshadow, white powder and lipstick. One even had a well-combed ponytail and it seemed clear to me that male grooming practices operated with a different set of boundaries between masculinity and femininity than in mainstream society. However, this offered no more freedom; as my guide informed me, at butler cafés masculinity is performed according to a set of explicit strict rules, with the men working there divided into a rigorous hierarchy (i.e. first, second, third footman), their positions within which the (culturally competent) customer can recognise in their attire and gestures.

Except for a few couples and (foreign) tourists (which I myself must have looked like), I quickly noticed how the other people dining there were predominantly female, ranging from their late teens to their early forties.

While some customers were actively interacting with the butlers, others seemed content to just observe them while being served. My guide told me that when he visited alone he could sense the fact that female customers often seemed surprised by his presence and he said that their stares made him feel uncomfortable. This again suggested to me that in this space it was not only the butlers serving the customers who must perform and present gender in the correct manner; customers also took on parallel responsibilities, in order for the fantasy to be played out. As a heterosexual woman in her early forties, I, for the first time in my rather random career as a customer at Japanese establishments specialising in gendered fantasy, fell within the exact target group (in terms of gender at least). However, this did not remove my sense of uneasiness, which I attribute to the fact that my sex and gender, as presented in mainstream society, were not enough to deliver my performance here. I sensed that there was something else going on of which I was not aware, which I was not culturally competent to fulfil, something I would probably have known if I had been a fan of *otome* or *yaoi manga*. But as my guide and I agreed while we might feel awkward in the moment, it was this very psychological distance that allowed us to undertake an analysis of gender and the work it requires in this context.

We ordered a three-course meal, but while the food presentation and the tea selection were more sophisticated than what I saw at Mai:lish, the quality did not quite match the rather high price and it seemed clear that people did not come to satisfy gastronomic cravings. Instead, the function of the meal seemed to be mainly that it enabled the butlers and customers to play their respective parts. As we waited for our tea, my guide explained that, as is also the practice in some maid cafés, Swallowtail issues point cards that give regulars various privileges, including, for example, the right to be called by any name they chose, or to select their own cup and saucer. Although these 'benefits' did not hold much attraction for me, I imagine that they were designed to make customers feel differentiated from other customers and to ultimately experience a more personal and intimate relationship with the butler serving them. While we ate, my guide continued to tell me more about the interactions he had observed during his previous visits. He explained that although a footman or a butler would be assigned to a specific table, he could still interact with other customers – on one occasion, my guide had even seen how simple eye contact resulted in a female customer clenching her fists in apparent joy, and on several other occasions he had observed how a light (and more or less accidental) touch exchanged between two butlers would spark reactions from women in the room, who seemed to get some emotional satisfaction from viewing this.

When our eighty minutes had passed, our butler escorted us to our 'waiting carriage' and we returned to the busy streets of Ikebukuro, where I immediately felt much more at ease than I had on the fantasy stage of Swallowtail. Here I knew how to be. As we made our way back to the station, my guide tried to make sense of our experience for me, but I was still not sure what to make of it. One thing was clear though: it was not only the men – the butlers and footmen – who had to perform in order for the fantasy to be completed. Customers – the *ojō-sama* – also had to perform according to a carefully choreographed and rule-based service exchange. And just as at my visits to the hostess club in 1995 and to the maid café in the early 2000s, I had failed; and this had prevented me from taking part in the fantasy and enjoying the experience – even though this time I came pretty close to belonging to the target audience.

As I continued my research on gender and female character construction in contemporary Japanese literature and visual culture, over the years my thoughts have kept returning to these sporadic experiences that I had as a culturally incompetent customer. Studies have of course long been undertaken of the specific types of spaces I frequented, and many are useful in making sense of (for example) why men might pay for women to act in highly choreographed ways – whether in the context of lighting cigarettes and pouring drinks as the Osaka hostess did for my host father, or in the context of dressing as cute maids from *manga* and *anime*, as the maid in Akihabara did for the single male customer I saw. As Patrick W. Galbraith (2011) has concluded, 'intimacy' and 'a place to belong' both seem to be important themes here: Yokoe-san, who took me to the hostess club he frequented with his work colleagues, may have found this during the Japan Inc. years, and the man, unknown to me, who drank cheap coffee alone (and who was, I therefore concluded, lonesome, making him fit the stereotypical idea of a customer at a maid café) may have found it, in the context of post-bubble Japan, when job security changed. But although I experienced this as it was playing itself out in history (or at least close enough to that point), I was not able to fully appreciate the gendered fantasy that was being performed and consumed. I attributed this to the fact that, as a heterosexual woman, I was not the target customer. Yet even when I visited a butler café, where I should have felt more at home, this was far from being the case. Here too, something prevented me from playing an active part in the fantasy. But while I never really explored this further, I always refused to interpret my experiences through the lens of the concept of 'weird Japan', through which Japanese spaces like these have, too often, been interpreted in Anglo-American discourse.

Then, a few years ago when I was invited to the Great Britain Sasakawa research day as a commentator on ongoing masters and PhD work, I noticed that a group of UK-based research students were working on various topics which asked many of the same questions about gender, fantasy and the people involved that had become stuck in my mind from my random experiences through the years. Jotting down the contact details of these researchers and PhD candidates, I invited them to present their work in more detail at a workshop in Newcastle. Since then, more people have joined the project. The idea of an edited book had already taken root in my mind that day in London, but although I was privileged to have the support of both the Great Britain Sasakawa Foundation and NIAS Press from early on, it would still be some years before the book materialised.

While my own work has focused primarily on gender and character construction in contemporary Japanese literature and visual culture, I have always understood this text-based discipline to be one that deals with people and ways of life. Working on a book that is framed around ethnographic and anthropological approaches to examining gender in contemporary Japan has been extremely enriching for me. The co-editor of this book, Fabio Gygi and I are extremely proud of the young scholars and research students included in this volume, who all managed to gain access to spaces not easily obtained. Through this volume, all of their hard work and skill enhance our knowledge of how gender works in contemporary Japan.

References

Allison, Anne. 1994. *Nightwork: Sexuality, Pleasure, and Corporate Masculinity in a Tokyo Hostess Club*. Chicago and London: University of Chicago Press

Patrick W. Galbraith. 2011. Maid in Japan: An Ethnographic Account of Alternative Intimacy. *Intersections: Gender and Sexuality in Asia and the Pacific* (25)'. intersections.anu.edu.au/issue25/galbraith.htm.

Acknowledgements

Gitte Marianne Hansen and Fabio Gygi

This volume emerged from a workshop held at Newcastle University in 2018. It brings together a group of promising young UK-based scholars who approach the topic of gender ethnographically. As editors we are first and foremost grateful to each of our authors, who all skilfully gained access to fields rarely accessible. Many have spent months or years gaining trust and/or learning how to position themselves as both researchers and participants in these particular cultural spaces.

Throughout the project, we are grateful to have been financially supported by the Great Britain Sasakawa Foundation. Many of our authors completed their fieldwork and PhD theses with a Sasakawa Studentship, and the foundation also generously funded both the initial workshop held at Newcastle University as well as contributing significantly to the final editing process. In addition to this financial support, we are also extremely grateful to have received continued support from NIAS Press, especially from Editor in Chief Gerald Jackson, who believed in the project from the start. We also thank NIAS Press gender series editor, anthropologist Monica Lindberg Falk (Lund University), who attended the workshop at Newcastle and who later – together with series editor anthropologist Wil Burghoorn (Emeritus, University of Gothenburg) – provided invaluable comments that helped tie the project together. Gratitude is also due to the two peer reviewers for the book as well as to the copy-editing team at NIAS Press.

Finally, we want to acknowledge anthropologist and artist Marcello Francioni, who kindly drew the intriguing front cover. Just as depicted in Francioni's image, we hope this volume will make clear how gender often requires precisely choreographed work.

CHAPTER 1

Gender as Work

Fabio Gygi and Gitte Marianne Hansen

This volume examines how different forms of gender are presented and commodified in contemporary Japan. It focuses on the deliberate work that goes into producing presentations of gender and on how the result of this work becomes an object to be consumed by others. Through ethnographic methods, we enter specific spaces where gender is a carefully choreographed performance to be sold, bought or negotiated. Each chapter is an invitation to join the ethnographers on the specific stages on which they themselves perform gender alongside their interlocutors. Readers of this volume will be taken along as the researcher provides service as bar staff in a Shinjuku gay bar; trains as a cross-dressing escort; waits for customers alongside sex delivery workers; joins a pornography fan community; records the life stories of transgender people; or listens to Kōenji street performers as they deliver both music and gender. Through access to these unique spaces, the edited volume examines gendered performances that are enacted, sustained, denied or disavowed surrounding particular kinds of transactions. It takes an ethnographic close-up look at how intimacy, agency and commodification create gender as a social and economic form in contemporary Japan.

We argue that what the customer pays for – in brothels, gay bars, at fan events, when hiring a cross-dressing escort or simply when throwing down a few hundred yen for a street performer – is a particular performance of gender. Rather than proposing a gender-*at*-work perspective (Ogasawara 1998; Macnaughtan 2020), the assembled chapters make the work *of* gender itself the focus of analysis. This has two crucial advantages over previously published literature on gender in Japan. Firstly, it allows a move away from sociological survey-style quantitative research that – while very important in order to address questions of gender inequality more broadly – too often simply assumes gender to be a fixed category (Steel 2019; Assmann 2020). Secondly, it enables a return to a perhaps older paradigm of gender, which puts performance over performativity (Butler 1990; 1993). In the spaces presented here, as in many everyday life scenarios, gender is the focus of a deliberate performance that involves complex cognitive, social and bodily skills. It is the affective effect of these performances that becomes the object of desire.

These new forms of commodification occur in the context of a global shift from manufacturing to service-based economies in developed countries. Michael Hardt and Antonio Negri describe it as a transition from material to immaterial forms of labour in post-industrial societies. In their 'immaterial paradigm' (2000: 112),[1] post-industrial work takes three forms: informatisation of production through robotics, the advent of symbolic–analytical services such as management and problem-solving, and affective labour, which produces 'intangible feelings of ease, excitement, or passion' (ibid.: 293). Analytically, affective labour is differentiated from the older notion of emotional labour by arguing that emotions are mental phenomena, while affect comes before emotion and is both more visceral and less contained. The contagious nature of affect turns affective labour into that which 'always directly constructs a relationship' (ibid.: 147), and thus opens the social up to be subsumed into the forces of capitalist production. This understanding is broader than Arlie Hochschild's earlier definition of emotional labour as 'the effort to induce or suppress feeling in order to sustain an outward appearance that produces the proper state of mind in others' (2012 [1983]: 7), but also less precise and more difficult to apply in concrete situations. An ethnographically meaningful distinction between emotional labour and affective labour is articulated in Elizabeth Wissinger's work on modelling in the U.S., in which she understands 'affect as a condition of emergence of emotion, and emotion as the capture, closure, and naming of affect' (2007: 260).

Emotional work is divided along gendered lines, in that those who perform the bulk of emotional labour are women, poorly paid, or not paid at all (Macdonald and Sirianni 1996). As Hochschild shows through the example of stewardesses, emotional labour is often understood to be feminised and requires the suppression of anger and aggression in the service of being nice and caring. Indulging and pampering male egos while suppressing one's own irritation is how Anne Allison (1994) describes the main task of

---

1 For a critique of the analytic distinction between the material and the immaterial see Yanagisako 2012.

working in a Japanese hostess club, for example. Several of the chapters that follow challenge the gendered assumptions about who has to undertake the emotional labour required, thus rendering it an important heuristic to compare the different stages on which this happens.[2]

While emotional labour becomes associated with femininity because it requires a deference to hierarchy and often remains unacknowledged, the notion of affective labour allows us to focus on how gender and its production are drawn into the sphere of commodification. Whether as care or sex work, the service industry packages it as immaterial commodity (one that is, however – and this is one of the blind spots in Hardt and Negri's theorisation – achieved by material means such as cosmetics, clothes, hair products and hormones). Superficially, this seems to respond to the feminist call for wages for feminised work (Federici 1975), but, in one of the many ironies of capitalist production, while gendered presentations become both work (as in individual effort) and labour (as in paid by wages), affective labour remains precarious with little job security and long-term stability. The costs on the other hand remain considerable: distinctions upon which the whole idea of modern work is based, between public and private, between work and leisure and between that which is paid for and that which is given freely are increasingly eroded. Life itself, its capacity for regeneration, reproduction and connection, is drawn into the sphere of production.

While the notion of affective labour provides a powerful critique of late capitalist production and consumption, the ways in which affect is described as circulating among anonymous 'bodies' has a disturbingly dehumanising effect. Human subjectivity is often relegated to the status of a mere side effect of affective contagion in such accounts. Against this post-human tendency, Gregory Mitchell proposes the notion of 'performative labour'. In his ethnography of male sex workers in Brazil and their customers, affective and performative labour are intertwined:

> [T]he frame of performative labour shifts focus away from intangible and often invisible affects that trouble the mind-body distinction and exist sometimes on the surface, sometimes below, sometimes ricocheting around

---

2   Although Hardt and Negri describe the rise of affective labour as a distinctly post-war phenomenon, Nakamura Miri has applied the term to maids in the age of Japan's opening to the West. Her argument is that the affective labour that maids performed became increasingly demanded from housewives, thus anticipating the rise of the 'professional housewife' in the post-war years (2015).

the room. Performative labor calls attention to the very visible products of labor: the masculinity that is embodied, commodified, and consumed.
(Mitchell 2016: 55)

While affect may be the driving force behind the dynamic of such encounters, the ways in which the promise of intimacy is commodified is better understood as 'a *commissioned performance* of masculinity, in which economic incentivization structures and guides the contours of idealised gender presentations available in a given culture's repertoire of masculinity' (Mitchell 2016: 38).

The chapters in this volume refer to these concepts to different degrees, but what brings the contributions together is a shared attention to the ways in which gender is created as an intersubjective artefact to be consumed by others. From gender presentation in everyday life to the gender display of male porn stars at female fan events, these performances unfold on a continuum from quotidian gender expression to highly controlled and commodified customer-tailored experiences.

The variety of phenomenological approaches chosen here make it possible for the ethnographer to participate as gendered subjects in the everyday life-worlds of the people and situations they study. Focusing on how gender comes into being in an intersubjective process allows the 'bracketing' – the intentional setting aside of assumptions concerning what is real – of both the notion of gender as a psychic reality and the view of gender as a biological fact. This is not to deny the importance of either, but to point out that in everyday life we do not have direct access to neither the interior aspect of gender identity nor to the genitals of persons.[3] What we do have access to as participants and observers and what we ourselves make available to others is our own and others' gender presentation. This volume therefore follows the ethno-methodological convention of talking about gender presentation rather than gender expression. While both terms suggest considerable agency on the part of the person expressing or presenting, 'expression' implies a stronger connotation of freedom to outwardly express an inward reality, something that in everyday life is constrained by culturally specific and normative ideas of how 'gender' should look.

The way gender is presented in everyday life in Japan – and elsewhere – is strongly inflected by the particular situation one finds oneself in. Gender is

---

3   In contemporary Japan, public baths and saunas are the exceptions, although they are almost always segregated into male and female spaces.

never what simply is – it is always something that ought to be in a particular way, thus always something that has to be achieved, that has to be created or modulated according to complex expectations of gendered behaviour that social others hold, be they present or imagined. What is particularly interesting about the chapters collected here is the level of consciousness individuals hold about the requirements of their staged performances. Unlike the gender performances that people (more or less) unconsciously undertake as part of their everyday lives, the individuals we meet here are highly aware of and consciously calibrating their performances as work, thus making visible some of the hidden assumptions of gender.

Doing gender: Phenomenology and ethnomethodology

The notion of gender in the social sciences was originally intended to point to the ways in which 'female' and 'male' were not natural, but socially constructed categories (Ortner 1974; Ortner and Whitehead 1981). Dislodging the natural (= material) underpinnings of gender was crucial to show that other configurations were possible. To do this, primacy had to be given to agency, subjectivity and discourse; hence the initially counter-intuitive formulation of 'doing gender' (West and Zimmerman 1987). Candace West and Don Zimmerman built their concept on an earlier body of scholarship in ethnomethodology that started with Harold Garfinkel. Arguing from a phenomenological perspective that starts from everyday social reality, Garfinkel argues that gender is not something given, but something that we attribute to people. His famous study of a transgender woman called Agnes defines gender as both the *result* of attributions made through interactions and as *device* that structures future interactions (1967: 116–185; for a feminist critique see Rogers 1992). In their seminal *Gender: An Ethnomethodological Approach*, the social psychologists Suzanne Kessler and Wendy McKenna maintain that '[e]veryone must display her or his gender in every interaction. This is the same as saying everyone must pass or everyone must ensure that the "correct" gender attribution is made of them' (1978: 126). The term 'pass' here refers to being recognised as the gender one is presenting as.[4] This

---

4   The term 'passing' has been widely used in American literature to describe the experience of someone of mixed racial background who is taken by others to be white or, more rarely, as black or belonging to a First-Nation. See, for example, works by James Weldon Johnson (1912) and Nella Larsen (1929). However, 'passing' is also used in the field of gender, but in the context of transgender experiences, the term is problematic as it suggests deception on the part of the person presenting as male or female.

is made possible by conventional gender markers, which they call 'cultural genitals', such as hairdos, gender-specific clothing, voice pitch, speech patterns and bodily comportment. Crucial to the stability of the gender system is the 'natural attitude', a set of assumptions about the world that to the holder appears as common sense. 'There are only two genders' and 'gender remains stable over time' are the most common and basic of these assumptions.

Once an attribution ('male' or 'female') is made, everyone participating in an interaction is involved in maintaining it, often with considerable cognitive effort: from editing out contradictory information to ignoring what the person themself is saying. Kessler and McKenna also point out that, from an ethnomethodological perspective, it is the continuous effort to construct and maintain gender as a stable entity that justifies the assumptions made by the 'natural attitude', and not the other way around. This counterintuitive point is supported by historical inquiries into the material culture of gender: the now internationally recognised gendered distinction of blue for boys/pink for girls, for example, is a recent innovation that becomes culturally institutionalised precisely at the juncture at which the assumed 'difference' (read 'inferiority') of women can no longer be held up by biological arguments (Paoletti 2012). In *Delusions of Gender*, Cordelia Fine notes with ironic relish how the colour code that is introduced to maintain the binary gender system is then re-naturalised when biologists try to explain these colour preferences as the result of 'evolutionary processes' (2010: 208).

Note that Kessler and McKenna maintain a strict distinction between gender presentation, gender identity and sexual orientation. Not to do so would mean to regress to the implicit assumptions of the sex/gender system, which Rubin has analysed as a nested system of categories that induce each other: biological sex determines gender determines sexual orientation (1975). Differentiating between these aspects of gender allows for a more fine-grained analysis of gender presentation in Japan that does not necessarily draw in gender identity or sexual orientation. There are, for example, forms of femininity specifically performed for other women, which are different from femininity performed for men, in the same way that there are recognised forms of masculinity that men produce for other men and others that are produced specifically for women to consume/enjoy. Neither of these impinge on the sexual orientation of the producers. Furthermore, different styles of gender presentation are often recognised as social categories of people: the *oyaji-gyaru* or *ossan-joji* ('geezer girl'), for example, is a young girl with the manners and habits of an older man and thus fits right in when out drinking or at karaoke with older work colleagues; *sōshokukei danshi* ('herbivore boys'), on the other hand, present as 'non-threatening' heterosexual men interested not so much in sex as in beauty products and self-expression (Deacon 2013). *Rōrukyabetsu danshi* or 'cabbage roll' boys,[5] by contrast, present as herbivores but are actually hidden carnivores. The *joshiryoku danshi* ('boy with girl power'), epitomised by the figure skater Hanyū Yuzuru, is yet another example in which youthful cuteness as a style of gender expression does not necessarily cast doubts on a person's gender identity or sexual orientation. These social categories do not, however, emerge from the social field as self-descriptions but are usually created by journalists and gain traction through media exposure. In Japanese discourse, they form a distinct category of their own: half social critique, half marketing language, they provide the means to navigate an increasingly fragmented social landscape.

Gender in and as theatre: Masculinity and femininity as kata

Each chapter in this volume examines specific spaces in which gender is performed and consumed in a highly conscious, often choreographed, manner suggestive of a theatrical stage. The term *kata* (lit. 'form') in Japanese is useful in considering feminine or masculine gender presentation as an ongoing, repetitive and deliberate performance. *Kata* are a series of precisely circumscribed movements and postures that form the core of any traditional art, whether spiritual, martial or aesthetic. Through the minute imitation of the teacher, the student's body is shaped into the appropriate form, 'so that the individual becomes the form and the form becomes the individual' (Yano 2003: 26). This is repeated until the skill becomes second nature:

> Once committed to muscle memory, skills and techniques become a palpable part of the self. Those who have put in their years of training, those who have tempered their skills to the point where skill is 'attached to the body' [*mi ni tsukerareta*], have also become more mature persons in that process.
>
> (Kondo 1990: 239)

---

[5] A cabbage roll is cabbage on the outside, meat on the inside, hence the moniker. The opposite is asparagus rolled in bacon (*Nikumaki asupara*). See Jolivet 2015.

Dorinne Kondo's description of the learning processes of master artisans also applies to gender socialisation: '*kata* of all kinds codify gender, in effect naturalizing behaviours and making infringements of them improper' (Bardsley and Miller 2011: 8). Implicit in this emphasis of imitation and repetition over cognitive understanding is the idea that the visible exterior, the bodily 'form', will in turn shape the mind (Yuasa 1990).

The expression of femininity and masculinity as *kata* is most prominent in the long and elaborate theatrical tradition of cross-gender performance that has received much scholarly attention from historians, theatre scholars and anthropologists (Isaka 2015; Stickland 2008; Leiter 2002; Kano 2001; Robertson 1998). Although it is too simplistic to suggest trans-historical continuities between pre-modern theatre and contemporary gender presentation in everyday life, there are four parallels that are worth considering: first, the close alignment of the theatre with sex work; second, an understanding of gender based on conventional signs; third, the independence of gender presentation from 'nature', sexual orientation and gender identity; and fourth, a heightened awareness of gender as performance.

Kabuki theatre serves as a case in point. While both 'boys' (*wakashu*)[6] and women performed female roles in early Kabuki, the close connection of this new form of theatre with prostitution soon led to a crackdown by the military administration, which banned female performers from the stage in 1629 (Shively 2002). After that, female roles were taken over entirely by *wakashu* actors whose feminine beauty was appreciated in contrast to the military masculinity of their suitors. Unsurprisingly, in 1652 *wakashu* actors were also banned for prostitution. After this, male actors (many of whom had been 'boy' actors) took over female roles and perfected the impersonation of women, in which dress, comportment, the use of voice, language and stylised movement

---

6 The category of 'boy' (*wakashu*) had considerable temporal elasticity in pre-modern Japan. It was usually the *genpuku* ceremony of 'shaving off the forelocks' (*kado o ireru*) that marked the beginning of adulthood. This ceremony could be held anytime from the age of 13 to 17 (Leupp 1997: 125). Before that, boys were eligible to enter a homosocial relationship that might or might not have involved sex: 'The adult male lover [the *nenja*] was supposed to provide social backing, emotional support, and a model of manliness for the boy. In exchange, the boy was expected to be worthy of his lover by being a good student of samurai manhood' (Schalow 1990: 27). Although the fluidity includes gender presentation, sexual orientation and sexual roles according to the power dynamics of the *wakashu/nenja* relationship, note that these relationships were socially institutionalised and regulated according to life stages. The temporal fluidity of gender should thus not be taken to indicate a greater freedom of choice, although *wakashu* had some leeway in choosing their *nenja*.

conspired to create not an illusion of femininity but an idealised, perfected version of it. Morinaga tries to grasp this by describing it as 'citationality' of gender,[7] '[f]or in the light of citationality, neither a pure original (a hypothetical original that cites nothing) nor a rigorously exact imitation (a perfect copy that does not differ from its original in any way)' exists' (2002: 273). She argues that male actors did not replace female actors to become *onnagata*, but that the *onnagata* is a result of making permanent the transient status of the *wakashu*. It was not the goal of the male actor to pass as women,[8] but to create an enhanced imitation. An able *onnagata* arouses heterosexual desire in the male audience and jealousy and a desire for imitation in women (Morinaga 2002: 269). It was thus bodies considered to be male that participated in the circulation of femininity as citation, so much so that when the early 20th century female Kabuki performer Ichikawa Kumehachi took on female roles, it was considered high praise when critics claimed she was playing women just as though she were a man (Isaka 2016: 19). Importantly, the historical acting technique was not based on 'completely becoming a character' or presenting a gender illusion, but on a careful layering of the actor's persona with the role being played. The role never obscured the actor completely. Thus, modern-day fans shout the name of the actor during particularly dramatic moments of the play (*ōmukō*), not the name of the character.

What *onnagata* did on stage, thus, was signifying femininity rather than becoming female (Barthes 1970). A performance was not successful because it created a convincing illusion, but because it rendered the performance and the skill involved visible; the audience enjoyed the performance as performance. This is particularly evident in the elaborate play with convention and parody common in the Kabuki repertoire. In *Onna Shibaraku* for example, a play about an evil warlord who has arrested and threatens to execute those who oppose him, the leading role of the tempestuous young man (the *aragoto*)

---

7   The concept of citationality of gender is based on Butler's application of Derrida's idea of citation (1981) to gender. Butler refers to this idea when she argues that gender is not a performance, as there is no subject that exists prior to the performance of gender (1991). She devises the term performativity to indicate that subjects come into being as gendered through acts of repetition that do not have an origin. Each of these acts instantiates and materialises gender.
8   Isaka explicitly speaks of '*onnagata* who pass' (2016: 37) but bases this entirely on a passage from the 1776 treatise *The Words of Ayame*: 'It is hardly possible for an *onnagata* to be considered proficient unless he spends his everyday life as a woman' (quoted in Isaka 2016: 40). While this means that ideally the *onnagata's* femininity extends beyond the stage, it does not mean that passing as a woman in everyday life was their goal (for a critique see Leiter 2017).

is played by an *onnagata*. After the curtain comes down, the *onnagata* remains upstage and reverts to being a model of dainty femininity, complaining that the sword is so heavy and the male costume so cumbersome. The *frisson* of this moment is entirely based on the fact that the audience knows that this is a man playing a woman playing a man. That is to say, the *onnagata* is practicing a *presentation* of gender, not a representation: 'representation is a form of expression that effaces its mediated nature, which looks immediate and thus realistic. In turn, presentation is a form of expression that openly recognizes its mediated nature' (Morinaga 2002: 265). The question of whether a gendered performance is taken at face value or whether it is enjoyed *qua* performance is relevant to several of the chapters collected here.

In her seminal *Acting like a Woman in Modern Japan* (2001), Kano Ayano documents the shift from a paradigm based on the conventional display of gender to the discovery of the body in theatre, a development triggered by the import of naturalistic acting styles from Europe and Russia. The gendered body becomes the new ground from which to build convincing, that is, illusionistic, performances of human behaviour. The goal of the actor in this naturalistic paradigm is 'to become' the character; to do this, they have to amplify what is already 'there', to use their body in a way similar to everyday life. In other words, 'nature' guarantees the verisimilitude of the performance through the implicit new assumption that everyday ways of behaving are inherently 'natural', and that the actor needs only to draw on their inner experience. The expressive spectatorship of the Kabuki stage in the Edo period, in which the audience co-creates the performance, is replaced by the appreciation of performance as interior experience: through a psychological 'suspension of disbelief', the spectator enters the imaginary world of the play and experiences the emotions portrayed as 'real'.

The complementary if not synchronous institution to Kabuki theatre is the all-female Takarazuka revue theatre, founded in 1913, which cultivated a similar cult around its stars embodying male roles (*otokoyaku*) (Robertson 1998). While Kabuki male actors created images of perfect femininity for a predominantly male audience in the Edo period, 'Takarasiennes' create images of dashing masculinity for a predominantly female contemporary fan community:

> To create appropriate representations of male and female characters on the Takarazuka stage, performers largely rely upon one or more of three

methods – the copying of traditional *kata* that signify masculinity or femininity in a theatrical context, the observation of real people in society, and the exercise of imagination. Like many 'traditions', *kata* have been invented, adapted and discarded at various times, and are mainly learned by mimicking the clothing, makeup, voice, gaze, posture, gait, singing/dancing style and mood of seniors in the Revue. Many Takarazuka *kata*, however, have become stylised to the extent that they no longer relate to 'real' gender in mainstream society, and have meaning only within the theatre's fantasy world.' (Stickland 2004: 187–88)

As in Kabuki, gender is created by the actor's performance and is supported by the audience through rapt attention, by weeping and clapping for their favourite stars: 'The audience is effectively watching two people in one body, and this adds to the potential alternative, "subversive" subtext underlying Takarazuka performances.' (Stickland 2004: 210)

It is important to note, however, that on top of belonging to different periods of Japanese history, male impersonations of femininity and female impersonations of masculinity are not symmetrical in terms of power. Many urban women in the Edo period looked up to the *onnagata* as perfect examples and studied their attitude and comportment, suggesting that it is only in its most artificial form – an artificiality that is never disguised or passed as natural – that femininity fully comes into its own. The opposite cannot be said of the *otokoyaku*. Although 'he' provides female fans with a view of men as gallant and dashing, it is not common for men to study their comportment and stance to enhance their masculinity. Robertson quotes from a revealing story about a male Takarazuka fan who describes what he finds attractive about the *otokoyaku*: 'Otokoyaku can't quite pass as men. When females wear male trousers their rear end is a dead giveaway.[…] In fact I find it thrilling to try to uncover the female in the man.' (Robertson 1998: 198) On one hand, then, there is the male-assigned performer who provides the perfect template for female behaviour and etiquette; on the other there is a performance that is (sexually) thrilling because it is betrayed by female 'nature'. In other words, within these two long established theatrical worlds, men succeed in being ideal women, while women try but fail at being ideal men. The same argument extends to sexual attraction and, implicitly, sexual orientation: both *onnagata* and *otokoyaku* should[9] appeal to men as women (Isaka 2016; Robertson 1998), thus recreating a sexual hierarchy undergirded by heterosexual male desire. Despite the possibility of a queer reading of these theatrical practices, mainstream interpretations lead straight back to the most basic tenets of the gender binary that renders women closer to nature and thus requiring close surveillance, while men forge culture out of chaos through acts of artifice.

While we emphasise that the notion of *kata* is useful in order to think about the specific gender presentations discussed in this volume, it is important to note some differences between the Kabuki and Takarazuka stage and the stages as they appear in each chapter. First of all, unlike Kabuki and Takarazuka actors, who perform gender on the theatrical stage at a distance, and with only strictly regulated interactions with their audiences, the cross-dressing escort, the male star at a porn event for female fans, or the street musician, for instance, perform on each of their stages *together with* their consumers. This means that their gender presentation is more situationally calibrated and necessarily includes a degree of spontaneous reactive behaviour not seen on the theatrical stage, where everything is choreographed down to the smallest detail. The various degrees of emotional ties that emerge between the paying customer and the bar staff in a gay bar, the cross-dressing escort or the sex worker, tend to 'break' the frame of (theatrical) performance. Takeyama Akiko, in her *Staged Seduction: Selling Dreams in a Tokyo Host Club* (2016), emphasises the importance of the stage and off-stage aspects of interaction, and this also applies to the chapters included in this volume. When the ethnographers and the participants in their fieldwork perform gender as a form of work in their specific contexts, the experience becomes personal in a way that it rarely is for an actor on a theatrical stage.

Performance versus performativity

Speaking of gender as performance may suggest a return to a theatrical metaphor of gender as role, with the implication that it can be taken on or off at will. West and Zimmerman (1987) have pointed out this weakness and

---

9 The fact that the majority of the Takarazuka fans are women would suggest that same-sex desire plays a part, a point made by Robertson (1998), but denied by Nakamura and Matsuo (2003), who prefer to see fandom as an asexual phenomenon. See Stickland (2004) for a more in-depth discussion.

argued that one's gender presentation is not only situational but constitutes a master identity that must be maintained across a vast gamut of social contexts. These include the rigid recognition of one's binary gender by institutions such as schools and hospitals, as well as by the state. Influenced by Foucault's contention that subjects come into being as a result of particular regimes of discipline and thus power, Butler argues that 'coherent gender, achieved through an apparent repetition of the same, produces as an *effect* the illusion of a prior and volitional subject' (1990: 24). In a famous passage from *Bodies that Matter*, she extends her argument: 'Subjected to gender, but subjectivated by gender, the "I" neither precedes nor follows the process of this gendering, but emerges only within and as the matrix of gender relations themselves' (Butler 1993: 7). Distinct from Austin's notion of performative acts, which require an uttering subject and intention, performativity for Butler is the repetitive iteration of a norm: 'This repetition is not performed *by* a subject: this repetition is what enables a subject and constitutes the temporal condition for the subject' (Butler 1993: 95).

While we agree with Butler that many aspects of gender are inextricably linked to becoming a gendered subject, we oppose a fatalistic reading of her work, which totalises gender as an all-penetrating regime of power on methodological and ethnographic grounds. Methodologically speaking, her hypotheses concerning gendered subjectivities are metaphysical rather than empirical. This does not render them invalid, but removes them from the everyday and fantasy arenas of gender that we are interested in. Like the 'natural attitude', the 'performativity of gender' thesis can be bracketed in order to see how power is ascribed and claimed, denied and reinforced in everyday interaction. The emphasis on gender as something we 'do' returns some agency to individual and collective actors, but does not in any way imply that actors are free to choose their own ways of performing gender. The work of gender is achieved as a collective intersubjective construction by many actors and is thoroughly infused with expectations, norms and powers of definition not necessarily held by the individual. A performance can fail to achieve an appropriate form of gender in the eyes of others. While a failed performance on stage will only throw doubt on your ability and identity as an actor, however, the stakes of performing gender appropriately in everyday life are much higher: failing to do so is likely to lead to ostracism, if not violence. In other words, the fact that gender is intersubjectively constructed in interaction does not mean that it does not have real consequences, or that the performance can be changed at a whim. Quite the opposite seems to be the case: the more social actors are aware of the artifice of gender, the more strictly they must perform it. That being said, gender as a binary category of person ('male'/'female') is not always the overarching principle that distributes power along gendered lines. In this we follow Barrie Thorne's account of gender in the schoolyard in *Gender Play* (1993), which through careful observation and analysis shows how the ability of the category 'boy' or 'girl' to structure interactions between children is switched on and off depending on the frames of action and play (chasing versus co-operative group work for example). In such a situational rather than a totalising reading, gender moves in and out of focus as a relevant social fact. In that sense, we are closer to Butler's *Undoing Gender* (2004) than to her *Bodies that Matter* (1993):

> If gender is a kind of a doing, an incessant activity performed, in part, without one's knowing and without one's willing, it is not for that reason automatic or mechanical. On the contrary, it is a practice of improvisation within a scene of constraint. Moreover, one does not 'do' one's gender alone. One is always 'doing' with or for another, even if the other is only imaginary. What I call my 'own' gender appears perhaps at times as something that I author or, indeed, own. But the terms that make up one's own gender are, from the start, outside oneself, beyond oneself in a sociality that has no single author.
>
> (Butler 2004:1)

The second objection is grounded in ethnographic reality. Rather than to take our cue from philosophical assumptions that are impossible to verify, the analyses assembled here take their cue from the experiences of those who consciously 'do' gender as part of their everyday lives. The ways in which some aspects of gender are negotiated in Japan allows some glimpses into conceptions that do not necessarily align either with the 'natural attitude', nor with the idea of performativity in which the subject comes into being in necessarily gendered forms. Rather, expressions such as '*onna o suteta*' ('I gave up being a woman') and '*onna ja nai jibun ni nareru*' ('I can become myself without being a woman') – see Mochigi 2019 – suggest that there is a gap between subjectivity and gender presentation, an awareness of the work that goes into passing as a gendered being, but also an awareness of the emancipatory possibilities that this entails.

Sincerity and authenticity commodified

Thinking of gender in everyday life as a kind of performance points towards both the artificiality of gender and the sanctioning of the performance by a given audience. By not relying on a notion of 'nature' to guarantee the 'reality' of gender, we can ask a series of questions that would make no sense if we took gender to be a biological fact: If there is a correct form of performing gender, what happens when gender is performed incorrectly? Is there such as thing as 'gender failure' (Coyote and Spoon 2014)? What are the parameters of sincerity for a gendered performance? Is it sincere because it instantiates a match between an external performance and an inner reality of gender? How do we account for the situational aspects of gendered performances? Furthermore, what happens if one ceases to assume that gender is stable over time and considers the temporal horizon of gender? Given the evanescence of human intention and emotion, the more exigent question to ask, then, is not whether something is natural, authentic or sincere, but how long one can keep it that way. This is what Goffman means when he argues that there is no gender identity, 'only a schedule for the portrayal of gender' (1979: 8).

As most chapters in this volume show, it is precisely the time limitation of the performance that is the condition of its sincerity. This may sound doubly paradoxical because of two implicit Eurocentric assumptions: a) that a person who is truly sincere does not have to put on a performance – 'one cannot at the same time both be sincere and seem so' as André Gide said (1930: 142); and b) that commodification and authenticity are incompatible, something we still tend to assume as academics trained in a Western Marxist tradition. Such mutual exclusionism renders us blind to 'the subtle ways in which people actually match their monetary transfers to their various social relations, including intimate ties.' Payments as such do not determine a relationship's quality, 'but the relationship defined the appropriateness of one sort of payment or another' whether it is made as a reward, as compensation, as an entitlement or as gift (Zelizer 2000: 818). Even when intimacy is commodified, it does not follow automatically that it is therefore 'insincere'. Prasad has argued that the gift is more likely to 'draw forth the ritualized pretence of sentiment', which usually camouflages strategic machinations on the part of the giver. The commodity form, on the other hand, 'offers freedom from the necessity of *appearing* selfless, generous, grateful, or otherwise sentimental and can therefore be construed as free from hypocrisy' (Prasad 1999: 185).

Defining the modern 'pure relationship' that is entered for its own sake as authentic (Giddens 1992: 58), does not automatically render commodified exchanges of sexual services 'inauthentic'. In *Temporarily Yours*, her ethnographic work on sex workers in North America, Sweden and the Netherlands, Elizabeth Bernstein introduces the concept of 'bounded authenticity':

> In contrast to the quick, impersonal 'sexual release' associated with the street-level sex trade, much of the new variety of sexual labour resides in the provision of what I call 'bounded authenticity' – the sale and purchase of authentic emotional and physical connection. [M]iddle-class sex workers' efforts to manufacture authenticity resided in the descriptions of trying to simulate – or even produce – genuine desire, pleasure, and erotic interest for their clients. Where in some cases this involved mere 'surface acting' [...] it could also involve the emotional and physical labour of manufacturing authentic (if fleeting) libidinal and emotional ties with clients, endowing them with a sense of desirability, esteem, or even love.
> (Bernstein 2007: 103–4)

For this to work as escape, fantasy and recreation, however, it is crucial to establish a clear sequestration of experience. The cut that stops the relationship between the worker and the client from contaminating everyday life is the monetary transaction, as the San Francisco-based sex worker and writer Carol Queen has argued: 'We create sexual situations with very clear boundaries, for ourselves and for our clients. In fact, one of the things that people are paying us for is clear boundaries [...] Same thing with seeing a psychotherapist; there you are paying someone to tell your secrets to, someone you can trust will not judge you and who at least won't interrupt you in the middle and start telling you their secrets. Instead, you are getting focused attention' (quoted in Chapkis 1997: 77).

Thus, the client can enjoy the performance as performance, without worrying about ongoing commitments, relationships of obligation and, furthermore, without the burden of having to be grateful for what one has received. That is not to say that clients have no obligations at all; as many of the chapters show, clients are also expected to act in certain ways and rules are often in place to ensure that consumers stick to their part. In that sense, experiences of 'bounded authenticity' are 'cost-efficient and well-suited to the structure of the modern corporation: temporary, detachable, and flexible' (Bernstein 2007: 175). It is not surprising, then, that sex work, which has been less stigmatised in Japan than in the West, is seen as an expedient means to earn significant amounts of money by many women who do not want to subject themselves to the drudgery of an 'office lady' existence (Koch 2020). But as Bernstein points out, 'those who participate most fully in the emotionally contained economy of recreational sex and bounded authenticity are also those whose psychic lives are most fully penetrated by the cultural logic of late capitalism' (2007: 176).

Takeyama provides an excellent example of this in her ethnography of host clubs in Tokyo (2016), where entrepreneurial male hosts turn themselves into commodities to entertain the romantic fantasies of female clients. She notes that the desire at the heart of the transaction tends to spill over the temporal boundaries:

> While the host club stage is physically bounded, the actors' exchanges extend well beyond the club and potentially transact in shared imaginary futures. Thus, the value of exchange stretches out over time and space. As a result, the relationship between reality and fantasy, commodity and gift, and profit-seeking capitalism and life-enhancing humanism becomes opaque and ambiguous in the quest for [a] hopeful future.
>
> (Takeyama 2016: 68)

In this case, the commodity form is split open by the desire to extend relationships in time and space, or rather to sustain a more ambiguous social space within which truth and reality are partly suspended: '[T]he clients I interviewed told me that they felt good about themselves, even though they knew their hosts' flattery and romantic gestures were merely a performance. In seduction, as is sometimes also the case in ethnography, it is not so much the truth that matters as the fantasy, the sensible experience, and the dream' (ibid.: 19).

This point is further supported by Kumada Yōko's ethnography of a 'delivery health service' in Tokyo that specialises in light SM. Anonymity is the most crucial element that gives both clients and sex workers a certain degree of freedom from shame, but also the potential to 'reinvent' themselves, or, as Kumada writes, to separate or connect aspects of the self (2017: 196–201). Anonymity also relieves both clients and sex workers from the imperative of a coherent self, an important precondition for sexual fantasy play, especially when the client wants to try something he thinks of as 'uncharacteristic' of himself. Her interlocutors, on the other hand, revealed different aspects of their selves in a strategic manner. Aya, who is a single mother, for example, carefully judged whether to reveal this fact to her customers. When clients spoke of their own children she often did, and this created a sense of solidarity and warmth. Other clients, she sensed, were put off by this 'smell of real life'. Whether the fantasy space remained contained or not depended on the concrete interactions and relationships of trust that emerged between them.

Following these cues, the present volume asks how this cultural logic of late capitalism shapes new social forms and new subjectivities surrounding gendered performances in different frameworks. Here the advantages of ethnography are clearly displayed. Rather than assuming what the appropriate relationship between privacy, intimacy and sexuality should be and then formulating a critique of the commodification of intimacy based on these assumptions, the contributions look at the lived experience of the providers and consumers of these experiences and assess each case as to the fulfilments and constraints it offers. They militate against the tendency to view commodification as something categorically negative, but interpret it as a nascent social form that allows for new ways of being and feeling. Following Maruta Kōji's ethnography on 'assisted dating' (2001), they ask: Who is selling what to whom? What is exchanged in these transactions? How does the exchange give form to fantasies, subjectivities and ways of being in the world? Instead of reducing complex realities to a facile critique of neoliberalism, the ethnographic portraits assembled here look in more detail at the trade-offs that people make between freedom, marketization, hierarchies and self-commodification. What emerges, then, is not just a more nuanced interpretation of social experience for those enmeshed in it, but also new ways to define established concepts, such as alienation, freedom and agency. Yes, one may not have the freedom to change an expected and standardised performance to fit one's needs, but one has the freedom not to mean it and still be paid for the work. Part of the reason why commodification is understood to be alienating is because we tend to assume that work necessarily draws in the whole person, an assumption that in turn is based on a mythology of the self as undivided, whole entity. If we took a more relational view of the self, we might find that a different kind of freedom can be found in the 'insincere' performance, a freedom that resides in the gap between external performance and inner feeling, a freedom from the imperative to be an authentic, sincere and coherent person at all times. Conversely, an initially stylised gesture can become filled with genuine emotion and a sincere gesture can become mannered and stylised over time.

Authenticity, the Japanese self and the limits of gender

It is crucial for a critical anthropology to take different ways of doing gender not just as local variations of a universal theme but as an invitation to rethink our own assumptions concerning the stability and inevitability of gender. Even in their most current iteration, popular Euro-American discourses on gender are still based on a 'depth ontology of the person' (Miller 2009: 16): they start with the assumption of a core personality that must be expressed in order to lead a meaningful life. The imperative to be an 'authentic self' pitches the individual against society and, at the same time, disregards the social nature of the imperative. Not to be true to oneself implies 'living a lie' towards others. From popular television programmes such as *Queer Eye for the Straight Guy* to the vast and dangerous landscape of self-help literature, we are interpellated from all directions to 'be ourselves' and 'to live our own truths' independent of the opinions of society; to submit to the imperative of authenticity more slavishly; to prostrate ourselves in front of the altar of the one true self.

In contrast, the Japanese social experience has a greater appreciation of the fact that to be oneself, one needs others. There is a heightened awareness of gender as not a natural given, but as something to be performed, something the individual must learn, perfect and manipulate in appropriate ways for a given situation. The Japanese examples brought together here allow glimpses of a different way of conceiving the links between freedom of expression and gendered performances. Persons are interpellated to gendered performances, but there is a sense shared by those interpellating as well as those interpellated that what is required is a performance *qua* performance, not an instantiation of nature. What emerges, then, is a gap between the gendered performance, which has to be correct and committed, but not necessarily sincere, and the psychic reality of gender, which is authentic, but whose expression cannot be forced. In the depth ontology of the person, freedom is understood as the freedom to express what one already is against social constraints (Nietzsche's dictum 'become what you are'), while in a more interdependent cosmology the imperative to self-expression can itself appear as a form of coercion.

Freedom can be found in the awareness of the performance as performance, that is, in the gap or the disconnect between the outward performance and the inner truth.

Here the issues of gender and presentation of the self meet with a rich literature on the 'relational self' in Japan, which is usually contrasted with American notions of personhood (Kondo 1990; Rosenberger 1992; Sugiyama 2004; Ozawa-de Silva 2008; Hansen 2016). Wim Lunsing succinctly summarises these findings:

> Japanese, indeed, seem to be relatively sophisticated in dealing with varying presentations of themselves in a variety of contexts and do not allow themselves to be led astray by the idea that they have to present unchangeable selves regardless of contexts. Their inner selves appear rather to be stronger precisely because they feel less of a need for confirmation by others, unlike for instance Americans who tend to present themselves all the time as if they were unchangeable and essential to the personhood, adhering to some identity or other. It seems to suggest that they are insecure about what they are and therefore seek confirmation from others continually.
>
> (Lunsing 2001: 331–32)

While we think of gender as relational, as embedded in social relationships and hierarchies, we also think of it as situational, that is, as being shaped by co-presence, even if the present others are not part of a social relationship or not human themselves. De-centring the human subject as that which 'has' gender, we understand the work of gender not only as presentation and attribution, but also, in the words of Jane Ward, as 'the act of giving gender to others', which consists in 'witnessing, nurturing, validating, fulfilling, authenticating, special knowing, and secret-keeping' (2010: 240). Ward describes this act as in itself gendered along a division of labour between male-identifying subjects whose masculinity is co-created by those identifying as female, but she also stresses that gender is always co-constructed and that everyone requires and gives gender labour. This emphasis on the collaborative nature of gender allows for a more dynamic understanding that does not shy away from conflict, power differentials and historical and cultural specificities.

Finally, we have to address the question of the limits of gender, as a social fact on one hand and as a theoretical concept on the other. Insofar as we understand gender as an intersubjective construct that involves many different agencies – 'a practice of improvisation within a scene of constraint' – gender carries only as far as the communities of practice implicated in its co-construction reach. This counterintuitive insight is particularly important for queer takes on gender. Constructions of gender are precarious to the degree that they cannot invoke support from the 'natural attitude'. This creates a gender hierarchy that privileges those who feel that their gender identity and their gender presentation match, or, in other words, those whose gender appears as 'natural'. Everybody else has to put in extra work to justify and legitimise their presentations of gender, extra work that accumulates in turn around racialised and gendered categories (Bailey 2013).

Conceptually, too, there are limits to the understandings that can be wrought from an intersubjective construction of gender. What can be said about the psychic realities of gender from this perspective is limited, for example. Nonetheless it allows us to ask 'heretical' questions: To what degree can gender presentation be separated from one's gender identity, and at what cost? Is gender detachable from personhood? And do we cease to be gendered when left to our own devices?

Fieldwork and embodiment

The chapters in *The Work of Gender: Service, Performance and Fantasy in Contemporary Japan* are written by junior scholars and are based on long-term fieldwork in Japan, mostly as part of their doctoral research. Each chapter looks at a particular situation in which work, gender, and commodification intersect; each then provides an analysis in terms of power, agency and fantasy. What all the chapters have in common is an unwavering commitment to ethnographic research. The insights presented here are the results of visceral encounters in the field that go beyond just interviews and observation. It may be a commonplace in anthropology by now to argue that the fieldworker's main instrument is their body, but we are still some way from letting the embodied nature of fieldwork register in our writing. All ethnography is necessarily affective, but affective ethnography, understood by Takeyama as 'the method and writing derived, in part, from affective modes of knowing' (2016: 20) is still a challenge to the imperatives of empirical objectivity. A hermeneutic phenomenological approach offers both a close examination of concrete bodily experience and an insight into how this positions the researcher as a gendered participant in a particular social field (Desjarlais 2003). Whether it is waiting for hours in the biting cold of Tokyo winters for an audience to gather for a street music performance, being groped and slapped in a gay bar, being drawn into the fan community at a porn event aimed at women – or, on the contrary, becoming the object of adoration of customers – or being misgendered on a regular basis in the field or in academia, the knowledge presented here is only made possible by rendering oneself open and vulnerable to encounters in the field. As readers, it behoves us to acknowledge the personal cost at which this knowledge is made available to us.

Another aspect of ethnographic research that is often suppressed is the role failures play in the creation and shaping of knowledge. In an age in which funding bodies want to know about expected results preferably before the project starts, the open-ended nature of fieldwork constitutes a considerable risk. Failure is not an option, or at least it is anathema to success in academia – or so the common perception goes. But as every ethnographer worth their salt knows, ethnography is just a long series of unfortunate events: failure to gain access, failure to gain the trust of gatekeepers, failure to be accepted as fieldworker/participant/friend, failure to perform according to taken-for-granted standards in the field, failure to understand what is at stake until it is too late; the list goes on. Despite this seemingly pessimistic view, we believe that failure is an essential part of fieldwork in the ethnomethodological sense: it is the failure of the ethnographer that creates a situation that forces participants to make explicit what happened and how things went wrong. The foreign body, in the broadest sense of the word, becomes the instrument that reveals how 'normality' is constructed. It is also the foreign body that becomes the target for 'normalisation': being physically corrected or shouted at, being excluded from proceedings, being shunned or joked about or rendered the material of countless anecdotes.

Guide to the chapters

In the second chapter, 'Serving Gender' by Marcello Francioni, it is service itself that becomes gendered, behind the counter of a gay bar in Tokyo's gay district. Although it is assumed that both customers and bar workers are sexually interested in men, the dynamics of service unfold around a masculinity/femininity binary. Ideal service at Eclipse, the bar Francioni worked at for almost a year, means allowing the customers to experience their masculinity by presenting a feminine, and therefore obedient, demeanour. The *miseko* strategically adopt linguistic gender presentations that would render them more feminine (using the personal pronoun *atashi* instead of *boku* or *ore*). The 'proper' gender presentation of staff would even be policed by the customers. In terms of space, too, gay bars create a homely atmosphere in which the master is the mama and the *miseko* act as surrogate daughters who are there to indulge the customer's every whim. The third element of the situational feminine gender of the gay bar experience is the sexually explicit banter, which often revolves around the real or imagined sex lives of the bar staff, who are presumed to be 'bottoms'. There are, however, important exceptions to this rule: Francioni documents how *miseko* who present a more butch masculinity get treated quite differently. Their gender presentation is less policed, but in line with gendered stereotypes they are assumed to be 'tops', bad listeners, and thus less in tune with other's desires.

Gay bar life as described by Francioni is less about liberation, or about shifting norms of gender, than it is about keeping up the power differential between customers, who after all pay for the service provided, and the service workers, who are expected to provide the emotional work to create a nurturing environment. The customer returns because of an increasing familiarity with the bar's personnel and style and the hope of recreating and increasing the indulgence he was granted previously.

The different perspectives of consumers and staff described by Francioni are also recognisable in several of the following chapters. In the chapter by Marta Fanasca, this is taken a step further: by training as a cross-dressing escort, Fanasca both became the object of her inquiry and the object of desire of those who booked dates with her. She describes in minute detail the process that she underwent to transform into a 'guy', from the haircut to the accoutrements such as binders to change her body shape, to masculine forms of language use and the creation of a masculine alter ego that corresponded to the fantasies of customers. This included forms of embodiment such as the use of a lower voice register and following a strict diet and exercise regime. Her descriptions of what happens during a 'date' shed a fascinating light on the construction of gender as a complex transaction: Fanasca quickly realised that her masculine gender presentation served as a foil for the clients' femininity and that both parties ended up deeply involved in re-creating romantic ideas of binary gender.

Unlike the hosts described by Takeyama (2016), cross-dressing escorts are forbidden to engage in sexual relationships with clients; the issue of drawing boundaries thus looms large. This requires delicate negotiations, during which the escort conspires to keep the fantasy of a future, more intimate, encounter alive in the mind of the client, so much so that the client becomes a regular customer and creates a steady stream of income for the escort. Here the temporal horizon of the transaction comes into sharp focus: the exchange of money may delimit the boundaries of the paid intimacy, but the fantasy and desire created extend beyond the commodified frame, with consequences that are again distributed unevenly in terms of power and dependency. The money flows to the successful purveyors of masculinity, while the clients sometimes end up with considerable debt. While male clients of hostess clubs can still put such entertainment on to corporate accounts (Allison 1994), female consumers bear the brunt of the financial burden and often find themselves in precarious situations as a result.

Even when it comes to the 'real thing' in terms of sex work, commodified experiences of intimacy have clearly demarcated boundaries, as Nicola Phillips argues in her chapter on the women who work for *Deadball*, a sex delivery service specialising in *busu* women (often a coded expression in Japan for chubby or middle-aged). With unprecedented access to the 'backstage' where the women on duty waited for customers, she informally interviewed 12 women in their 40s and 50s about their motives and the nature of the service they provide. The women working for *Deadball* cultivate a deliberately amateurish image that suggests the experience of intimacy provided is more authentic than a 'clinical' encounter with a professional sex worker. The authenticity of the connection is further supported by the fact that negotiations over the precise nature of the act (anything short of vaginal intercourse) are done by the back office on behalf of the workers, thus outside the frame of 'bounded authenticity'. What customers expect and what they pay for is not a polished and thus perhaps intimidating performance, but an experience of connection and closeness through relatability. Interestingly, the felt authenticity of the encounter is not diminished by the fact that clients pay the women directly.

While at *Deadball* it is the women who are providing the service, in the fan communities that emerge around pornography aimed at women, youthful men become the object of the female gaze, as Maiko Kodaka shows in her chapter. The titillating spectatorship of the fans initially suggests that gender roles are reversed, that male bodies and a kind of masculinity specifically performed for women become the object of female desire. Shared desire for the *eromen* creates a community of fans in which they can open up about their own perceived shortcomings and openly discuss sexual desires and experiences. But Kodaka also shows how the fandom creates a safe space in which fans who lack self-esteem can experience the thrill of being flattered and feeling feminine, thus recreating a disempowering notion of gender. What the *eromen* are paid for, then, are acts of 'giving gender' to the fans, who often interpret these acts as personal attention. Like Fanasca, Kodaka observes that the 'bounded authenticity' created by the fantasy space creates emotional attachments that tend to extend beyond the boundaries of the commodified experience and leads some of the fans to incur considerable debt in the process of repeating it.

Performances of a different kind are the subject of Robert Simpkins' contribution on gendered spaces of street music on the streets of Kōenji, West Tokyo. While at first glance the street musician's ethos seems to be defined by a search for authentic artistic expression, a closer analysis shows that in order to be successful one has to calibrate one's performance in ways that conform to police surveillance, neighbourhood noise awareness and public expectations. But street performance is not just a question of how to occupy a space, it is also a question of how to co-create the space in which to enjoy music in the first place, that is, the skill of turning random passers-by into an audience. While male performers often display a carefully cultivated carelessness, female street musicians are more stringently 'policed' by the public male gaze in ways that renders them more vulnerable. They thus negotiate the spaces of performance and interactions with the public in ways that solicit a non-threatening experience by taking into account the business of a station exit, the number of people on the street and their proximity to the police.

The final contribution, by Lyman Gamberton, takes us back to the original question of the work of gender in an everyday context. His project investigates how transgender individuals negotiate their everyday lives and future gender trajectories in light of the draconian gender reassignment law that enforces a conservative and stereotypical understanding of the gender binary and the gender/sex system. Starting from an auto-ethnographic account of how he managed his own gender presentation as a white trans man in a Japanese context, Gamberton describes the experiences of gendering and misgendering that his informants encounter in everyday life. He illustrates the many ways in which the gender binary haunts every attempt to free oneself from it, even in the most progressive of contexts. For example, it is often assumed in the trans community that trans men are interested in women, thus recreating a heteronormative idea of transitioning. These strictly binary parameters of transitioning are ultimately dictated by the state and transcend the everyday life of trans people. In this system, to refuse full medical transitioning is akin to renouncing one's claim to transgender identity. This is also where the ethnomethodological approach with its focus on everyday acts of doing gender reaches its limits: when it comes to structural inequalities, the micro-focus alone will not suffice.

As traditional notions of gender are interrogated and gender inequality is challenged, anthropology has shown that gender varies widely in different contexts. Conversely, links between gender and a biological understanding of sex are currently reinvigorated by the nascent neuroscience of gender. Gender thus remains a moving target and that is why its constructions and performances provide a rich and important field of analysis for the anthropology of Japan and beyond. The ethnographic work assembled here shows – for better or for worse – that 'femininity' and 'masculinity' remain salient ideals around which people create life and fantasy worlds. And although many of these fantasy worlds are accessible through monetary transactions, the source of their value remains social: it is to be found in the desires of others. This renders them profoundly human, despite the argument that all forms of commodification are essentially alienating. There is misery to be found in authentic human relations and a great deal of joy in the artificial paradises of commodified experience. It is our hope that this collection will inspire more research into the complex and fascinating thing we call the (gendered) human condition. The work of gender is never done.

References

Allison, Anne. 1994. *Nightwork: Sexuality, Pleasure and Corporate Masculinity in a Tokyo Hostess Club*. Chicago: University of Chicago Press.

Assmann, Stephanie. 2020. Gender and the law: Progress and remaining problems. *In* Jennifer Coates, Lucy Fraser and Mark Pendelton (eds), *The Routledge Companion to Gender and Japanese Culture*, 157–67. London; New York: Routledge.

Bardsley, Jan and Laura Miller. 2011. Manner and mischief: Introduction. *In* Jan Bardsley and Laura Miller (eds), *Manners and Mischief: Gender, Power, and Etiquette in Japan*, 1–28. Berkeley: University of California Press.

Bailey, Marlon M. 2013. *Butch Queens up in Pumps: Gender, Performance, and Ballroom Culture in Detroit*. Ann Arbor: University of Michigan Press.

Barthes, Roland. 1970. *L'empire des Signes*. Genève: Editions d'Art Albert Skira S.A.

Bernstein, Elizabeth. 2007. *Temporarily Yours: Intimacy, Authenticity and the Commerce of Sex*. Chicago: University of Chicago Press.

Butler, Judith. 1990. *Gender Trouble*. London; New York: Routledge.

———. 1991. Imitation and Gender Insubordination. *In* Diana Fuss (ed) *Inside/Out: Lesbian Theories, Gay Theories*, 13–31. London; New York: Routledge.

———. 1993. *Bodies that Matter*. London; New York: Routledge.

———. 2004. *Undoing Gender*. London; New York: Routledge.

Chapkis, Wendy. 1997. *Live Sex Acts: Women Performing Erotic Labor*. London; New York: Routledge.

Coyote, Ivan E. and Rae Spoon. 2014. *Gender Failure*. Vancouver, British Columbia: Arsenal Pulp Press.

Deacon, Chris. 2013. All the world's a stage: Herbivore boys and the performance of masculinity in contemporary Japan. *In* Brigitte Steger and Angelika Koch (eds), *Manga Girl seeks Herbivore Boy: Studying Japanese Gender at Cambridge*, 129–76. Wien: Lit Verlag.

Derrida, Jacques. 1981. *Dissemination*. Chicago: University of Chicago Press.

Desjarlais, Robert. 2003. *Sensory Biographies: Lives and Deaths among Nepal's Yolmo Buddhists*. Berkeley: University of California Press.

Federici, Silvia. 1975. *Wages against Housework*. Bristol: Falling Wall Press.

Fine, Cordelia. 2010. *Delusions of Gender: The Real Science behind Sex Differences*. London: Icon Books.

Garfinkel, Harold. 1967. *Studies in Ethnomethodology*. Malden, MA: Polity Press.

Giddens, Anthony. 1992. *The Transformation of Intimacy: Love, Sexuality and Eroticism in Modern Societies*. Cambridge: Polity.

Gide, André. 1930. *L'Immoraliste*. Paris: Mercure de France.

Goffman, Erving. 1979. *Gender Advertisements*. London: The Macmillan Press.

Hansen, Gitte Marianne. 2016. *Femininity, Self-harm and Eating Disorders in Japan: Navigating Contradiction in Narrative and Visual Culture*. New York and London: Routledge.

Hardt, Michael and Antonio Negri. 2000. *Empire*. Cambridge, MA: Harvard University Press.

Hochschild, Arlie R. 2012 [1983]. *The Managed Heart: Commercialization of Human Feeling*. Berkeley and London: University of California Press.

Isaka Maki. 2016. *Onnagata: A Labyrinth of Gendering in Kabuki Theater*. University of Washington Press.

Johnson, James Weldon. 1912. *The Autobiography of an Ex-Colored Man*. Boston: Sherman, French & Co.

Jolivet, Muriel. 2015. *Confidences du Japon*. Bordeaux: ELYTIS.

Kano Ayako. 2001. *Acting Like a Woman in Modern Japan: Theater, Gender and Nationalism*. New York: Palgrave.

Kessler, Suzanne and Wendy McKenna. 1978. *Gender: An Ethnomethodological Approach*. Chicago: University of Chicago Press.

Koch, Gabriele. 2020. *Healing Labor: Japanese Sex Work in the Gendered Economy*. Stanford: Stanford University Press.

Kondo, Dorinne K. 1990. *Crafting Selves: Power, Gender and Discourses of Identity in a Japanese Workplace*. Chicago: University of Chicago Press.

Kumada Yōko. 2017. *Sei-Fūzoku Sekai wo Ikiru 'Onna no ko' no Esunogurafi: SM/Kankeisei/'jiko' ga Tsumugu Mono* (trans. *A World as Woven by Sexual Play: An Ethnography of 'Onnanoko' or Female Workers in the Japanese Sex Industry*.) Tokyo: Akashi shoten.

Larsen, Nella. 1929. *Passing*. New York: Knopf.

Leiter, Samuel L. 2002. *Frozen Moments: Writings on Kabuki, 1966–2001*. Ithaca, NY: Cornell University Press.

——— 2017. Onnagata: A labyrinth of gendering in Kabuki theater, by Maki Isaka. (Review) *Journal of Japanese Studies* 43 (2): 423–27.

Leupp, Gary. 1997. *Male Colors: The Construction of Homosexuality in Tokugawa Japan*. Berkeley: University of California Press.

Lunsing, Wim. 2001. *Beyond Common Sense: Sexuality and Gender in Contemporary Japan*. London: Routledge.

Macdonald, Cameron L. and Carmen Sirianni. 1996. The service society and the changing experience of work. *In* Cameron L. Macdonald and Carmen Sirianni (eds), *Working in the Service Society*, 1–28. Philadelphia: Temple University Press.

Macnaughtan, Helen. 2020. Gender at the workplace. *In* Jennifer Coates, Lucy Fraser and Mark Pendelton (eds), *The Routledge Companion to Gender and Japanese Culture*, 168–78. London and New York: Routledge.

Maruta Kōji. 2001. *Dare Ga Dare Ni Nani wo Uru No Ka? Enjokōsai Ni Miru Sei/Ai/Comyunikēshon* (trans. *Who is Selling What to Whom? Sex, Love and Communication as seen through Assisted Dating*.) Osaka: Kansaigakuin daigaku shuppankai.

Miller, Daniel. 2009. *Stuff*. Cambridge: Polity.

Mitchell, Gregory. 2016. *Tourist Attractions: Performing Race and Masculinity in Brazil's Sexual Economy*. Chicago: University of Chicago Press.

Mochigi. 2019. *Gei-Fūzoku No Mochigi-San* (trans. *Mr. Mochigi from the Gay Brothel*) Tokyo: Kadokawa.

Morinaga Maki. 2002. The gender of *onnagata* as the imitating imitated: Its historicity, performativity and involvement in the circulation of femininity. *Positions: East Asia Cultures Critique* 10(2): 245–84.

Nakamura, Karen and Hisako Matsuo. 2003. Female masculinity and fantasy spaces: Transcending genders in Takarazuka theater and Japanese popular culture. *In* James E. Roberson and Nobue Suzuki (eds), *Men and Masculinities in Contemporary Japan: Dislocating the Salaryman Doxa*, 59–76. London; New York: Routledge.

Nakamura Miri. 2015. The cult of happiness: Maid, housewife and affective labor in Higuchi Ichiyō's 'Warekara'. *The Journal of Japanese Studies* 41 (1): 45–78.

Ogasawara Yuko. 1998. *Office Ladies and Salaried Men: Power, Gender and Work in Japanese Companies*. Berkeley: University of California Press.

Ortner, Sherry B. 1974. Is female to male as nature is to culture? *In* M. Z. Rosaldo and L. Lamphere (eds), *Woman, Culture and Society*, 68–87. Stanford: Stanford University Press.

Ortner, Sherry B. and Harriet Whitehead. 1981. *Sexual Meanings: The Cultural Construction of Gender and Sexuality*. Cambridge: Cambridge University Press.

Ozawa-de Silva, Chikako. 2010. Shared death: Self, sociality and internet group suicide in Japan. *Transcultural Psychiatry* 47 (3): 392–418.

Paoletti, Jo B. 2012. *Pink and Blue: Telling the Boys from the Girls in America*. Bloomington: Indiana University Press.

Prasad, Monica. 1999. The morality of market exchange: Love, money and contractual justice. *Sociological Perspectives* 42(2): 181–214.

Robertson, Jennifer. 1998. *Takarazuka: Sexual Politics and Popular Culture in Modern Japan*. Berkeley: University of California Press.

Rogers, Mary F. 1992. They all were passing: Agnes, Garfinkel, and Company. *Gender and Society* 6 (2): 169–191.

Rosenberger, Nancy R. 1992. Introduction. *In* Nancy R. Rosenberger (ed.), *Japanese Sense of Self*, 1–20. Cambridge University Press.

Rubin, Gayle. 1975. The traffic in women: Notes on the 'political economy' of sex. *In* Rayna R. Reiter (ed.), *Toward an Anthropology of Women*. New York and London: Monthly Review Press, 157–210.

Schalow, Paul Gordon. 1990. Introduction. In *The Great Mirror of Male Love*, 1–46. Stanford: Stanford University Press.

Shively, Donald H. 2002. Bakufu versus Kabuki. *In* Samuel L. Leiter (ed.), *A Kabuki Reader: History and Performance*, 33–59. Armonk, N.Y: East Gate Books.

Steel, Jill. 2019. Introduction: Changing women's and men's lives in Japan. *In* Jill Steel (ed.), *Beyond the Gender Gap in Japan*, 1–24. Ann Arbor: University of Michigan Press.

Stickland, Leonie. 2004. *Gender Gymnastics: Performers, Fans and Gender Issues in the Takarazuka Revue of Contemporary Japan*. PhD thesis submitted to Murdoch University, Perth.

——— 2008. *Gender Gymnastics: Performing and Consuming Japan's Takarazuka Revue*. Melbourne: Trans Pacific Press.

Sugiyama Lebra, Takie. 2004. *The Japanese Self in Cultural Logic*. Honolulu: University of Hawaii Press.

Takeyama Akiko. 2016. *Staged Seduction: Selling Dreams in a Tokyo Host Club*. Stanford: Stanford University Press.

Thorne, Barrie. 1993. *Gender Play: Girls and Boys at School*. New Brunswick, N.J: Rutgers University Press.

Ward, Jane. 2010. Gender labor: Transmen, femmes and the collective work of transgression. *Sexualities* 13(2): 236–54.

West, Candace and Don H. Zimmerman. 1987. Doing gender. *Gender & Society* 1(2): 125–51.

Wissinger, Elizabeth. 2007. Modelling a way of life: Immaterial and affective labour in the fashion modelling industry. *Ephemera* 7(1): 250–269.

Yanagisako, Sylvia. 2012. Immaterial and industrial labor: On false binaries in Hardt and Negri's trilogy. *Focaal: Journal of Global and Historical Anthropology* 64: 16–23.

Yano, Christine R. 2003. *Tears of Longing: Nostalgia and the Nation in Japanese Popular Song*. Cambridge, Mass.: Harvard University Press.

Yuasa Yasuo. 1990. *Shintairon: Tōyōteki Shinshinron to Gendai* (trans. *Discourse of the Body: The Eastern Mind-Body Theory and the Present.*) Tokyo: Kōdansha.

Zelizer, Viviana A. 2000. The purchase of intimacy. *Law & Social Inquiry* 25(3): 817–48.

CHAPTER 2

Serving Gender

Performing Gender Roles at a Gay Bar in Tokyo's Shinjuku Ni-chōme

Marcello Francioni

'Sometimes I don't know whether I'm supposed to be a boyfriend or a mother to my customers...'

My manager, Tazu, confessed this to me one weeknight, when I visited a more than usually deserted Zenith bar to interview him. As he paused for a second, all I could hear was the music in the background. It was loud, almost deafening, compared to the quiet conversation we were having, as if the bar wanted to show us that it was ready for a busy night of drinking, chatting and general shenanigans.

Almost six months had passed since I started working as a bar help (*miseko*) at Zenith, a tiny gay bar on the fifth floor of a large ex-residential six-storey building on the corner of one of the main crossroads that punctuated the compact landscape of Tokyo's most popular queer nightlife area, Shinjuku Ni-chōme. Zenith bar had ten employees, a high number considering its minuscule size, but only a handful were regularly helping Tazu – customers addressed him as *mama*, 'mother', or *masutā*, 'master' – behind the counter. For a period, I was one of them, alongside assistant manager (*chi-mama*) Tatsuki and fellow bar helps Katsu and Yagi. Tazu had accepted me at Zenith aware that it would be for the sake of my research. Although he seemed supportive of my endeavour to learn about the culture of Ni-chōme, I often got the impression that he did not fully understand the point of my fieldwork. Most crucially, he did not understand why I found gay bars in Tokyo of any interest. He remarked with a sigh that I should focus on more beautiful, worthwhile aspects of traditional Japanese culture.

Nevertheless, most gay bars in Ni-chōme, Zenith included, have a way of serving and a style of social drinking that are considered specifically Japanese;

in fact, my interlocutors called these venues Japanese-style bars (*nihon-shiki bā*) and described the bar scene as a sub-culture (*sabu-karuchā*) with a history of its own. At Japanese-style gay bars, the preferred way of drinking involves the purchase of a bottle of spirit (usually Japanese barley vodka, called *shōchū*) to be kept at the bar and accessed during each visit for a set price (*setto ryōkin*), rather than ordering one drink at a time, as is usual at Western-style cocktail bars (*shotto bā*, lit. 'shot bar'). On top of that, Japanese-style bars have developed a sophisticated etiquette for serving. Staff members are encouraged to toast and drink with the customers and are required to entertain them across the counter (unlike hostess bars, most Japanese-style gay bars do not allow one-to-one service at the table), often for several hours, through sustained conversation, with the support of the karaoke machine and several drinks. The first time we ever talked, Tazu claimed he chose me because I represented an interesting addition to Zenith bar, keeping him from getting bored with the routine and keeping the customers interested in the bar.

The night Tazu confessed to me that he didn't know whether he should be a boyfriend or a mother to his customers, we were talking about customers and the best way of dealing with them. Maybe because there was no-one else at Zenith at the time, he sounded more patient than usual. I could hear a note of compassion in the otherwise unfazed tone of his voice – he had clearly perceived my difficulties in navigating a space so new to me and my confusion concerning customers' ever-changing and unexpected requests, which went far beyond serving drinks and chatting. Some wanted their drinks refilled, fast; some wanted me to make them laugh; others wanted me to play seduction games, give them compliments or show them some skin; some, finally, wanted me to listen to their stories and simply nod.

I believe that Tazu made the confession to me because he wanted to share some of the hardships he believed to be part of his work – and at that point, of mine, too. His words stayed with me for months and helped me make sense of a vital part of service in nightlife – one which, no matter how many customers and service professionals I talked to, I had the hardest time mastering. What represented successfully delivered service? Was it about selling drinks, a relationship of diffused mother-like care, the promise of so erotic involvement from a boyfriend – or all the above, depending on the situation? Moreover, on what basis was I, as well as all the other staff members, assigned such roles?

Figure 2.1 – A view of the building where Zenith bar was in Shinjuku Ni-chōme.

When Tazu decided to let me go and fired me, right before the end of my fieldwork at Zenith bar, he confessed to a customer in my presence that many aspects of my training had not been brought to completion. I could clearly hear a mix of sadness and disappointment in his voice. My position as a half-baked bar help stemmed from my difficulty in adjusting to the way my body was constantly scrutinised, ranked, sexualised and commodified, and to the way my words and actions behind the counter had to live up to the expectations built around how my physicality was being perceived.

For several reasons – my origins, my background, the fact that my immersion in Tokyo's gay bar life was possibly too short for me to find ease amidst the many dynamics already at work – I initially resisted performing the role I was being assigned, a highly gendered and sexualised one about which none of the staff members (including Tazu) had much say vis-à-vis the customers. Inspired by this experience, this chapter explores how commodifiable binary gender and sexual roles are combined and projected onto three aspects of staff-customer interactions in order to shape pleasant experiences for customers at Japanese-style gay bars in Ni-chōme. These aspects encompass the perception around the bodily presentation of staff members; their use of gendered language; and their participation in sexual innuendo. Ultimately, by looking at the frames of reference, what I call the fantasies, deployed to rank staff members and guide the performance of service, I would like to explore the relationship between participants in Japanese-style gay bar culture and the structures of gendered power at work in Japan at large, whether that be one of resistance or complicit reproduction. The data presented have been collected through semi-structured interviews and participatory observation while working as a bar help as part of my fieldwork in Tokyo from September 2016 to September 2017.

Service as Endless Availability

No account of Japanese-style gay bars, or of Japanese nightlife (*mizu shōbai*) at large, can avoid a discussion of the service industry and its main feature, availability. The phrase 'service industry' (*sābisu gyōkai*) was frequently applied by my staff interlocutors to describe their line of work. Out of the officially estimated total workforce of 66 million in Japan, 44 million are registered as employees of private companies in the tertiary sector. If we add public sector employees we reach 71% of Japan's workforce (almost 47 million). Although the service industry is generally understood as a synonym for the tertiary sector in Anglophone contexts, in Japan the term 'service industry' refers to a smaller section inside the tertiary sector, in which there is face-to-face interaction with clients or customers in hospitality and retail, as opposed to white-collar office work. It would be a stretch indeed to assume that almost half of the Japanese living population is employed to directly interface with the remaining half.[1] Service (*sābisu* or *sekkyaku*, lit. 'dealing with customers face-to-face') is a key concept in contemporary Japanese economy and I will start with its definition to tease out some points directly relating to my fieldwork. The Digital Daijisen Dictionary states:

Sābisu (service)

[name] (often verbalized)

1. Spending one's energies for the sake of others. [...] 'During the weekend I take care of my family (*kazoku sābisu*).'

2. In sales (*shōbai*), to make the customer welcome (*motenasu*). Also, the several kinds of acts of care performed for the customer [...].

---

1 Data source: www.stat.go.jp/english/data/shugyou/pdf/sum2017.pdf and Table 1 www.stat.go.jp/data/roudou/sokuhou/tsuki/index.html (last visited 13 July 2020).

3. In sales, the act of giving discounts or adding free items (*o-make*) to a purchase. [...].[2]

Firstly, the household appears along the workplace as environments where service is performed, through the expressions *katei-sābisu* ('devotion to one's family', or 'family-servicing') and *sābisu-seishin* (lit. 'spirit for service', or 'attentiveness').[3] Definitions of *sābisu* summon a mixture of work(place) and house(work), making servicing others (*motenasu*) an all-encompassing practice of everyday life in Japan.

Second, point three introduces *o-make*, a sales strategy by which the purchaser gets more for what he is paying. Thus, at Japanese-style gay bar customers pay a 'cover charge' (*setto ryōkin*) for seating, bottomless nibbles, use of the karaoke machine, access to their kept bottle of alcohol or one drink and different mixers to choose from (mostly cold tea – see Ishida 2006; Sunagawa 2015). Since no breakdown of the charges is provided, customers need not bargain in making requests that go beyond being served drinks, and they are rarely turned down. All these points highlight the fact that service in Japan centres around the display (and commodification) of one's availability vis-à-vis the needs of others, even the anticipation of those needs. In terms of the level of availability, moreover, the line between 'customer' and 'family' is often blurred. As Amy Borovoy states when discussing the co-dependent relationships of alcoholic Japanese men and their indulgent wives, 'service entails a great deal of attention to detail. Attentiveness is seen as a virtue and obliviousness as rude and selfish, particularly in women' (2005: 97).

If service entails an all-encompassing availability toward the customer that tends to blur the line between the domestic and public, we might think service is boundless. However, limits to service exist and they are influenced by the sector at large, the laws at work and the worker's level of commitment. As Tazu once said to me, as long as no sex and violence is involved the rest is up for negotiation at Zenith bar. Under the current Japanese legislation on sex work,[4] in fact, sexual interaction between staff and customers is strictly prohibited at drinking venues (*nomiya*) such as Japanese-style gay bars.

---

2 kotobank.jp/word/サービス-186588.
3 www.weblio.jp/content/サービス.
4 *Fūzoku-eigyō-tō no Kisei oyobi Gyōmu no Tekiseika-tō ni kansuru Hōritsu*, often shortened as *Fūeihō* (1948).

Figure 2.2 – An example of what customers get with their "cover charge".

There is no correct way to deliver service, I was told many times by nightlife professionals. Since every customer had different needs, no step-by-step guide to service existed. Nonetheless, service providers employed recurring strategies. Through the consumption of alcohol, customers seemed to gravitate towards staff members displaying a seemingly unshakable availability and willingness to deliver the best service possible. Being available entailed numerous small acts being continuously reiterated by the staff in order to create and maintain a regime of 'total care' (Borovoy 2005: 82) whereby the customer feels special, if not spoiled, as he would be by his mother or boyfriend. In Japan, in fact, intensely attentive care is connected to mothers and wives in the household but not to fathers, as well as to romantic partners performing a caring role, who therefore are seen as mother-like. As I was often reminded, alcohol is nothing but an excuse for service at gay bars, since most customers choose to drink either draught beer or the same cheap brand of *shōchū*. Rather, customers seemed interested in interacting with the staff and with one another. In fact, due to its traditional role in fostering homosociality in Japan (see Christensen 2014), alcohol may be considered the only constant in service.

At Zenith, some customers wanted to be entertained by the staff, whereas others wanted the staff to simply be present as they entertained themselves. According to Tazu, service in nightlife boiled down to the concept of *tanoshimaseru*. As a causative of the verb *tanoshimu* (to have a good time), it implies both 'to (actively) make someone have a good time' and, more saliently here, 'enabling someone to have a good time'. The constant, therefore, was not the content, but the modality through which service is offered. Unsolicited acts of availability such as placing an ashtray in front of a customer who was known to smoke even before he takes his cigarettes out were considered signs of good service. Similarly valued was keeping in store, for instance, a frequent customer's favourite nibbles, silently providing a tall glass of water or serving instant noodles to a drunk customer, remembering a regular's mixer of choice, or lining up a customer's go-to duets on the karaoke machine. These acts were paired with other acts of psychological availability that pertained to the entertainment and the validation of the customer. Singing together and telling funny stories pertain to the former. Examples of the latter were flattering, flirting and letting customers know that the staff was always on their side and ready to listen, no matter how immature, unreasonable and unproductive their stance might appear.

Because of the rhetoric of committed availability in Japanese nightlife, the ways in which service providers offered themselves, their help, positive affirmation, voices and bodies, engendered temporary relationships characterised by heavily polarised power dynamics, where one party's role was to ensure that the other party was having a merry experience, thus channelling the 'spirit of service'. Customers in Japan are considered to be temporarily occupying a higher status and must be treated with utmost regard because of their interest in the venue and their economic investment. When talking to them, the honorific register (*keigo*) is the preferential mode of interaction. As the Japanese saying has it, the customer is a deity. In the case of Japanese-style gay bars, customers also differentiated themselves on a socio-economic level. There was a significantly higher proportion of university graduates among customers than among service providers, and occupationally most customers identified (either concretely or aspirationally; see Cook 2016) with the image of the Japanese salaryman – a full-time employee with a life-long contract at a private company.

The Gay Salaryman Doxa and the Pyramid of Desirability

With the high expectations surrounding service, one of my biggest struggles in the field was understanding the unfixed nature of the service sought by customers and honing the skills required of service providers to navigate the power dynamics at work. Here I wish to focus on one of these power configurations, namely gender, and on its role in service at Japanese-style gay bars.

If we were to attempt a tentative definition of gender, this might go something like this: Gender (like race) is an interactional mode that creates unequal power dynamics among bodies by leveraging specific biological traits (i.e. sexual organs or skin colour) as a source for differentiation in order to value and rank said bodies. The power imbalance generated by such ranking is reinforced by the expectations around the way bodies should act, talk, dress, move and sexually engage because of that very configuration.

Successfully 'doing gender' (West and Zimmerman 1987) requires a skill set that allows individuals to occupy specific subject and object positions (Boellstorff 2003). They learn to carry their bodies through the world, talk and move in a way that attempts to satisfy both them and their surroundings, even when it feeds into a pre-existing system of oppression that does not fully benefit them. Every small action, word or piece of adornment is as essential as the very ideal people try to model themselves on, and behind every movement or word lies the threat of failing at one's gender and revealing the ultimately fabricated nature of gender and the fragility of individuals' sense of self – what Judith Butler (1990) describes as 'performativity'.

At bars like Zenith, the positions emerging through service were not a reflection of the lived experiences of the interactants and did not carry as deep an existential weight. Quite the contrary: my interlocutors were often openly dismissive of the way in which staff members, in particular, personally identified. In fact, in order to fit into the business model of gay bars – which involves the provision of commodified merriment for the customers – the positions of staff members had to be bent into more static roles to be swiftly assigned and performed within a single interaction. Thus, once they had paid their cover charge customers reserved for themselves the right to classify and rank the bodies of staff members based on their presentation, as I will discuss below, and to require them to act, talk and engage in sexual innuendo accordingly. Zenith's customers, Tazu revealed, came to the bar because they wanted to *drink a lot and sing a lot*. And that is what they did. Having a good time and interacting with people seemed the main driving force bringing customers to Zenith, rather than meeting new romantic or sexual partners – something they could more comfortably find on the many online dating applications available to gay men in Japan. Whether in their everyday lives customers choose their romantic or sexual partners in such a rigid fashion is in fact beyond discussion here. If anything, it was difficult to observe customers' real-life tastes because, once in a relationship, most tended to desert the bar to enjoy life as a couple.

In order to understand how these roles worked, we need to know the *how* and the *what*, namely how roles were assigned and what their content or frame of reference was. Roles were cast along two strict binary axes (the *how*), the former being that of gender presentation, *masculine* vis-à-vis *non-masculine* and the latter being that of sexual role, *top* (*tachi*, the penetrative role during intercourse; lit. 'sword') vis-à-vis *bottom* (*neko*, the receptive role; lit. 'cat'). Sexual roles were assigned based on the appearance and gendered aura emanated by an individual, rather than on their actual tastes and experiences. The two axes were always paired up so that masculine was necessarily top, non-masculine was necessarily bottom; and so that masculine/top was necessarily romantically and sexually interested in non-masculine/bottom and vice versa. The casting of these roles onto the staff then allowed customers to occupy the diametrically opposite role in the binary. In a way, this may be considered a queer version of Butler's 'heterosexual matrix' (1990: 151), a heteronormative matrix of sorts. Ultimately, the assignment of these roles created a *pyramid of desirability*. Those at the top enjoyed the most freedom of movement, action and speech, and the least amount of labour was required of them. The closer we get to the bottom, the more individuals are controlled in their movements, actions and speech and the greater is the amount of labour required of them. Customers at Japanese-style gay bars always occupy the top position by virtue of the fact that they are paying for service, regardless of whether they are masculine or non-masculine. Always one step below the customers, staff members were instead assigned fixed roles and ranked following rigid binary gender lines. As I will show, masculinity was identified with prestige and non-masculinity was attributed a lack of prestige that had to be compensated for through more labour. It goes without saying that this pyramid of desirability reflects the microcosm of Japanese-style gay bars in Tokyo and other urban centres in Japan. Beyond gender presentation, sexual positions and language, other coordinates such as nationality, ethnicity and race may be included (see Baudinette 2016) in an attempt to better understand Ni-chōme and the entertainment business in Japan at large.

I should explain the use of the term *non-masculine* here, instead of *feminine, effeminate* or *femme*, as opposed to masculine. There are two reasons for using this term: one is ethnographic and one historical. On the one hand, during my fieldwork, individuals who were assigned a non-masculine role at Zenith actively resisted identification as feminine or femme. They lacked female genitalia, to begin with. They did not present as women and they reacted negatively to any association between themselves and womanhood, a trend that Ishida and Murakami (2006) also noticed in Japanese gay media starting from the 1970s. The link between biological sex, gender identification and sexual role was so strongly felt that a customer of Zenith presenting as what in an Anglophone context could be called 'trans-femme' refused to be labelled as woman/feminine – the term used, *josei*, carries both meanings in Japanese, just as the Chinese character for 'sex' and 'gender' (*sei*) is the same. He would remind the customers around him that, although he only performed the receptive role in sex and presented in a feminine way, he still possessed male genitalia and therefore was not a woman.

Non-masculine-performing staff and customers were jokingly or derogatorily labelled *onē* ('fairy', 'nelly'), *okama* ('fag') or *onna* ('woman'), all terms linking non-masculinity to sexual receptiveness, while masculine-performing individuals were described using terms such as *yarashii* ('dirty-looking'), *otokorashii* ('manly') or simply *otoko* ('man'). On the other hand, as Pflugfelder (1999) has shown, Japan has a long history of male-centred conceptualizations of gender and sexuality, starting from the pre-modern era. In this context, male/masculine has been contrasted with non-masculine genders, such as woman and young males (*wakashū*), in a binary opposition that has always included one masculine party, and in which each party has a specific sexual role to play. Individuals classed as 'masculine' performed the penetrative role, while those classed as 'non-masculine' played the receptive role.

What then was the frame of reference (the *what*) for the attribution of roles? What fantasy, what agreed-upon 'story' about what it means to be masculine or non-masculine in Japan infused the roles and oriented how bodies were ranked at Zenith bar along the pyramid of desirability that I have suggested was in operation there? Unexpectedly, my interlocutors' most frequent reference for their interactions inside the bar was the hegemonic conceptualization of gender that characterised the era of the Japanese economic miracle until the burst of the economic bubble (1960s–1990s). This pervasive fantasy, labelled by Romit Dasgupta (2003) 'salaryman doxa', dictates that the ideal man (corresponding to the masculine role at the bar) is the main breadwinner for his nuclear family and is specifically identified as a 'salaryman'. The ideal woman (corresponding to the non-masculine role at the bar) is a full-time housewife in charge of childrearing. The ideal man is of few words; his movements are limited and he does not express many emotions. The ideal woman is talkative, emotional and constantly moves around. Inside the household, the ideal man is taken care of and is the object of attention, while the ideal woman takes care and gives attention. Inside the household, sex is geared toward procreation; therefore, the salaryman seeks to be taken care of sexually outside the household, as an act of consumption, at venues where he can purchase the company of a flirtatious girlfriend (in a hostess bar) or sexual release *per se* (in a massage parlour, *sōpurando*). This rigid binary division of spaces (man belongs inside the office, woman inside the home or the bar) and distribution of labour (man should be served, while woman serves) rewarded lifestyles that revolved around rigid heteronormative and reproductive aspirations, while other life-paths, such as single-parent households, full-time participation in the work-force for women and, clearly, non-straight relationships, were silenced.

The literature on gender in Japan has long stressed these idiosyncrasies around men's and women's expected roles in society and it was indeed also reflected in the lived experience either of the customers of the Zenith bar or of Japanese citizens at large. From the women's liberation movement of the 1970s (Rosenberger 2001; Lebra 2007) to women's mass entry into the white-collar workforce in the 1980s, the gender segregation of labour never perfectly matched the idealised gender roles promulgated by the Japanese nation-state and the corporate-industrial sector. In fact, the presence of women as a non-regulated workforce outside the household propped up Japan's economy at various critical historical moments, both in wartime and during the economic miracle. However, at the Zenith bar there seemed to be an attachment – or perhaps it was a nostalgia? – for these idealised gender relations, despite the fact that these gender relations were actually extremely fragile and outdated, especially after the bursting of the economic bubble (Roberson and Suzuki 2005; Gill 2015). This attachment seems rather ironic given that these gender relations did not seem to directly benefit the patrons of a gay bar like Zenith.

It is clear that the fantasy around gender roles continues to carry considerable power and that it shapes the subjectivities of women in Japan. It limits their access to the workplace and their prospects of building durable careers (Kondo 2009), affecting their perception of what they can and should achieve, since the expectations around their role even outside the household unfailingly cast them as providers of motherly care to the point of reproducing family-like dynamics of indulgence, or *amae* (Kumagai 1981) – so much so that Michiko Asai describes Japan as a country of 'children who depend on and yearn for maternal love and nurturance' (1990: 868; also see Yoda 2000).

The customers of Zenith reflected these same expectations of their own roles. A same-sex-attracted, male-bodied customer at Zenith bar would, for example, state with dreamy eyes that his ideal man was the stereotypical Japanese 'dominant husband' (*teishu kanpaku*), thus placing himself in the role of subservient housewife – and the staff had to pick up on that information in order to deliver the service best suiting his needs. That meant finding the best match to perform for the customer in this binary, heteronormative nostalgic fantasy of Japanese gender relations. This someone had to tick three boxes – bodily presentation, language use and sexual interaction. He had to look the part, that is, his bodily presentation had to read as masculine according to the fantasy. He also had to talk the talk, that is, not use (hyper) feminine language. Finally, he had to engage in sexual innuendo, playing the part of someone who takes the penetrative role in sex (top).

In the next three sections I will explore these three realms – bodily presentation, language and sexual innuendo – and their specific points of reference inside the world of the gay salaryman doxa. These are: the divide between *gachimuchi* (burly) and non-*gachimuchi* body types; Japanese language ideology and the use of the dialect of Japanese-style gay bars, known as *onē-kotoba* (lit. 'fairy speech'); and finally, the image of the hostess as sexual temptress.

The Consequences of the Body

Tazu knew that a balanced ratio of masculine-performing to non-masculine-performing staff members would be the easiest bet to satisfy Zenith's customers and provide them with the ideal boyfriend material, so he kept that in mind during the hiring process. The first step toward ensuring that the staff inhabited the right binary gender and sexual roles was to find staff members whose bodily presentation (frame, hairstyle, clothing style, mannerisms) would be easily read; and who could perform well as either masculine or as non-masculine.

Around the same time I started working at Zenith bar, Tazu had just hired another bar help, called Katsu. He was a burly but extremely placid man in his early thirties whose company and understated service style customers seemed to enjoy. Customers started commenting on his impassible calm so often that Tazu gave him the nick-name of Daibutsu ('Big Buddha'). Both physically and in the way he dealt with customers, Katsu resembled another more experienced member of staff at Zenith, who was called Yagi. As far as body type went, both Katsu and Yagi were referred to and described themselves as *gachimuchi*. Among Japanese gay men this term refers to a solid-looking man, neither slim nor fat, similar to a rugby player type in the Euro–American context. Katsu's hair was always buzzcut and Yagi's was shaved, and both had some facial hair. Their clothing style featured baggy jeans or joggers, hoodies, plain T-shirts, sneakers, few if any accessories, backpacks as bags and mountain-wear jackets (although neither hiked). Their style was not the glamourous, beautified image of the host, not afraid of waxing, perfumes and make up (Miller 2006; Takeyama 2010), that heterosexual women in contemporary Japan seemed to find desirable. Rather it referenced an older image of masculinity, displaying the burly roughness and scruffiness of a construction worker (*tobi*) or of a sportsman, someone with untouched body hair and who smelt like a male (*osu*; see Mackintosh 2009). It was hardly an uncommon style, as most gay men in the area were either sporting it or were attracted to it – a linguist would call it unmarked. It was so common, in fact, that in Ni-chōme the phrase *ikanimo-kei* (lit. 'He's-clearly-[gay]-style') was used to describe gay men who adopted it.

Both Katsu and Yagi were quiet characters. Their movements were slow and limited behind the counter. However, Tazu would not scold them for this, and he did not insist that they be faster or sharper, or that they perform more than one task simultaneously. During the farewell night for his 'retirement' from nightlife (*sotsugyō*, lit. 'graduation'), Yagi sat on the stool behind the counter for most of the night serving drinks and chatting, a cigarette hanging from his lips. The customers did not show any sign of concern; indeed, for hours they admired him and showered him with compliments about how masculine (*otokorashii*) he looked. Following the binary distribution of sex

Figure 2.3 – Katsu behind the counter at Zenith bar.

and gender, Katsu's and Yagi's bodily presentations and their static working style revealed that they were inhabiting the masculine role. The expectations around their role behind the counter were coupled with assumptions regarding their sexual preference, as I will explore later. Their penetrative role in sex was a given they never challenged.

On the other hand, the rest of Zenith's regular staff during my fieldwork – that is, Tazu, Tatsuki and I – did not fit into Katsu and Yagi's *gachimuchi* type. None of us had a sturdy frame; we were either slim or petitely framed. Our clothing included more variation and experimentation with cross-gendered clothing and make-up. Tazu and Tatsuki did drag in their professional lives, so their facial hair came and went, as it did for me. Customers expected the three of us to be especially cheerful and chatty, the life of the party. When my energy was low, Tazu would scold me fiercely for bringing down the level of service. Customers would urge Tazu, Tasuki and me to make them laugh and would complain loudly if one of us was not bubbly enough.

The three of us used dynamic hand gestures and facial expressions to emphasise our emotional reactions. When laughing, Tazu would not just laugh; he would cover his mouth with both hands while bursting into a laugh, his eyes wide open with surprise, akin to the way Japanese women are expected to (over)react in social settings. When annoyed or frustrated, Tazu would also amplify that state and would act like a stereotypically short-tempered old man from a TV comedy skit (*iraira oyaji*), shouting furiously at the bar helps and throwing things around. Whenever a customer bought a bottle to keep at the bar, Tazu would urge me to thank them by shouting as loudly as possible, so that the whole bar would hear over the music and the chatter.

Our movements had to be swift and precise, we were supposed to multi-task and to always be moving even in what was a tiny working space. Once, while I was washing the glasses that piled up with alarming speed, Tazu and a couple of customers commented that I should do that quickly so as to resume regular service immediately, all the while keeping the conversations going and making the least amount of noise. Seeing me slightly unsure about how to move during my very first shift, a customer got frustrated and dryly commented to Tazu that I looked too idle (*hima-sō da na*). Tazu defended me, saying I was only doing what I could for the moment. That was the last time he defended me. From the following shift on, he expected me to quickly learn the ropes and how to perform my (non-masculine) role. Finally, during my farewell party, I spent the night incessantly entertaining the customers, chatting, singing karaoke, thanking them and taking pictures with them. I even felt that it was necessary for me to come up with a stunt of sorts and wore a vintage white hospital gown for the customers to sign. As non-masculine-performing staff members, Tazu, Tatsuki and I were being sexually typecast by customers (and by Tazu) as sexually passive, regardless of our actual preferences.

The way in which bodies presented themselves and were interpreted and the way members of staff interacted with customers through language and sexual innuendo were an essential part of gendered service at Zenith, but that did not imply in any simplistic way that any service provider was equally required or able to successfully perform both masculine and non-masculine roles in response to a customer's request. Bodies like those of Katsu and Yagi, for example, were more susceptible to being marked and inscribed as masculine; therefore, as staff members, they were assigned the masculine role through interaction with customers seeking a match to their own non-masculine persona – and vice-versa with masculine-performing customers seeking a non-masculine match (Kodaka in this volume).

Ultimately, serving gender at Zenith required service providers to tap into their common knowledge (*jōshiki*) of Ni-chōme-specific codes and mainstream Japanese discourses around gender, to adapt to the gender and sexual role they were asked to perform while interacting with the customers in their exterior appearance, in their movements and in their words. If staff members managed to create a cycle whereby, upon having their bodily presentations and mannerisms read by the customers as masculine or non-masculine, they matched the expectations that were generated with 'correct' behaviour, immediately generating positive feedback for following these shared standards, their service could be considered successful.

Masculine- and non-masculine-performing staff members were expected to orient their whole working behaviour following their gendered fantasy, rather than simply adjusting the amount and intensity of their spoken interactions and speed of their movements. Masculine-performing service providers were expected to carry out the same amount of practical serving, minus the rush – that is, to display the same level of material availability as non-masculine ones by pouring drinks, emptying ashtrays, opening bottles. Nonetheless, the expectation for their psychological availability to be integrated into their work – what Arlie Hochschild (2012) termed *emotional labour* – was clearly lower compared to the expectation in relation to non-masculine-performing staff. Tazu reinforced this by claiming that 'top' (i.e. masculine) staff members were bad listeners, as they wanted to talk over the customers. On the other hand, bottom (i.e. non-masculine) members were better active listeners – just like a woman would be, Tazu claimed – and knew how to give good advice. I have never seen any customer asking Katsu and Yagi for advice, while countless times Tazu and Tatsuki were asked to listen to often convoluted dilemmas and offer some help. Masculine-performing staff members could afford to actively engage with the customers to a lesser extent.

Often Tazu confessed that he dreamed of managing a bar whose staff only consisted of handsome but quiet masculine-performing bar helps to whom customers would be drawn. Their masculine bodily presentation, backed up by low expectations around psychological availability, would be a guarantee of a pleasant enough experience (*tanoshimaseru* – an actively passive stance) to keep customers satisfied. Non-masuline-presenting staff members, by contrast, were expected to make themselves appealing by compensating for their non-masculine bodily presentation, language use and sexual role. The fact that they were required to be always actively engaging, listening and conversing with the customers, and emphasizing their emotional stance behind the counter, pointed to the fact that their presence in itself was not enough. They needed to actively make the experience pleasant (*tanoshimaseru* as a passively active stance).

Talk the talk

It wasn't just looking the part that mattered: the roles at Zenith bar also had to fit into the gender fantasy at play linguistically. In this section I will look at the relationship between language and service. I will focus firstly on the role of first-person pronouns and end-phrase particles from *onē-kotoba* (lit. 'fairy speech') in shaping masculine and non-masculine language personae for staff and customers alike. I will then proceed to compare the use of *onē-kotoba* with another element of language central to the service sector, namely expressions of politeness, and the use of honorifics in particular, in reinforcing the pyramid of desirability.

Onē-kotoba (literally 'older sister speech') is a variant of Japanese that originated in Japanese-style gay bars. It interpolates elements stereotypically belonging to Japanese Women's Language (*joseigo*) with Japanese Men's Language (Maree 2013). Fushimi Noriaki (1991) and Ōzuka Ryōji (1995) have argued that *onē-kotoba* represents nothing but a parody of the gendered variants of Japanese. My data, however, seem to point toward a different interpretation, as I will show.

The fantasy around gendered language that underpins *onē-kotoba* is the same as that which accompanied the building of Japan as a nation-state. Starting from the Meiji period, policy makers, as well as distributing labour along gender lines, also clearly defined how women and men were supposed to segregate the way they spoke, in order to propel modernization – Kathryn Woolard and Bambi Schieffelin (1994) call this *language ideology*. The speech of upper-class Tokyoites was elected to a class-less national standard and then subsequently differentiated into two contrasting gendered variants. Japanese Women's Language is characterised, syntactically, by the attribution of feminine-specific deictics and end-phrase particles; pragmatically, by indirectness, verbosity, a proclivity for emotional speech, politeness and the frequent use of honorifics in everyday life – as well as an overall tendency towards hyper-correction (Okamoto 1995; Okamoto and Shibamoto-Smith 2004). By contrast, Japanese Men's Language features, to a lesser degree, masculine-specific deictics and end-phrase particles. Pragmatically, it promotes directness, a preference for explicit talk (including matters related to sex) and an avoidance of verbosity, emotional speech and honorifics unless strictly necessary. While a clear distinction between male and female language has waned in the Japanese spoken by younger generations, residues of it survive through contemporary prose and television and in the speech of older generations such as the mothers and fathers of the customers at Zenith bar. The way in which service providers have tapped into this fantasy around language can be gauged by the degree to which service providers 'talked the talk' of Ni-chōme's Japanese-style gay bars. In this case, how and when they employed features typical of *onē-kotoba* such as first-person pronouns and end-phrase particles.

Proficiency in *onē-kotoba* was not a prerequisite for working at or frequenting Japanese-style gay bars. Customers and service providers all showed varying degrees of engagement with it, but more experienced bar-goers, especially those in their late thirties to mid-fifties, tended to use it more frequently. Younger customers were more tentative about using it, possibly because of a lack of confidence in their proficiency in it. But customers' expectations around binarily gendered behaviour required staff to adjust their speech style by resorting to *onē-kotoba* to mark a non-masculine role, or by avoiding it to signal a (linguistically unmarked) masculine role.

When asked what pronoun he would normally use to refer to himself, Tazu replied that he usually chose *boku* (a masculine pronoun, not too informal) at the bar, to demonstrate his authority as a manager, while at home he was *ore* (a hyper-masculine pronoun, extremely informal), because, he said, 'I'm an old man (*jiji da kara*)'. Tatsuki immediately interjected, adding that at times Tazu had to drop the more masculine persona for a customer who fancied him particularly and use *atashi* (a hyper-feminine pronoun) instead, to make himself look 'cuter' (*kawaii*).

I can recall more than one instance of customers' preferences leading to staff members altering their use of first-person pronouns. One night I was visiting Zenith as a customer and I found myself sitting next to a regular customer whom I knew already, a burly salaryman (he fit the *gachimuchi* type) in his early 50s. While he was having a lively conversation with Tazu, the man asked Tazu's opinion on the topic they were discussing. Tazu began his reply with '*Boku wa...*' ('For me...') and that generated an explosive reaction from the customer, who shouted at him: 'What is this *boku*! Use *atashi*!' ('*Boku janē yo! Atashi darō!*'), using the hyper-masculine negative conjugation *V-nē* (instead of *V-nai*) and the modal *darō* (instead of the less informal *deshō*). Tazu, who was leaning on the draught beer dispenser, stared at the customer blankly for a while and then immediately switched his expression into an exaggerated laugh, covering his mouth and apologizing: '*Gomennnasai! Boku yutchatta!*' ('I'm sorry! I said *boku* by mistake!'). When he did this he used the feminine verb contraction *V-tchau* (which implies having done something by mistake) instead of the non-contracted form *V-te shimau*. Not all such episodes were so sudden. Tazu was often simply reminded jokingly by customers that, as the non-masculine-performing manager, he should use the pronoun *atashi*. What is clear from this is that customers were highly sensitive to the 'proper' gendered language use and self-attribution of gender on the part of members of staff.

It is also worth considering the way in which another member of staff, Tatsuki, used gender language. When asked about the terms that he used to refer to himself, he replied that he mostly used *atashi* at work, both at the bar and at his drag gigs. However, he confided that he found it difficult to find a self-reference term that really worked for him in the daytime world. When he was working as a hair-dresser he told me that he resorted to the less markedly masculine *watashi*. The customers, he continued, reacted positively to this, as they perceived him to be projecting a polite image rather than a non-masculine one – *watashi* is in fact mostly used by men in formal settings. In comparison, masculine-performing Katsu and Yagi only used *boku* to refer to themselves both in the bar and outside of it, and neither showed hesitation in doing so nor were they ever made the objects of policing comments from customers.

The frequency with which the *onē-kotoba* feminine end-phrase particles *wa, wa yo, wa ne* and the copulae *N+nano, N+yo* were used was also interesting. I never heard Yagi use any of these and Katsu, too, used them extremely rarely. On the other end, Tazu and Tatsuki, like many other non-masculine-performing staff members whom I observed at other bars in Ni-chōme, used them quite frequently, along with many catch-phrases that were popular at the different bars in Ni-chome at the time of my fieldwork, which Katsu and Yagi never used. Although catch-phrases are not feminine per se, they did require little choreographies, exaggerated facial expressions in order to evoke a reaction in the customers. They were an expression of emotional work; and in that, they generally attributed to non-masculine roles.

On the other hand, I found that the linguistic feature that most commonly defines the service industry, the use of politeness forms including honorifics, was not as marked in gay bars as it is in general within the industry. Japanese gay bars represent a relaxed environment that does not require both staff and customers to adhere to the strict use of polite language found in other service sectors such as shops, where staff undergo intensive training on the correct use of honorifics. Customers generally did not use the formal or the honorific register when addressing the staff; and among customers, formal speech was only used in first encounters. After that, by contrast with the strict superior-inferior rules (*jōge-kankei*) governing the use of honorifics in the daytime world, fellow customers communicated with each other in the informal register even when a clear age gap was present. Staff members, on the other hand, used a mixture of honorifics and informal language, especially toward regular customers, while reserving more crystallised honorific phrases for use in welcoming customers, serving them drinks, thanking them and sending them off. This use of language could be described as *sābisu keigo*, or a less rigid version of the honorific language used across several segments of the service industry, gay bars included.

Nevertheless, as far as the frequency in use of honorifics is concerned, I observed no great difference between staff members in masculine and non-masculine roles. All customers were equally treated as situationally occupying a higher status regardless of their gender role, or sex. Female-bodied customers were treated just as politely. Other general rules of politeness applied to the behaviour of all staff members equally. There was, for example, a reluctance to contradict or silence one's interlocutor, which, in the context of service, was a strict prohibition vis-à-vis customers. This was so much the case that when masculine-performing bar help Katsu disrespected a very demanding and rude customer by inviting him to get lost (*shineba dō?*), Tazu immediately fired him in front of the whole bar.

Gendered self-reference terms and end-phrase particles were the main areas of language involved in the characterization of staff members as having masculine or non-masculine roles. They helped define the roles of members of staff as gendered speakers, without explicitly addressing their relationship with their interlocutors, namely the customers. A customer's gendered persona would thus emerge implicitly, in binary contrast to that of the staff member.

On the other hand, expressions explicitly in response to customers' actions or referencing their higher position (when a customer entered the bar, bought a bottle, offered a drink, paid and left) abandoned any gendered difference and used honorific language. Masculine- and non-masculine-performing staff members alike focused on stressing the customers' higher position through an evenly distributed use of polite forms.

To sum up, I would suggest that *onē-kotoba* should not be regarded as a tool used by non-straight Japanese people to parody traditional Japanese gendered language structures. I found that it was mostly deployed at Ni-chōme's Japanese-style gay bars to align, on a linguistic level, the gender and sexual roles staff members were typecast into based on their bodily presentations, dismissing their own linguistic identifications. Masculine-performing staff members did not use *onē-kotoba*, while non-masculine-performing staff members were required to use it. Honorifics and politeness forms were ultimately used as an equivalent and alternative to *onē-kotoba* to reinforce the pyramid of desirability. When honorifics and politeness were not used to explicitly signal that customers occupied the top of the pyramid, customers were able to enjoy their privileged position by witnessing their gender and sexual role emerge as a reflection of the staff's gendered use of language.

Sexual Innuendo as Availability

At the conjuncture of bodies and language, of material and psychological availability, is another strategy that allows service to make use of gendered fantasies at gay bars. This is sexual innuendo. By showcasing sexual availability, namely one's availability to engage in sex innuendo, flattery and some light touching (which never led to any sexual act), staff members at Zenith were able to enrich the experience of service for their customers by performing a more rounded boyfriend role, which was not devoid of sexual interaction. Although Japanese gay bars are not allowed to provide the up-close, one-on-one entertainment of bar and dating services centred around hostesses and hosts (see Fanasca in this volume), staff at Japanese-style gay bars were nevertheless expected to engage in the same type of flirtatious behaviour, both on the giving and receiving ends.

I was initially slightly reluctant to recognise my own role of staff member as that of a sexually available hostess-like presence – until one night, while serving a customer, I ironically compared my role with that of a hostess (*kyaba-jo*) in Ginza, in her life of luxury. Tazu immediately scolded me harshly: 'You haven't got it yet, you idiot? (*Nannimo wakattenai, koitsu?*) You are a hostess, so act like one!' There was a significant gap in hourly pay between a hostess, who can earn up to thousands of pounds in one night, and a gay bar help like me, earning at most £40 (ca ¥5,000) a night. Nevertheless, it made me think about how hostesses behave. As Anne Allison (1994) argues, hostesses need to entice, awaken desire and add spice to the perceived dullness of the everyday company life of their salaryman customers – the same customers who populate Zenith bar. Hostesses cannot be afraid to talk dirty or to use their own and others' physical appearance to create a connection, and they need to behave confidently in the context of the debauched drunkenness and grotesque aspects of nightlife. Hostesses (and some bar helps, too) are individuals no-one would marry, because their sexual appetites appear too vast to be tamed and contained, yet they are the ones to have around (and to have an affair with) because they know how to ensure a jolly good time.

Displaying availability to partake in sexual innuendo and sex talk along rigid binary lines helped staff better perform their gender roles and provide better service, which was also sexually charged. Sex talk usually started with innocent surveys of the kind of man the other party liked, then it moved on to one's preferences in bed and quickly escalated to very intimate questions about penis size (if the counterpart was masculine-performing) or level of anal sensitivity (if he was non-masculine-performing). The talk usually went both ways across the counter. Staff members asked the customers about their tastes and experiences, while also sharing their own experiences and engaging with the customers' most private questions. An open attitude was always welcome and a staff member with juicy sex stories was adored by the customers, especially if there were graphic details involved.

Tazu had an interesting approach in this regard. He would recollect sex stories about his past adventures at gay cruising saunas in vivid and precise detail (possibly a sign of well-rehearsed tales). The famous 24 Kaikan, just a few blocks away from the centre of Ni-chōme, was the main stage for many of his stories. Although he had recently announced that he was no longer interested in sex, he had garnered a reputation as a 'perv' (*hentai*) and customers still held him to those standards of graphic lewdness in his story-telling.

Tatsuki, too, was quite graphic in what he came out with. More than once, he claimed that his favourite genre of porn was a series of movies featuring groups of 'tops' taking turns penetrating a young, smooth 'bottom' who had just injected drugs and lost consciousness. I could not hide my expression of surprise. This jarred with the clean-cut boy image I had of Tatsuki. I felt the urge to ask him if he meant it seriously. He looked lost for a second, as though the option of disclosing details of his actual sex life to complete strangers had never crossed his mind and added with an understanding smile: 'Yeah, as a fantasy!' ('*Fantajī toshite ne*').

At the same time, Tazu tried to draw other staff members to the *hentai* side, by depicting them as sexually voracious and by making up sex stories about them right in front of the customers. Whenever I was working at Zenith, one of the first things he and Tatsuki would ask me was when I had sex last, and one evening Tazu looked at me and stated in front of the customers:

> You have the face of one of those guys in porn movies who stand right beside the other two fucking and when the top takes his cock out, he grabs it and sucks on it before putting it right back in the bottom's hole.

I was taken aback, as I had never expressed any interest in performing such an act. Nonetheless, the customers on the opposite side of the counter enjoyed that indirect confession, laughing and clapping their hands, regardless of my acknowledgement of it as true.

The protagonists of such sexually-charged stories were always non-masculine-performing staff members at Zenith, in other words Tazu, Tatsuki and myself. Katsu and Yagi were rarely asked about their sex life. Apart from asserting, and often having asserted for them, that they were 'tops', the two were never made subjects of any extemporaneous sexual episodes. Conversely, as earlier stated, non-masculine-performing members of staff were only read as 'bottoms' (*neko*) or 'insatiable bottoms' (*bari-neko*).[5] This division between masculine/'top' and non-masculine/'bottom' was held so strongly that, whenever a non-masculine-performing staff tried to challenge the label of being sexually receptive, he was met by a harsh reaction from the customers. More than once, when asked about my preferences in bed by Sakai, Tazu's former employer and now fellow bar manager, my answer got corrected by a dry and severe: 'So you're a bottom, don't lie (*dakara, neko deshō*).' Tazu went so far as to state that before hiring me, he had only been

---

5   As Pflugfelder (1999) shows, in the early 20th century the receptive role in male–male sexual acts in Japan shifted from the young male (*wakashū*) to the inverted, that is a male with a (heterosexual) female psyche – a conceptualization that has survived to this day alongside the Western-imported model of LGBT sexual identity.

able to gather staff members who were tops (such as Katsu and Yagi) – who, he believed, did not make for good business. My alleged bottom-ness together with my non-masculine demeanour and bodily presentation had given him hope for the bar.

Another strategy used by non-masculine-performing staff members to mark their availability was actively complimenting customers on their physical appearance (*kawaii, kakkoii*) and commenting on their sex-appeal (*eroi*). By contrast, masculine-performing service providers were not expected to offer compliments, but to receive them happily, just as Yagi did during his farewell party. Allowing crotch and ass groping, the touching of nipples and the uncovering of bodily parts were other, more daring, techniques to initiate a seduction game with customers. Here again it was the non-masculine-performing customers and service providers who took the initiative in these interactions, while masculine-performing counterparts were expected to be touched, groped and undressed without resisting. Customers asking to have sex with the staff and Tazu jokingly offering to sell the staff members' bodies to increase sales was the apotheosis of such behaviour.

All these modes of connecting with customers and presenting oneself as intimate with them allowed the bar staff to construct themselves as sexually open and available in the eyes of customers, always following a binary gendered division of desire. Customers could attempt a move on staff or entrust them with the goriest and most detailed sex story without being judged, as well as expecting the same level of content back. The availability, intimacy and openness helped create and nurture a productive tension that was based on desire, spicy confessions and inches of skin exposed. Takeyama labels this mode of interaction 'staged seduction' and describes it as 'the commercially staged force that seduces people into acting on their desires for self-satisfaction, as well as for meeting others' ends: increasing business profits and fulfilling their roles as citizens' (2016: 4). The sexual tension generated around the endless possibilities and experiences that were intimately shared with staff members generated an almost endless source of entertainment and, most importantly, gave customers a reason to become regulars.

One Step Further

Why do Japanese-style gay bars provide entertainment infused with binary gendered expectations surrounding care and intimacy as part of their service?

Why do customers at the Zenith bar enjoy a game of care and seduction whose rules – that is, the fantasies it feeds off – seem as outdated as the end-phrase particles used in *onē-kotoba*?

When Tazu confessed to me that one of the hardest parts of his job was not knowing whether he should act as a mother or a boyfriend to his customers, I initially thought he was simply referring to the extent to which some needy customers felt entitled to be taken care of and therefore how emotionally exploitative the service industry was, at times. Later, it made me wonder what mothers and boyfriends represented for the customers and for service providers such as Tazu. These figures – or better, roles – stood for one-on-one relationships in his cutomers' private lives in which customers were culturally allowed to be on the receiving end of a profusion of care without any expectation that they should reciprocate. Expectations around the direction of care in Japan still tend to follow strict gendered lines, in which the non-masculine party (for the most part, women) needs to be the care provider in the domestic sphere. This attitude was reflected in the way in which fantasies around romantic and sexual relationships are envisioned at Japanese-style gay bars like Zenith bar, filtered through the lens of commodified interaction. There, the mother role was merged with the role of materially, emotionally and sexually caring boyfriends performed by non-masculine-performing staff members vis-à-vis the customers. This in turn took the pressure off the masculine-performing staff members, who did not have to perform the same level of emotional and sexual labour.

The enforcement of these gender roles along rigid bodily, linguistic and sexual lines reproduces what I have called the pyramid of desirability inside Japanese-style gay bars. Customers at the Zenith bar occupied the top position, and this allowed them to have the staff engage in gendered interactions with them. They ranked staff members' bodily presentations and controlled their participation in the use of *onē-kotoba* and in sexual innuendo. Masculine-presenting staff performed in a masculine way by avoiding non-masculine language, acting as 'tops' and showing interest in non-masculine-presenting, *onē-kotoba*-talking customers acting as 'bottoms' – and vice versa for non-masculine-performing staff and masculine-performing customers.

Times have changed immensely since the economic miracle, particularly since Japan entered a phase of economic stagnation in the mid–2000s. However, the fantasies around a gendered distribution of material, emotional and sexual labour and around gendered language differentiation that infused my interlocutors' interactions – namely the salaryman doxa, Japanese language ideology and the image of the hostess as temptress – seemed to still hold a great deal of imaginative power. They also point to the aspirational middle-class lifestyle centred around the reproduction of heteronormative nuclear households that dominated Japan throughout the economic miracle.

As university-graduate company employees during the day, or as individuals aspiring to that status, customers at Zenith bar participated in that fantasy, at least publicly. Privately, though, they did not partake in the corresponding nuclear family system. Therefore, rather than thinking of Zenith bar as a substitute for a home environment – it lacks the 'bright atmosphere' of a Japanese home (Daniels 2015: 3) as well as the privacy, the intimacy, the responsibilities, the routines and the upkeep of a real household – we may think of it as a third space (Oldenburg 1989), neither private nor public, that feeds on commonly agreed-upon tales around the roles that individuals in Japan have traditionally been expected, and in some cases may still be expected, to perform vis-à-vis one another and around how these dynamics should take place in the nuclear home – as well as at the bar as its commodified substitute.

The creation of such a space allows customers to witness and inhabit, at a relatively low cost, a multi-faceted fantasy that covers the parts of that pre-stagnation era middle-class aspirational life that they do not get to fully experience first-hand because they are not participating in the marriage institution. We can say that the binarily gendered pairs created across the counter encapsulate wider discourses on the reproduction of the Japanese nation-state (see also Takeyama 2016).

One last remark needs to be made here. Be it in the amount of chatter and flirting or in the display of emotional reactions or of emotional availability vis-à-vis customers, Japanese-style gay bar staff – and customers too – play on the tension between being passive and being active that always exists at the core of binary gender discourses. It is hard to say whether attachment to these corporate fantasies of care, sex and language on the part of customers at these bars represents a heartfelt call for unity in an 'imagined community' (Anderson 1983: 49; also see Moriyama 2012) of excluded salarymen (Fushimi 2000; McLelland 2005) – or a parody-like take on that very exclusion by means of reversal.

It is certainly the case that, on the one hand, the roles at Zenith bar expose the innate contradictions of the very fantasies they reproduce, and to a certain extent they do queer (Sedgwick 1990) the heterosexual matrix, as Butler might say. After all, these are male-bodied men playing now bossy husband and busy housewife, now complacent salaryman and flirty hostess – and they are very serious about it. On the other hand, the efforts that were put into using these tensions to reinforce the bar's internal pyramid of desirability on a material, linguistic and sexual level show the undeniable pervasiveness of these fantasies and possibly betray a nostalgic attachment that Japanese (gay) men feel for a Japanese society that grants male-bodiedness centre stage. Economic stagnation has brought the idea of masculinity at the core of the miracle into crisis, and so has the economic model of Japanese-style gay bars, which revolve around providing commodified care and merriment for working men. Even though their participation in a hegemonic position is necessarily limited, the yearning, as bell hooks (1990) describes it, for such a position may be the reason behind the choice made by these Japanese (gay) men to hang onto these outdated fantasies – which are perhaps best described as delusions.

References

Allison, Anne. 1994. *Nightwork: Sexuality, Pleasure, and Corporate Masculinity in a Tokyo Hostess Club*. Chicago IL: University Press.

Anderson, Benedict. 1983. *Imagined Communities: Reflections on the Origin and Spread of Nationalism*. London: Verso.

Asai Michiko. 1990. Kindai kazoku gensō kara kaihō *wo* mezashite (trans. Towards an emancipation from the illusion of the contemporary family). *In* Ehara Yumiko (ed.), *Feminizumu Ronsō 70-nendai kara 90-nendai he* (trans. *Debates on Feminism from the 1970s to the 1990s*), 87–117. Tokyo: Kōsōshobo.

Boellstorff, Tom. 2003. Dubbing culture: Indonesian gay and lesbi subjectivities and ethnography in an already globalized world. *American Ethnologist* 30(2): 225–42.

Borovoy, Amy. 2005. *The Too-Good Wife: Alcohol, Codependency, and Politics in Postwar Japan*. Berkley CA: University of California Press.

Butler, Judith. 1990. *Gender Trouble: Feminism and the Subversion of Identity*. New York: Routledge.

Christensen, Paul. 2014. *Japan, Alcoholism, and Masculinity: Suffering Sobriety in Tokyo*. Lanham, MD: Lexington Books.

Cook, Emma. 2016. *Reconstructing Adult Masculinities*. London: Routledge.

Daniels, Inge. 2015. Feeling at home in contemporary Japan: Space, atmosphere and intimacy. *Emotion, Space and Society* 15: 47–55.

Dasgupta, Romit. 2003. Creating corporate warriors: The 'salaryman' and masculinity in Japan. *In* Kam Louie and Morris Low (eds.) *Asian masculinities: The meaning and practice of manhood in China and Japan*, 118–134. London: Routledge.

Fushimi Noriaki. 1991. *Puraibēto Gei Raifu* (trans. *Private Gay Life*). Tokyo: Gakuyō Shobō.

———. 2000. Queer Japan 2: Hentai Suru Sarariiman (trans. *Salarymen Doing Queer*). Tokyo: Keisō Shobō.

Gill, Tom. 2015. *Yokohama Street Life: The Precarious Career of a Japanese Day Laborer*. Lanham, MD: Lexington Books.

Hochschild, Arlie Russel. 2012. *The Managed Heart. Commercialization of Human Feeling*. Berkley CA: University of California Press.

hooks, bell. 1990. *Yearning: Race, Gender, and Cultural Politics*. Boston: South End Press.

Ishida, Hitoshi. 2006. Interactive practices in Shinjuku ni-chōme's male homosexual bars. *Intersections: Gender, History and Culture in the Asian Context* 12: 1–21. Available from: intersections.anu.edu.au/issue12/ishida1.html [Accessed 14 September 2021].

Ishida, Hitoshi and Murakami Takanori. 2006. The process of divergence between 'men who love men' and 'feminised men' in postwar Japanese media (trans. by W Lunsing). *Intersections: Gender, History and Culture in the Asian Context* 12 (12). Available from: intersections.anu.edu.au/issue12/ishida.html [Accessed 14 September 2021].

Kondo, Dorinne K. 2009. *Crafting Selves: Power, Gender, and Discourses of Identity in a Japanese Workplace*. Chicago IL: University Press.

Kumagai Hisa A. 1981. A dissection of intimacy: A study of 'bipolar posturing' in Japanese social interaction – *amaeru* and *amayakasu*, indulgence and deference. *Culture, Medicine and Psychiatry* 5(3): 249–272.

Lebra, Takie. 2007. *Identity, Gender and Status in Japan*. Folkstone, Kent: Global Oriental.

Mackintosh, Jonathan D. 2009. *Homosexuality and Manliness in Postwar Japan*. New York: Routledge.

McLelland, Mark. 2005. Salarymen doing queer: Gay men and the heterosexual public sphere. *In* Mark McLelland and Romit Dasgupta (eds), *Genders, Transgenders and Sexualities in Japan*, 96–110. New York: Routledge.

Maree, Claire. 2013. *'Onē-Kotoba' Ron* (trans. *On Onē-Kotoba*). Tokyo: Seidosha.

Miller, Laura. 2006. *Beauty Up: Exploring Contemporary Japanese Body Aesthetics*. Berkley CA: University of California Press.

Moriyama Noritaka. 2012. *'Gei Komyuniti' no Shakaigaku* (trans. *A Sociology of the 'Gay Community'*). Tokyo: Kōsōshobo.

Okamoto Shigeko. 1995. Tasteless Japanese. Less 'feminine' speech among young Japanese women. In Kira Hall and Mary Bucholtz (eds), *Gender Articulated: Language and the Socially Constructed Self*, 297–325. New York: Routledge.

Okamoto Shigeko and Janet S. Shibamoto Smith (eds). 2004. *Japanese Language, Gender, and Ideology: Cultural Models and Real People*. Oxford: University Press.

Oldenburg, Ray. 1989. *The Great Good Place*. Boston MA: Da Capo Press.

Ōzuka Ryōji. 1995. *Ni-Chōme Kara Uroko* (trans. *Opening One's Eyes to Ni-chōme*). Tokyo: Shōeisha.

Pflugfelder, Gregory M. 1999. *Cartographies of Desire: Male–Male Sexuality in Japanese Discourse, 1600–1950*. Berkeley CA: University of California Press.

Roberson, James and Suzuki Nobue (eds). 2005. *Men and Masculinities in Contemporary Japan: Dislocating the Salaryman Doxa*. New York: Routledge.

Rosenberger, Nancy R. 2001. *Gambling with Virtue: Japanese Women and the Search for Self in a Changing Nation*. Honolulu: University of Hawai'i Press.

Sedgwick, Eve Kosofsky. 1990. *Epistemology of the Closet*. Berkley CA: University of California Press.

Sunagawa Hideki. 2015. *Shinjuku Ni-chome no Bunkajinruigaku: Gei Komyuniti Kara Toshi wo Manazasu* (trans. *The Cultural Anthropology of Shinjuku Ni-chōme: Looking at the City from the Perspective of the Gay Community*). Tokyo: Tarōjirō Editasu.

Takeyama Akiko. 2010. Intimacy for sale: Masculinity, entrepreneurship and commodity self in Japan's neoliberal situation. *Japanese Studies* 30(2): 231–246.

———. 2016. *Staged Seduction: Selling Dreams in a Tokyo Host Club*. Palo Alto CA: Stanford University Press.

West, Candice and Don H. Zimmerman. 1987. Doing gender. *Gender & Society* 1(2): 125–151.

Woolard, Kathryn A. and Bambi B. Schieffelin. 1994. Language ideology. *Annual Review of Anthropology* 23(23): 55–82.

Yoda Tomiko. 2000. The rise and fall of maternal society: Gender, labor and capital in contemporary Japan. *South Atlantic Quarterly* 99(4): 865–902.

CHAPTER 3

(Re)searching (for) Identities

Crossdressed Ethnography in a *Dansō* Escort Company

Marta Fanasca

Introduction

Imagine a cosy coffee shop in a tall building in central Tokyo: wooden tables and comfortable seats, dim lights, cool jazz as soundtrack. A couple is seated slightly out of sight of other customers. The man is very charming in his fashionable clothes, luxurious brand accessories, his hair carefully styled. Maybe he is not very tall, but he is still very attractive, and he is enveloped in the scent of sophisticated cologne. He moves his hands elegantly as he pours milk and stirs the lady's coffee, smiling at her all the time. She is significantly older than him, a bit chubby, and wears a pinafore dress adorned with ribbons and crochet here and there and a light pink cardigan, giving her a somewhat childish appearance. They make a strange couple. Perhaps she is his mother? No, the glances, the small intimate gestures are those of a couple. She talks at length about her work and how it has become terrible recently, explaining that her boss bullies her every day, and her colleagues never invite her out or organise events that include her. She feels like nobody loves her and sobs silently; she is on the verge of crying. During this conversation, he never takes his eyes off her, listening to her words carefully, with a sympathetic expression on his beautiful face. Then he takes her hands and pulls them close to his lips, saying 'I care about you. You are the most important person in the world to me,' and he delicately kisses her hands. A phone call interrupts the magic moment. He answers quickly, muttering only a few words, such as 'wakarimashita' (I see), and then hangs up. 'What do you want to do? Our time is almost over...' he asks her. 'Let's go.' She takes the bill and steps towards the cashier, while he collects her bags and discreetly waits a few steps behind while she pays. The couple walks out together; she hangs on his arm. A light rain starts falling as they walk under the same umbrella, very close to each other. As they reach the subway station, they hug for a long time, a rare sight in fast-paced Tokyo. Then she descends the steps, turning around two or three times to wave goodbye, as if she wants to carry his smile home with her. He waits and waves back until she disappears from his sight. Then he takes out the phone, makes a call and announces 'The date is over; I am coming back to the office'.

Should you spot a similar scene in Tokyo, you are probably witnessing a date between a *dansō* – a female-to-male (FtM) crossdresser escort – and his client; such dates are the service provided by *dansō* escort companies. This kind of entertainment business originated in 2006 in Japan, in the midst of what I call the '*dansō* movement', a wave of different *dansō*-related forms of businesses that had at their core FtM crossdressing women but were not related to the LGBTQ+ scene. In fact, the second half of the 2000s saw the birth of *dansō* cafés in which crossdressing women, usually – but not necessarily – dressed as charming butlers served female customers; the stage debut of *dansō* boybands such as the Fudanjuku and The Hoopers; and the first *dansō* escort agency, 'With the Garçon' (no longer in existence).

Apart from the few *dansō* who also work as idols, models or musicians (whose popularity can be more widespread), the *dansō* escort business generally caters to a niche clientele. Cafés and especially the escort service mostly target women, some of them embedded within the *otaku* – or to be more precise the *fujoshi* – culture.[1] Still, the *dansō* business is flourishing. This can be seen in the overall increase in the number of crossdressers, the rapid growth of side activities they engage in (including special events, gigs and collaborations between various *dansō* units and public events such as comic fairs) and the steady increase in the numbers of clients. When I first

---

[1] *Otaku* is commonly used to describe individuals with obsessive interests, mostly (but not exclusively) in *anime* and *manga*. The term is often linked to the neighbourhood of Akihabara, where most of the *manga/anime*/games-related shops and entertainments are located. While *fujoshi* was first intended as the female equivalent of male *otaku*, it has come to define female fans or creators of works centred on male–male romance. For a fuller explanation of *otaku* culture and the shifting perceptions of *otaku*, see Galbraith and Schodt (2009) and Itō, Okabe and Tsuji (2012).

began my research, Dreamland, the *dansō* escort company I worked for, had only four crossdressers and no more than 15 clients. During my fieldwork, however, these numbers increased to 15 crossdressers serving more than 120 clients (most of them regular customers).

In this chapter, I analyse *dansō* escort services and discuss my ethnographic approach to *dansō* gender performance. From September 2015 to July 2016 I worked in a *dansō* escort company as a crossdresser escort myself. I thus had the daily opportunity to observe escorts while they were working and during their free time. I, like my escort informants, experienced the creation and performance of a masculine identity. My research is based on semi-structured interviews with both crossdressers and clients as well as on participant observations. My aim was to understand the phenomenon of *dansō* escorting, focusing particularly on the performance of gender and identity in relation to self-expression and the commodification of intimacy.

This chapter contributes to knowledge in the field of Japanese studies and anthropology by presenting a theoretically engaged discussion of how a male gender identity is created, performed and negotiated in the *dansō* escort business. Specifically, it shows gender 'at work' for the sake of clients but also as a form of self-expression for a specific sector of non-cisgender individuals in contemporary Japan. I will also debate my position, on the verge between being an insider and an outsider, contributing to the understanding of the research field as a process where different variables interact and merge.

In addition, the chapter highlights the strategies I adopted to access the field, to deal with my own 'otherness' (Lunsing 2001; White 2003) and to negotiate my position as insider and outsider, as researcher and practitioner, as a woman but also as a man. I focus on the physical and psychological challenges that I faced in terms of gaining access to the field, highlighting the process of creation and performance (Butler 1990) of a male gender identity. I explain how I started to mould my male alter ego, André, how I worked on my body to make it look more masculine and how I merged real and fictional aspects of myself to plausibly perform my *dansō* character. Following this, I focus on features that defined me as an outsider, and how, rather than allowing these to be limitations, I turned them into useful tools with which to gather information.

I begin by describing my physical and psychological efforts to reveal how gender 'works' and how it is 'worked' out in the crossdresser escort business. Considering inside and outside as a blurred and shifting positions rather than a fixed dichotomy, allowed me to place myself differently while doing research and this led me to an enhanced understanding of the phenomenon of *dansō* escorting, taking into consideration variables such as ethnic and cultural background, education, gender and sexual identity. I conclude by addressing the negative issues that I faced when stepping into the realm of the escort business as a fieldworker and the negotiations required to successfully complete my research, managing my position amongst my informants and vis-à-vis the context in which we were operating.

Research Site: Akihabara and the *Dansō* Escort Company Dreamland[2]

Akihabara, a district in central Tokyo, is known worldwide for its high concentration of *manga, anime* and games shops. Nowadays, Akihabara is both the *otaku*'s homeland and one of the core centres of 'Cool Japan', the nation-based brand project that works to create and promote various forms of Japanese (pop) culture and subculture abroad. In this context, Japanese perspectives on Akihabara are divided: while it often represents a sort of 'sacred space' (Nobuoka 2010) for consumers of *manga, anime* and games, for those critical of popular culture and subculture Akihabara is also the place where *otaku* cultivate and indulge in their 'antisocial' hobbies (Kam 2013). The word *otaku* took on a specific negative meaning in 1989, the year when it was used by various media to describe Miyazaki Tsutomu, the sociopathic killer of four girls between four and seven years old. After the crime, it became known that Miyazaki had little social life, and upon entry into his room police found not only child pornography but also anime (Kinsella 1998). Following the media coverage, *otaku* came to refer to antisocial dangerous males. However, it should also be noted that it is precisely through their supposedly antisocial hobbies (such as an interest in visiting 'maid cafés'[3]) that *otaku* cultivate their own kind of sociality. Since the Miyazaki incident, *otaku* identity and its link to Akihabara has, however, changed, moving in recent years to become more playful and less antisocial. Akihabara as a neighbourhood has also developed, with some defining it as 'a "pure consumer" space, an extension

---

2   Dreamland is a pseudonym. All the names of people and companies quoted in this chapter are pseudonyms adopted to protect my informants' privacy.
3   Maid cafés are establishments where staff dress in Victorian maid-like costumes and act as if they are serving a master upon his return to his mansion. See Galbraith 2013.

of the private (disconnected) "pleasure room" into public space' (Galbraith 2009: 21). The push from the Japanese government to use characters from *anime* and *manga* as Japanese cultural ambassadors played a pivotal role in moving the image of *otaku* away from more controversial associations, at least for non-Japanese consumers.

Understanding this emphasis on Akihabara as a district of pleasure and consumerism is fundamental when seeking to understand the role the neighbourhood plays in recent forms of affect-oriented services, to which the *dansō* entertainment belongs. Contemporary capitalism has a strong focus on the production of immaterial goods, including information, communication and affect, and so-called immaterial labour and 'affective labour' are considered two of the main aspects of this (Lazzarato 2008; Coté and Pybus 2007; Hardt and Negri 2000: 292). The affective aspect of immaterial labour engages with specific feelings and emotions including well-being, excitement and relaxation. To cater to the affective needs of *otaku* men, various business forms arose focusing on alternative and commodified forms of intimacy, such as maid cafés. While the affective entertainment industry was aimed mostly at a male clientele during the first half of the 2000s (Azuma 2007), from 2006 onwards services aimed at female customers also entered the industry. Together with butler cafés where male staff dress in Victorian attire for a largely female audience, *dansō* escort companies and *dansō* cafés can be understood as the female-oriented counterpart to the maid cafés and other services aimed at male clients. Akihabara is no longer directed towards the most extreme and antisocial aspects of *otaku*, but towards a milder, colourful pop culture available for consumption by anyone and everyone.

The concept of emotional labour (Hochschild 1983) is especially fitting when describing the *dansō* escort job. Crossdresser escorts must perform feelings such as empathy, affection and even love to inspire an emotional response from clients. When performing emotions, *dansō* resort to both surface and deep acting to better profit from clients' feelings.[4] While in a surface performance a worker acts to modify only the outward expressions of his or her feelings (without changing their inner emotions), deep acting involves the sphere of the worker's inner feelings, meaning that emotions are self-induced and external representation is based on modifications of

---

4   For more information on crossdresser escorts' emotional labour and its negative backlash, see Fanasca 2018, chapter 5.

what is felt inside. Both are used by *dansō* to help clients develop feelings of affection. Through these forms of acting, customers obtain the emotional engagement that is what they primarily desire through dating *dansō* escorts, and as a result they are likely to become regular customers, consequently increasing escorts' earnings.

Feminist scholars have highlighted the way in which the commodification of emotions is divided along gender lines, with women primarily performing emotional labour for male consumers, something that reveals women's subordination to the patriarchal capitalist system (Takeyama 2010). Within the affective labour market, this suggests a possible link between the (performance of) male gender and a tendency to profit from the exploitation of women's need for emotional experiences. From this perspective, the work of *dansō* escorts is similar to that of male hosts (Takeyama 2016), who are often presented in Japanese media as predatory individuals well-known for deceiving their female clients in order to monetise their affections (see Takeyama 2005: 204).

On Dreamland's website the business advertises itself as the most famous *dansō* escort company in Japan and from my experience it is certainly a leader in its field (for a detailed description of the function of Dreamland and its escort service see Fanasca 2019a and 2019b). Dreamland's boss, Mr Hirota, came to the industry after working for a number of years in the adult entertainment business. Located only a few minutes from Chūō Dōri, Akihabara's main street, the company does not appear on maps showing the entertainment premises in the neighbourhood (such as maid cafés). The building is not located in the very heart of Akihabara – in fact Akihabara is not even the closest station – and Dreamland can thus be said to be both inside and outside Akihabara. This borderline position reflects the liminal status of Dreamland's crossdresser escort service well. Being in Akihabara creates a link with the *otaku/fujoshi* culture while keeping a safe distance from the sexual and especially the homosexual entertainment world, both of which are primarily based in Shinjuku (see Francioni in this volume). Since homosexuality in Japan is subject to a powerful social stigma, Mr Hirota's decision to place his business in Akihabara disconnects *dansō* crossdressing from any link to LGBTQ+ culture, a link which could potentially disengage the clientele. However, the kind of service Dreamland provides is nevertheless closer to services offered by host clubs than by maid cafés, since the commodified intimacy provided in both cases includes highly intense emotional experiences (Takeyama 2016).

Dreamland's double status – both related to Akihabara's pop culture and at the same time resembling other forms of commodified intimacy services – is also reflected in the mixed range of its customers. According to my informants (both crossdressers and clients) and as observed during my participant observation, self-identifying *fujoshi* clients represent a minority of the total pool of Dreamland's customers. Presented as a non-threatening entertainment type that anyone can consume, *dansō* escort companies are openly promoted as guide services. The link to Akihabara and cosplay mitigates the possible homoerotic aspects that crossdressing might otherwise suggest and the renewed image of Akihabara itself distances the *dansō* business from the dark side of *otaku* culture.

Ensuring that transgressive or alternative subcultures are made 'safe', with the aim of capitalising upon them, is a well-known trend (the punk movement is a perfect example, see Moore 2005), and this is exactly what Mr Hirota has done to promote his business and to attract a wider range of customers. *Dansō* mix *otaku* culture, androgyny and eroticism, but none of these features is too extreme and they will therefore not scare away clients who do not recognise themselves under labels such as *fujoshi* or 'lesbian'. Because Akihabara is a place that allows unconventional identities to exist, a place where playing with identity is accepted as part of a larger 'performative play' industry complex, it is the perfect setting for a *dansō* escort business. Without generating too much uproar, cosplayers, maids and clients can perform different selves during the limited time they spend in this part of Tokyo. Akihabara represents an unrivalled opportunity to play with gender within a safe space, an exploration of the self, framed within a playful atmosphere. Here, switching gender identity is a form of play rather than an act of subversion and is conceived of as independent from the socio-political activism of the LGBTQ+ community.

'Inside' or 'Outside'?

When undertaking ethnographic work, researchers are considered insiders when they belong to the field – that is, to the same 'group' as their informants – and outsiders when they do not. Groups can be based on gender, gender identity (see Gamberton, this volume), sexual orientation (see Francioni this volume), ethnicity, social background or occupation. For my project

I had to consider the pros and cons of the two types of ethnography, and this meant entering the heated debate that has flourished within the field of anthropology over the past twenty years (Gregory and Ruby 2011; Sherif 2001). I will sum up the discussion and my specific considerations here.

Insiders, it has been argued, have advantages in terms of obtaining access to the field and recruiting informants; they can better understand the needs and issues that their informants (especially those belongings to marginalised groups) face, and thus better represent them from an ethical perspective (Bridges 2001). Because of their greater knowledge and awareness about the field, insiders may, however, run the risk of taking for granted information and may overlook data that forms part of understandings shared within the group (DeLyser 2001). The insider position can furthermore potentially put researchers at risk, for example if they develop bonds with their informants that are too close, thereby gaining access to highly intimate information that researchers may not be at ease with. Some scholars have supported the outsider position, arguing that it enables researchers to approach a given topic without pre-existing assumptions, and thus providing a means of undertaking in-depth investigation of a phenomenon through 'naïve' questions (Tang 2007). Thus 'the outsider's advantage lies in curiosity with the unfamiliar, the ability to ask taboo questions, and being seen as non-aligned with subgroups, thus often getting more information' (Merriam et. al 2010: 411).

In the context of Japan, the concepts of 'inside' and 'outside' cannot be assessed without taking into account the well-established debate around the concepts of *uchi* (inside)/*soto* (outside), which define social relations and social spaces in Japan (Kondo 1990; Martinez 2006). *Uchi* is the private area, including one's house, one's family, the group to which one belongs and even the inner self itself. *Soto* is what everything else is called – that and those which do not belong or cannot access the *uchi* sphere. *Soto* is the outer appearance of things and people. As Joy Hendry (1995) has argued, in order to understand Japanese society it is vital to assess the way in which *uchi* and *soto* shape the social in relation to spheres of belonging. The concept of belonging structures groups of insiders and outsiders and defines the position of the researcher vis-à-vis informants and the field itself.

From the beginning of my research, it was clear to me that I needed to obtain an insider position, at least from a spatial perspective, to understand the functioning of the escort company, especially when this is behind closed doors. I was not only looking for the opportunity to participate in dates, but also for information on the preparations made by escorts before dates, as well as information about their relationships with colleagues. I wanted to know more about escorts' private lives, which I assumed would be hidden from the eyes of an outsider. In order to get insights into the training *dansō* undergo before they meet clients and to access information shared only between crossdressers and other staff at Dreamland, it was necessary for me to be admitted into the escort company. After a careful evaluation of my options (taking on the role of customer, meeting crossdressers only for interviews, asking to be admitted to the escort company as an observer etc.), I concluded that the best option would be for me to be admitted into the escort company as a practitioner. Taking on a position as *dansō* escort myself would offer the widest range of insights into the company and into the industry and I therefore decided to work for Dreamland as a crossdresser escort myself. This meant that I had to work on my body, my appearance and my personality in order to craft a male identity suited to the job. Positioning myself so that I could seek to understand the practice of crossdressing from a bodily perspective through first-hand experience meant that I would be able to meet informants in a unique space. Thus, guided by my crossdresser informants, I made gender and its performance my work.

As Adler and Adler (1987: 8) have pointed out in relation to research focused on subcultures or unconventional groups, 'researchers must assume social roles that fit into the worlds they are studying'. To gather data about gender identity, sexual orientations and private lives of crossdressers and about the nature of their relationships with customers, it was necessary for me to fit in within a *dansō* company, to go through the same experiences as my informants, to demonstrate that there were similarities between them and me and to build relationships based on mutual knowledge and reciprocal trust.

I was, however, perfectly well aware of the impossibility of becoming a complete insider: my facial features, my cultural background and my reason for crossdressing (which was obviously different from that of other crossdressers) gave me a borderline identity that constantly moved me back and forth between *uchi* and *soto*. But while I was different from my informants in many ways, it should be noted that the same researcher can simultaneously occupy an insider and an outsider position. For instance, researchers investigating marginalised ethnic groups are insiders if they belong to that same ethnic group, but may at the same time be classified as outsiders in terms of, for example, social and educational background (Hayfield and

Huxley 2015). Hence, fieldwork is often a continuous process where the researcher constantly moves from the outside to the inside and back again (Jankie 2004) – and this was my own experience.

In the context of *dansō* escorting, there are different degrees of *uchi* and *soto*. The space of Akihabara defines the first grade of *uchi*-ness, since both clients and escorts can go on dates here without any problems. Hardly anyone would see anything strange about the couple within this space, while the same privacy cannot be guaranteed in other places in Tokyo. The escort company itself represents the second degree of *uchi*-ness, in that both escorts and clients are part of the same business, meaning that they know and accept rules that are different from those that operate in society in general. And finally, the *dansō* escorts represented a further, third layer of *uchi*-ness, as they themselves form a community, one that neither clients nor non-crossdressing Dreamland staff are part of. As a foreigner, I was an outsider in Japanese society; but with their unconventional choice in terms of gender, so were my informants, who expressed feelings that were different from those expressed by members of mainstream society. Through the act of crossdressing, we thereby all came to belong to the same group. At every interaction, the distinction between *uchi* and *soto* changed, and I as a researcher needed to be able to move across these boundaries in order to effectively navigate the FtM escort business. Crossdressing with my informants and being available to talk about my sexual orientation moved me several times from the *soto* to the *uchi* sphere.

Through my research experience in this field, I thus came to understand how inside and outside are never stable standpoints, but are, instead, constantly transitioning positions that must be negotiated. The idea that the 'field' of ethnographic research constitutes a spatially bounded place in which the researcher holds a clearly defined identity has been refuted (Friedman 2005), and my experience contributes to the questioning of fieldwork as a specific space, converging toward Burrell's (2009) view of the research site as a continuous process where space, body and feelings are conflated. Specifically, in my case, gender became a site for investigation, discussion and negotiation. As I will explain, how to approach the creation of a gender identity, the meanings attached to it, the ability or the necessity to move between various gendered version of the self – all of these represented my research 'field'.

During my fieldwork I constantly negotiated my position, emphasising or reducing those physical, social, cultural and psychological features that represented points in common or differences between my informants and me.

I worked constantly to adapt my body and my behaviour so as to achieve the standard expected by the company and so as to be accepted by my informants. At the same time, I worked on my undeniable otherness, trying to make its features appealing to my co-workers and customers. I aimed to establish a relationship of mutual trust and through this relationship to obtain relevant information.

Accessing Dreamland

I go to a hair salon close to my house, in North-Eastern Tokyo, bringing with me a flyer for the crossdresser escort company where I will be starting work the following week. At the salon, I ask the shy girl in charge of cutting my hair to turn me into a cool guy ('kakkoi otoko no ko ni naritai'), showing her the flyer with the pictures of my colleague to give her an aesthetic reference. I need to fit into the Dreamland environment, so it is not enough to look 'like a man', but specifically to look like the kind of men my co-workers embody, and whom clients want to date. She has a look at the flyer, nods and starts her work. While she is cutting my hair we talk a bit. She is full of praise for my very long, dark brown hair, asking me why I want such a radical change in style. I explain my research project to her, and she comments, with a profusion of 'sugoi' and 'kakkoi' – both terms that can be translated as 'cool' in English. At the end of the session, I look at myself in the mirror: I like the haircut, it is pretty cool, and exactly the style my co-workers will appreciate. It enhances my cheekbones and without make up I look very androgynous. She has done a good job. I am not very tall; I am slim with small shoulders, and obviously I do not have facial hair. It would be difficult for me to pass as a man in the UK. However, the final result is more than satisfactory for Dreamland's standards of masculine beauty. I send a picture of my new haircut to the LINE chat I share with my dansō colleagues, and they enthusiastically approve. The first step on my path toward masculinity is taken.

Now I have to work on my chest. I have no idea how to hide the female shape of my upper body. In a big department store, I look for something that could work. I find a so-called koshi sapōto, a waist support made from elastic strips with a Velcro closing, used by the elderly to keep their backs straight. At home, alone in my room and in front of the mirror, I try to hide the female curves of my chest, experimenting with different ways of placing the elastic strips on my body. Initially it is difficult to work out how to wear them: they are pretty tight, the Velcro is itchy and they tend to lose their grip on my skin when I move. Nevertheless, after a bit of practising and wearing a close-fitting jumper, the result is impressive: with no make-up, my freshly cut short hair and now with my breasts hidden under the grip of the elastic strips, I fail to recognise myself. I have become André.

I first manged to establish contact with Dreamland thanks to some acquaintances who had previously worked as crossdresser escorts. As requested by the management, I sent pictures of myself wearing male clothes, which fortunately resulted in an invitation to a job interview. The interview was primarily a way for management to judge whether I appeared to be in line with Dreamland aesthetic criteria. The weight of prospective escorts must be no more than their height expressed in cm minus 100 (for example, the maximum weight for someone 160 cm tall was thus 60 kg). In general, Dreamland staff consisted of slender individuals with a minimum height of 158 cm. In addition to checking whether I fitted into the required physical proportions, the interview was also intended to assess my language proficiency. In this line of work it is essential to be able to speak fluently with customers in Japanese. I was also asked about my desire to crossdress, and carefully informed of the limitations that working for Dreamland entails. Specifically, I was told that escorts are forbidden to wear female clothes in Akihabara, to hang around the neighbourhood with friends (both during and outside working hours) or to exchange contact details with customers with the intention of meeting privately. After accepting these conditions, I was admitted to Dreamland as a trainee *dansō*.

From the start, I was clear about being a researcher from a European university and I was glad to find that neither Mr Hirota nor the other crossdressers found this a problem as long as my observations, questions or interviews would not disrupt the working routine. When I began meeting clients, I came out as a researcher to them in our first meeting as well. During dates, I explained my research and my double identity did not really raise concerns with them either – my *dansō* identity interested them much more than my academic background. When I was conducting interviews with clients, I met them dressed as André, but provided them with business cards detailing my real name and affiliation. Before recording, I obviously also asked informants for verbal or written consent.

To access Dreamland, one must enter the office code on the doorphone and state one's surname or, in the case of workers and returning customers, their nickname (the first sign of the highly performative roles played by both

Figure 3.1 One of crossdressers' shared wardrobe. **Colour**, p. 217.

crossdressers and clients). The apartment that functioned as the company office had a narrow corridor leading to one door on the left and one at the end. The boss and his assistants had their desks in the room at the end, and it was also here that clients would interact with reception staff while booking or paying for dates. Out of bounds to clients, the room on the left was exclusively for *dansō*: it was here crossdressers spent most of their time, waiting to be booked or hanging out in their spare time between dates (this setup mirrors that of the health delivery service as described by Phillips in this volume). The room contained two big sets of lockers and a large wardrobe where *dansō* stored their suits, coats and other clothes only worn on request, such as *yukata* (a summer kimono made of cotton) (Figure 3.1). Each escort also had a locker in which he could store personal belongings (Figure 3.2). This

Figure 3.2 Two *dansō* waiting for customers in the office near the lockers. **Colour**, p. 218.

room was the setting for most of my observations and interactions with my crossdresser informants.

While working at Dreamland, I consciously worked to adapt my behaviour so that it was similar to that of my co-workers to reduce the problem of reactivity, and I was also conscious that I needed to avoid any artificial behaviour that might derive from my identity as a researcher. I wondered whether *dansō* informants would feel at ease when interacting with me – a researcher specifically there to observe (and perhaps, they might worry, to judge) their life choices – and whether client informants would feel able to discuss their lives and actions with me – a stranger who was not part of the world they share with *dansō*. Presenting an identity on my part that was too detached might, I considered, affect my informants, causing them to act less openly because of the differences between myself, as researcher, and them. My aim was thus to be involved with Dreamland not only as a researcher, but also as a practitioner, as someone who was learning about *dansō* crossdressing by doing it.

Therefore I took my escort role seriously. I worked on myself both physically and psychologically in order to be able to successfully perform this masculine role. For me, as for my informants, performing masculinity did not involve a process of surgical modification of the body or hormone injections, but was mostly a matter of *mi ni tsukeru*. Translated as 'wearability' (Allison 2009) or 'embodiment' (Otsubo 2003), *mi ni tsukeru* literally means 'to put onto the body' and refers to the acquisition of skills and knowledge, with the idea being that what one learns is so interiorised that it becomes part of the body performing it. I have adapted this concept to describe the acquisition by *dansō* of the knowledge and skills necessary to perform a suitable masculine gender identity proficiently (Fanasca 2019a). *Dansō* learn how to walk, talk and present themselves aesthetically following a series of behavioural, aesthetic and linguistic practices that are marked as masculine in the Japanese context. Creating a male gender identity was thus linked to the development of the ability to behave following patterns of masculine behaviour that are already widely shared in Japan.

As I explained at the beginning of this section, I started my transformation by working on my appearance. Generally speaking, *dansō* working for Dreamland perform a beautified and androgynous masculinity,[5] in line with the latest trends of male fashion and beauty. Gaining access to Dreamland as a practitioner was predicated on my possession of the necessary 'bodily capital' (Wacquant 2004), allowing me to perform my male escort role in line with Dreamland's standards. But this was not enough in itself. To perform male identity meant that I had to constantly work on my body and on my behaviour to ensure that I satisfactorily created and embodied a male gender identity.

After that first visit to the hairdresser, I kept my hair short for the whole period of my fieldwork. Before entering the field, I had very long, straight hair, which I sacrificed in order to work as crossdresser escort. I learned how to carefully style my short haircut with wax and gel. The result of this change affected me for a long time and now, years after my ethnographic work ended, I still prefer short haircuts (Fig. 3.3).

I also started to train daily in order to align my masculine self with the canon of masculine beauty that Dreamland's clients find aesthetically pleasant. As reasonably muscular but slender bodies were appreciated, I shaped my

---

5   For a full discussion of 'beautified masculinity' see Miller 2003.

Figure 3.3 Me posing as André in a promotional flyer for Dreamland. **Colour**, p. 219

muscles by following a fitness routine involving cardio and weight lifting, but made sure not to develop a physique that was too bulky. To support my workout and better conceal my female curves, I also followed a protein-based diet and refrained from consuming carbs and sweets as best I could. It was an intense process that affected my appearance very obviously: my muscles, feeble to begin with, became much more defined, especially on my arms and shoulders; and while my usual weight was around 50kg, it dropped to around 45kg during my time in the field.

I also trained my voice with the aim of speaking and singing in deeper tones. I practised outside working time – alone, with my *senpai* (veteran colleagues), and with other Japanese friends. I often booked karaoke booths, where I studied a repertoire of songs that I could perform in a masculine register with clients. All these changes were necessary to fit neatly into the escort role and they required constant effort. I focused on developing a masculine conversation style mostly resorting to a plain and 'masculine' Japanese, avoiding the *–masu* stems of the verbs, using instead a higher number of contracted words and tenses, presenting myself with the rather rough male pronoun *ore*. I became so accustomed to speak this way that it required additional effort to use a more polite Japanese when interacting in contexts outside the Dreamland environment. To change register became a necessary gender negotiation that required my attention to be correctly assessed at every social interaction.

Thus, to sum up: My being a woman, my age, my body, were all features in line with Dreamland's requirements, but I also worked to enhance those aspects of my appearance and to self-present according to the kind of masculinity sought after at Dreamland.

Creating a *Kei*: Creating André

Along with the necessary physical changes, I also had to develop my male self psychologically. I had to create the kind of man I wanted to embody, keeping in mind that the final aim of this crafted self was to attract clients. This brought out what was, I realised, a pivotal point of difference between myself and other *dansō* in terms of the gender work of *dansō* escorts. Although for many of them the possibility to dress as men and to perform a male role not only in their private life but also in the workplace was considered the best way to express their *hontō no jibun* – their real self – while working, this "real" self was subjected to several negotiations to meet clients' desires. As I was only crossdressing for research purposes and not to express my 'real self', this angle on the situation was lacking in my personal experience.

The male characters that *dansō* create for their job are a mixture of 'honest' self-expression, mirroring their selves in their private lives, and specifically developed aspects of behaviour and aesthetics. Each crossdresser crafts a character for himself that expresses his own preferences, abilities and features; but at the same time these selves must be performed in a way that charms customers and generates their interest, including potential feelings of love and affection. Crossdressers therefore often rely on a *kei* ('type') with which Japanese women are likely to be familiar already. *Kei* is a suffix that defines a set of physical, aesthetical and psychological features representative of a specific class of individuals. A *kei* can be inspired by samples from fictional worlds, typically *manga* and *anime*, or by well-established categories of actual men. A *dansō* might, for example, choose to present himself as a 'Prince Charming' type (*ōji kei*), a 'mischievous little brother' type (*shōta kei*) or a 'studious' type (*megane kei*). While there is a good deal of freedom in doing this, it is important that *dansō* avoid choosing roles they are ill-fitted to play, as this will shine through – a shy person is unlikely to be able to perform the role of a flirty guy convincingly, just as a less well-educated person may find it difficult to embody the studious type.

In my case, I decided to adopt the role of a friendly and slightly flirty Italian guy, to match the stereotypes that I expected my clients might have about Italian men. Although I did worry whether using a stereotypical Italian persona for the sake of clients might be ethically questionable, I felt that this character, with his friendly, straightforward approach, was consonant with my 'off-stage' self. It did seem to me that my informants appeared to find the character I created pleasant. I called myself André, a name I chose for its European sound and for its link to the character André in Ikeda Riyoko's *manga Versailles no Bara*, which prospective clients were likely to know.

My choice also fell on André because I felt it would be impossible to pretend that I was Japanese. Hence, I tried to turn my different background in my favour. All my Japanese informants showed a very positive evaluation of my home country, thus I strategically played on being Italian to create contact points with them, opening up spaces for friendly conversations, and consequently increasing our mutual knowledge. By answering questions about Italian food, football and fashion brands, I achieved my aim of appearing friendly and talkative. Through my conversations with crossdressers (in the idle time spent in the office or in gatherings outside working hours) and with clients (during dates or public Dreamland events) as André, I was able to obtain longer interviews, since most informants did not feel embarrassed, as they might have had I been a stranger.

Crossdresser escorts are required to take the lead in conversation, to make clients feel at ease and to avoid awkward silences. Life in Italy was a topic I often resorted to when holding conversations with clients and topics ranging from places to visit in Italy (a common travel destination for my clients) to suggestions about good Italian restaurants in Tokyo helped me to successfully navigate through dates. This then created the basis for additional dates together. Frequent meetings meant that I was able to make more observations and that I had better opportunities to establish intimate relationships with clients, and this helped smooth out any tension during interviews.

As for my co-workers, I often invited them for homemade Italian meals at my place, which they accepted enthusiastically. This gave me the opportunity to observe my informants in an informal and friendly setting, out of sight of clients, Mr. Hirota or of strangers. Hosting parties at my house helped me to develop good relationships with other crossdressers, and this meant that when I asked them for interviews, we already considered each other to be good co-workers, if not friends. A form of 'deep hanging out' (Bernard 1994; Geertz 1998; Kawulich 2005), this interaction was extremely useful as it allowed me to observe performances of masculinity on the part of my *dansō* co-workers in various situations, including reciprocal interactions in informal contexts. The insights generated helped me understand how my colleagues shaped their own specific performances of masculinity, not only in relation to clients but also vis-à-vis each other, and this provided me with the opportunity to observe how they managed the boundaries between their working and their private personae.

An important finding I drew from my 'deep hanging out' with *dansō* co-workers was that performances of masculinity on the part of colleagues outside work were different from the male characters they crafted and performed for clients. Private meetings, including *nomikai* (drinking parties) at my place, were an excellent opportunity to observe *dansō* in a context where they presented a less contrived expression of themselves. In such settings they appeared to behave more freely, expressing their true personalities. Through situations outside work, I saw the personalities of the different *dansō* emerging, showing their personal interpretations of masculinity, whether this involved being caring or talking dirty.

Some of them were openly talking about their sexual conquests, while others were very shy about this topic. Some presenting themselves as a Prince Charming type with clients, were sometimes indulging in strongly sexist comments about customers, or women in general. All these behaviours were expressions of my informants' personality.

While working as a *dansō* escort I also collected information about clients, how they acted and how they presented themselves to their escorts. It became clear to me that on a date, clients were performing what Jane Ward calls 'gender labour' (Ward 2010) – a term that 'describe[s] the affective and bodily efforts invested in giving genders to others or [...] helping others achieve the varied forms of gender recognition they long for' (ibid.: 237). When meeting crossdressers on dates and at events, clients almost always wore dresses and skirts. In most cases, the feminine clothes they wore expressed a delicate femininity, as they were in pastel colours, especially pink and ivory white, with girlish decorations (ribbons, glitter, hearts, etc.). All the customers used discrete make up and generally acted in ways that emphasised being 'weak and feminine', something that was in contrast with the manly appearance of crossdressers. By enhancing their own femininity, customers thus endorsed the performance of masculinity put on by the *dansō*. They also demonstrated their support for a binary gender system, in which they took active part alongside the crossdressers. As a couple, a *dansō* and a client embody the two genders, through stereotypical femininity – which is *kawaii* ('cute', see Kinsella 1995) – on the one hand; and an androgynous, beautified masculinity on the other.

It must be stressed that while crossdressers present themselves as of masculine gender they do not deny their birth assignment as female, a feature that differentiates *dansō* from transgender people. When asked about how they defined themselves, they would use the term *dansō*. change to: To them this seemed to be the best way to define their gender identity, since neither 'male' or 'female' seems appropriate. Clients do not recognise crossdressers as men or women either, but as *dansō*. *Dansō* is, thus, an 'in between' category. In her investigation of *dansō* working in crossdresser cafés, Michelle Ho (2020) defines *dansō* as non-binary and she uses the plural pronoun ('they') to refer to informants. I find this problematic as it appears to be a projection of anglophone LGBTQ+ activism onto a non-Western local embodiment of non-conforming gender identities. I found in my own research experience and in my informants' words that crossdressers use the term *dansō* to define themselves and that they referred to themselves and other crossdressers with the singular male pronoun, *ore* (see also Gamberton in this volume for a discussion of pronouns and trans people in Japan).

The Commodification of Identity

I found that for clients, the identity performed by crossdressers during dates represented 'the best partner a woman can dream of'. They regarded *dansō* as protective, kind and charming, and considered them to be masculine in the way that a perfect man should be masculine. They did not find them threatening, as many clients said they find biological men to be. My client informants also told me that because crossdressers are biologically women, they are capable of understanding a woman's psychology and emotions better than a man could. *Dansō* thus embody the best features of both genders, and according to clients this particular feature is what makes them *risōtekina otoko* or ideal men. In the company of *dansō*, female customers felt loved and protected, and they felt that they did not face the risk of being misunderstood, seduced and deceived, as they might be by a biological man (whether a non-commodified partner or a male host). This positive perception of *dansō* escorts echoes the stereotypical conceptions about men and women that both clients and escorts clearly endorse through their behaviour.

However, this ideal male identity is subject to rules defined by the market, as it is performed for a specific aim (to satisfy clients) and for a fixed price (30-minute dates range in cost from 1650 to 3300 yen, depending on the escort's rank). It is performed, then, in the context of a commodified date. During such a date, the crossdresser escort must adapt, at least partially, to his client's requests and accommodate her desire for a specific masculine *kei*. While *dansō* frame their personality through their self-presentation on the company website, in order to give customers an idea of what to expect by booking them, they must also show an ability and a willingness to adapt and to satisfy a wider range of requests, since this may lead to higher earnings. Hence, crossdressers are often ready to sacrifice what they consider more sincere expressions of their self for the benefit of specific customers. In order to lure a client, it is not unusual for crossdressers to change *kei* depending on what the client desires. As Haruka, a top star escort, explained when I asked him about his *kei*:

> What *kei* am I? I'm flirtatious. I don't know, I don't have a real *kei*, I want to be cool. Since I want to show off, I am basically a narcissist. I want to be myself. Yes, I want to be what I really am. I don't have a *kei*, and I don't want one. But when the customers ask me what *kei* I am, I say: 'What *kei* do you like? I can be whatever you want', and I make an effort to be the type they like. If you like the prince type, well, I can be your prince [...]. My real self and the character I play for work are basically the same person, but one costs you 4000 yen an hour.

For Haruka, crossdressing is a way to be himself, yet he also adapts his personality and his performance of masculinity to fit in with customers' requests for a specific *kei*. He only makes this effort to perform a specific character when he is paid to do so. The money transaction thus marks the difference between a less performative expression of personality and a specific *kei* performed to meet the request of a particular paying customer. Taking all of this into account, the self-presentation of *dansō* can on the one hand be understood as fictional, aimed at satisfying the requests clients make, but on the other hand it is also individual. Thus, *dansō* escorting forms part of the affective industry, straddling fantasy and the material world. Part of the pleasure it provides is arguably due to this overlap.

At the same time, it seems almost contradictory that in order to even get the opportunity to express what they define as their 'true self', *dansō* must perform more contrived versions of themselves. While, as Takeyama (2016) observes, men become male hosts in order to pursue success and self-realisation, including high financial rewards unachievable elsewhere, money is not a key factor for my *dansō* informants. In this business, earnings are highly unpredictable, with low-ranking crossdressers earning less than 10,000 yen a month and top star escorts between 150,000 and 300,000 yen per month. This is very different from the high income of successful male escorts. This occupation is chosen because it strongly matches *dansō*'s needs for self-expression. Working as a *dansō* is pivotal in my informants' lives in terms of their construction of a gendered identity, and the term *dansō* is the label by which they identify themselves. To do *dansō* is pivotal, in my informants' life in terms of the construction of their gendered identity, as the word '*dansō*' itself becomes the label they use to identify themselves. The articulation of *dansō* as a *doing* support the articulation of *dansō* as a signifier for a mode of *being*. To crossdress not only in their private time but also for their job provides *dansō* with the possibility to present themselves as gender masculine also in the workplace, which most of the traditional, corporate job would not allow them. Moreover, it helps them to structure their identity by being part of a group, of a community with shared interests in which building their identity through confrontation and identification with the other members, but also as a working category.

Conclusion: The Rules of the Game

Being part of the *dansō* escort world meant that I had to accept its rules. This included accepting several things that I experienced as rather negative, especially with regard to managing interactions with customers (Allison 1994; Parreñas 2011). Because of this, I found it essential to be able to negotiate my position and detach myself when I needed to do this. In this concluding section, I detail some of the difficulties I experienced during my fieldwork.

In order to work as a crossdresser escort, *dansō* must come to terms with the need to lie to customers. To develop a successful career, escorts develop intense and intimate relationships with clients, which often resemble love relationships. Clients who are deeply in love book escorts more frequently and for longer. They also buy various merchandise related to their love object. The earnings of a *dansō* depend heavily on his ability to maintain several of these 'love' relationships simultaneously. While Dreamland emphatically encourages the development of romantic relationships, the company does not allow the development of love affairs outside the framework of paid intimacy, and sexual services are strictly forbidden. Escorts who fail to follow the rules are subject to immediate dismissal and clients who pursue sexual relationships are banned from Dreamland.

Escorts, according to my data, are not interested in contravening the rules, firstly to not run the risk of losing their job, and secondly because they are not typically sexually attracted by their clients. In my sample, only 5 crossdressers out of 14 were lesbian, while the other were not (or not exclusively) attracted to women. In general, *dansō* do not find their clients attractive as they can be a fair bit older than them, and clients often do not match stereotypical canons of feminine beauty in Japan (they often have weight or skin problems) that *dansō* seems to appreciate. I did not encounter any *dansō* who was sexually aroused by his clients.

However, clients who are deeply in love are quite likely to ask for meetings that are not booked through the company, kisses or even sex. This means that successful *dansō* often face having to refuse clients, which is quite challenging as they must avoid offending them and disrupting the fantasy world in which the relationship is rooted, since this would endanger future revenue. *Dansō* often refuse forbidden requests by referring to the company rules, saying, for example, 'I would do it, but that is against the rules'. Thus escorts skilfully switch the blame to the company, thereby avoiding taking responsibility for their refusal, which might otherwise hurt the feelings of their customer. This excuse, moreover, also allows customers to believe that there may be a possibility to consummate their love in the future, something that is sometimes implicitly suggested by the crossdresser himself in order to keep a client's desire alive and thus to keep a loyal customer.

Lying and refusing prohibited requests are especially necessary when providing so called 'boyfriend experiences', the service that most explicitly requires *dansō* to fake feelings of love toward customers.[6] Even though clients

---

6   For a study on the provision of fake emotions and performed love stories (*gijiren'ai*) see also Takeyama 2016.

are aware of the highly performative nature of escorts' declarations of love, not all *dansō* are willing to lie and to perform this role. Whether a *dansō* is willing to take on this role or not is associated with whether a *dansō* is high- or low-ranking (in terms of success and earnings). Some escorts avoid declarations of love which are not genuine and/or refuse to provide boyfriend experiences because they do not wish to take advantage of the emotional weaknesses of clients. With this sense of empathy, however, comes significant economic disadvantage. I knew some *dansō* who overtly took advantage of their clients' emotional dependence on them, with the aim of increasing their earnings. They managed this by detaching themselves, emotionally, from their clients' painful experiences of love.

Escorts also have to detach themselves if clients start to 'spiral down' due to their relationship with a crossdresser, a situation I had to manage myself during my fieldwork. I witnessed the case of a client spending all her savings on her favourite escort for dates, dinners and presents. She was working part time and barely able to survive on her income. During one date with me, a day that her favourite was not available and she did not want to be alone, she complained about her current economic situation. I not only felt deeply sorry for her, but also guilty that my hourly fee contributed to her problems. However, to keep doing this job, a *dansō* must be able to detach himself from the inability of some people to safely enjoy the escort service as a commodified experience rather than a 'real' relationship.

Detachment is also necessary if long periods of time pass without customers. A lack of booked dates undermines escorts' self-confidence. Having no reservations not only means having to accept a lack of earnings and formal recognition of the efforts one puts into getting customers, but also having to deal with the thought that one is not loveable or charming enough to attract clients. During my time in the field, I saw how this can easily sneak into escorts' minds, often leading to various mental health issues, such as anxiety and depression. It is pivotal here to remember that *dansō*'s social recognition happens through the market, and their sense of self is created also through their occupation. This is not the case for those with other queer identities, who do not need to perform a specific job to define themselves. In most cases, *dansō* are fully able to identify as such through their work as *dansō* escorts. Crossdressers are required to constantly negotiate between their private selves and their working personae, but the two positions overlap and influence each other, often making it challenging for *dansō* to draw a clear demarcation line between their working 'I' and their self outside the escort business. Hence, a lack of clients represents a serious blow to many *dansōs'* self-confidence.

While I could not fully share my colleagues' feelings in this regard, I did find it difficult to accept that in the *dansō* escort business individuals are often judged and valued for their aesthetic appearance and performed identities rather than for their sincere personalities – which would potentially destroy clients' fantasies. I only fully understood and mastered managing negative comments on my look and personality after having been the subject of more or less harsh critique from colleagues and clients. I learned to react without feeling personally offended, taking these comments as 'part of the game' instead. The criticisms were, I realised, not about me, but about a performed identity of mine that I developed specifically for clients – an identity with which I did not identify. My position (and in this case, its privileges) was fundamental in dealing with my feelings. The coping strategy I resorted to when I felt that my sense of identity and my own self-evaluation were under scrutiny was to detach André – myself as *dansō* – from Marta, my real self. When things for André became hard, I had a place to escape to – my 'real' life. I had the option of stopping crossdressing at any time if I wanted to. I crossdressed for research, while my informants crossdressed to express themselves. I felt lucky that I had a way out, an option not available to them. For my crossdresser informants there was no other way forward but to keep expressing their 'real' selves through work, which meant accepting the commodification and exploitation of their identity, their own exploitation of other people's feelings, and the market rules that dominate the escort business. For them, gender represents their work, is the key to their self-expression, and is an unavoidable site of constant tension and negotiations, to be reshaped at every social interaction.

References

Adler, Patricia A. and Peter Adler. 1987. *Membership Roles in Field Research*. Thousand Oaks, CA: Sage Publications, Inc.

Allison, Anne. 1994. *Nightwork: Sexuality, Pleasure, and Corporate Masculinity in a Tokyo Hostess Club*. Chicago: University of Chicago Press.

———. 2009. The cool brand, affective activism and Japanese youth. *Theory, Culture & Society*, 26(2–3): 89–111.

Azuma Sonoko. 2007. Goshujinsama inai no basho: dansō kosupure kissa wo meguru jendāronteki kōsatsu (trans. A place with no masters: a discussion of gender in a *dansō* cosplay cafè). *Imēji toshite no 'Nihon'* (trans. *Imagined Japan*). Retrieved from ir.library.osakau.ac.jp/repo/ouka/all/13192/2004_05-1.pdf. [Accessed 30 September 2021].

Bernard, H. Russell. 1994. *Research Methods in Anthropology: Qualitative and Quantitative Approaches* (second edition). Walnut Creek: AltaMira Press.

Bridges, David. 2001. The ethics of outsider research. *Journal of Philosophy of Education*, 35(3): 371–386.

Burrell, Jenna. 2009. The field site as a network: A strategy for locating ethnographic research. *Field Methods*, 21(2): 181–199.

Butler, Judith. 1990. *Gender Trouble*. London: Routledge.

Coté, Mark and Jennifer Pybus. 2007. Learning to immaterial labour 2.0: MySpace and social networks. *Ephemera*, 7(1): 88–106.

DeLyser, Dydia. 2001. 'Do you really live here?' Thoughts on insider research. *Geographical Review*, 91(1–2): 441–453.

Fanasca, Marta. 2018. *Walk like a Man, Talk like a Man: Dansō, Gender, and Emotion Work in a Tokyo Escort Service* (Ph.D. dissertation, University of Manchester).

———. 2019a. FtM crossdresser escorts in contemporary Japan: an embodied and sensorial ethnography. *Asian Anthropology*, 18(3): 154–169.

———. 2019b. Crossdressing Dansō: Negotiating between stereotypical femininity and self-expression in patriarchal Japan. *Girlhood Studies*, 12(1): 33–48.

Galbraith, Patrick. 2009. Moe: Exploring virtual potential in post-millennial Japan. *Electronic Journal of Contemporary Japanese Studies*. Retrieved from www.japanesestudies.org.uk/articles/2009/Galbraith.html. [Accessed 30 September /2021.

———. 2013. Maid cafés: The affect of fictional characters in Akihabara, Japan. *Asian Anthropology*, 12(2): 104–125.

Galbraith, Patrick and Frederick L. Schodt. 2009. *The Otaku Encyclopedia: An Insider's Guide to the Subculture of Cool Japan*. Tokyo: Kodansha International.

Geertz, Clifford. 1998. Deep hanging out. *The New York Review of Books*, 45(16): 69–72.

Gregory, Eve and Mahera Ruby. 2011. The 'insider/outsider' dilemma of ethnography: Working with young children and their families in cross-cultural contexts. *Journal of Early Childhood Research*, 9(2): 162–174.

Hardt, Micheal and Antonio Negri. 2000. *Empire*. Cambridge, MA: Harvard University Press.

Hayfield, Nikki and Caroline Huxley. 2015. Insider and outsider perspectives: Reflections on researcher identities in research with lesbian and bisexual women. *Qualitative Research in Psychology*, 12(2): 91–106.

Hendry, Joy. 1995. *Understanding Japanese Society*, 2nd edition. London: Routledge.

Ho, Michelle 2020. Queer and normal: *dansō* (female-to-male crossdressing) lives and politics in contemporary Tokyo. *Asian Anthropology*, 19(2): 102–118.

Hochschild, R. Arlie. 1983. *The Managed Heart: Commercialization of Human Feeling*. Berkeley: University of California Press.

Ito Mizuko, Okabe Daisuke and Tsuji Izumi (eds). 2012. *Fandom Unbound: Otaku Culture in a Connected World*. New Heaven: Yale University Press.

Jankie, Dudu. 2004. 'Tell me who you are': Problematizing the construction and positionalities of 'insider'/'outsider' of a 'native' ethnographer in a postcolonial context. Kagendo Mutua and Beth Blue Swadener (eds.) *Decolonizing Research in Cross-Cultural Contexts: Critical Personal Narratives*, 87–105. New York: Suny University Press.

Kam H. Thiam. 2013. The common sense that makes the '*otaku*': Rules for consuming popular culture in contemporary Japan. *Japan Forum* 25(2): 151–173.

Kawulich, B. Barbara. 2005. Participant observation as a data collection method. *Forum Qualitative Sozialforschung / Forum: Qualitative Social Research*, 6(2), Art. 43. Retrieved from nbn-resolving.de/urn:nbn:de:0114-fqs0502430. [Accessed 30 September 2021].

Kinsella, Sharon. 1995. Cuties in Japan. In L. Skov and B. Moeran *Women, media and consumption in Japan*, 220–255. Honolulu: University of Hawai'i Press

———.1998. Japanese subculture in the 1990s: Otaku and the amateur manga movement. *Journal of Japanese Studies*, 289–316.

Kondo, K. Dorinne. 1990. *Crafting Selves: Power, Gender, and Discourses of Identity in a Japanese Workplace*. Chicago: University of Chicago Press.

Lazzarato, Maurizio. 2008. *Immaterial Labor*. On-line article. Retrieved from: www.generation-online.org/c/fcimmateriallabour3.htm. [Accessed 30 September/06/2021].

Lunsing, Wim. 2001. *Beyond Common Sense: Sexuality and Gender in Contemporary Japan*. London: Kegan Paul.

Martinez, P. Dolores. 2006. When *soto* becomes *uchi*: some thoughts on the anthropology of Japan. *In* Joy Hendry and Heung Wah Wong (eds), *Dismantling the East–West Dichotomy*, 51–57. London: Routledge.

Merriam B. Sharam, Johnson-Bailey Juanita, Lee Mingh-Yeh, Kee Youngwha, Ntseane Gabo, Mazanah Muhamad. 2001. Power and positionality: Negotiating insider/outsider status within and across cultures. *International Journal of Lifelong Education*, 20(5): 405–416.

Miller, Laura. 2003. Male beauty work in Japan. *In* J. E. Roberson and N. Suzuki (eds), *Men and Masculinities in Contemporary Japan: Dislocating the Salaryman Doxa*, 37–58. New York: Routledge.

Moore, Ryan. 2005. Alternative to what? Subcultural capital and the commercialization of a music scene. *Deviant Behavior*, 26(3): 229–252.

Nobuoka, Jakob. 2010. User innovation and creative consumption in Japanese culture industries: The case of Akihabara, Tokyo. *Geografiska Annaler: Series B, Human Geography*, 92(3): 205–218.

Otsubo Makito. 2003. The embodiment of tools – Interpretation through the theory of life. *Proceedings of the Annual Conference of the Japan Institute of Design*, 50: 12–21.

Parreñas, S. Rachel. 2011. *Illicit Flirtations: Labor, Migration, and Sex Trafficking in Tokyo*. Stanford: Stanford University Press.

Sherif, Bahira. 2001. The ambiguity of boundaries in the fieldwork experience: Establishing rapport and negotiating insider/outsider status. *Qualitative Inquiry*, 7(4): 436–447.

Takeyama Akiko. 2005. Commodified romance in a Tokyo host club. *In* Mark McLelland and Romit Dasgupta *Genders, Transgenders and Sexualities in Japan*, 216–233. London: Routledge.

———. 2010. "Intimacy for sale: Masculinity, entrepreneurship, and commodity self in Japan's neoliberal situation." *Japanese Studies* 30(2): 231–246.

———. 2016. *Staged Seduction. Selling dreams in a Tokyo host club*. Stanford: Stanford University Press.

Tang, T. S. Denise. 2007. The research pendulum: Multiple roles and responsibilities as a researcher. *Journal of Lesbian Studies*, 10(3–4): 11–27.

Wacquant, L. Loïc. 2004. *Body and Soul: Ethnographic Notebooks of An Apprentice Boxer*. New York: Oxford University Press.

Ward, Jane. 2010. Gender labor: Transmen, femmes, and collective work of transgression. *Sexualities*, 13(2): 236–254.

White, Merry Isaacs. 2003. Taking note of teen culture in Japan: Dear diary, dear fieldworker. *In* T. C. Bestor, P. G. Steinhoff and V. Lyon-Bestor (eds), *Doing Fieldwork in Japan*, 21–35. Honolulu: University of Hawaii Press.

CHAPTER 4

Professional Amateurs

Authenticity and Sex Work in a 'Delivery Health' Shop

Nicola Phillips

Downtown Uguisudani is an unglamorous corner of northern Tokyo, a stone's throw away from Ueno station. Narrow roads crisscross beneath the expressway, which casts a dark shadow over fast food eateries and grey office blocks. As most Tokyo natives will know, there is really only one reason to come here. If Kabukichō is the kingpin of Japan's illustrious sex and entertainment industry, Uguisudani is a somewhat sadder cousin: everything is smaller, older and less glamorous, promising cheap thrills for even less money. Located just two kilometres from the original licensed pleasure quarters of Yoshiwara, it is home to hundreds of legal establishments offering sexual services at affordable prices. Simply step into a dedicated information booth near the station and use one of the ageing public computers to filter the available services, based on your interests, location and price range. Once you have found a service, scroll through some of the icons of available women and call the office to arrange an appointment. All that is left to do is to check into one of the many cheap and unassuming love hotels in the area. However, these are not the flamboyant love hotels with water beds and mirrored ceilings depicted in tabloid newspapers. Instead, think beige walls, linoleum floors and PVC corner sofas. Hired by the hour, these unassuming rooms serve as the ephemeral workplace for the largest sector of legal sex work, 'delivery health' call-girls.

It was a cool spring afternoon and I had arranged to meet the owner of a local delivery health agency for a tour of the office. As we stepped inside a dank lift that smelt of stale cigarettes, Shinohara-san explained that the name of his company, Deadball, comes from the baseball term meaning 'a ball out of play'.

Having been a regular customer of the legal sex industry himself, he had seen a niche in the market for an agency that specialised not in the young, glamorous, skinny women who are typically the face of Japan's sex industry, but in the plain, the old, the chubby. Deadball has now expanded to four branches in Tokyo and one in Osaka, but the scale would be difficult to guess from the cramped office. We stepped out of the narrow corridor into a converted apartment from the seventies: three small rooms lined with tatami mats and separated by paper sliding doors. Four employees sat at computers in the central room, manning the active Twitter accounts, editing the videos for the Deadball YouTube channel and fielding calls from clients. In the other two rooms, women of all ages sat on cheap *zaisu* chairs on the floor, heads pointed down towards their phones or up towards the television showing an innocuous panel programme on mute. The women looked bored, or tired or both, but nodded politely as I greeted them. Truth to tell, there was not much to see, but Shinohara-san made sure to point to the government-issued licence that had pride of place by the door. 'We do everything here by the book', he tells me pointedly.

The process for hiring a delivery health worker is simple. When a client calls in, their phone number is routed through the agency's database system. If they've used the service before, their details will appear, including whether or not they've been blacklisted at the request of a worker. Assuming all is well, staff then run through the standard services, known as 'courses' (*kōsu*), and the client may request a particular woman, as well as provide details of preferred services and his location. Typically, this is a local love hotel. The call ends, and the staff relays the information to the employee who has been requested, who then goes out almost immediately to her client. During the short time I was in the office, a call came in. After a few minutes of discussion, a staff member called out lazily to the room: 'Inoue-san'. To my surprise, a woman in her seventies shuffled forward. She wore a light grey pinafore, a frayed pink cardigan and thick, white tights. The staff member said to her brusquely, 'So, you'll be meeting Tanaka-san at 4pm at the Hotel Raymond.' 'Where's that?' replied the woman. 'When you leave the office, turn left. Walk down three blocks, turn right and carry on until you hit the main road. You know the bridge?' The older woman nodded slowly whilst pulling a face of utmost concentration. 'It's just on the other side of the bridge. In the Yamanashi building, third floor, room 219.' I vaguely wondered why she didn't just use her phone to look up the hotel. 'I better get going straight away then. Thank you very much.'

She ruffled through her handbag and extracted an old-style flip phone (pink with a dangling phone charm), a small notebook and a pen. She lifted her reading glasses, which hung around her neck on a cord, and steadily made a note – 219. Then she bowed again and excused herself from the office to go to her first appointment of the day.

And in this slow manner rush hour began.

The Order of Play at Deadball

In line with the baseball theme, Deadball uses a whole range of metaphors and euphemisms related to baseball on its website to describe the services on offer. All the women are referred to as 'players' and they are divided into different categories: from the most expensive 'super major league players' to the 'regular players', down to the cheaper 'rookie players.' The company assigns a woman to a category based on her appearance, her age and her experience in the sex industry. Younger women who are more conventionally attractive command higher rates, though the take-home pay is still low at 4,000 ¥, around $35. There is a whole host of 'playtime' options to choose from, but the two most popular are the 'set course' of 70 minutes and the 'homerun course' lasting 100 minutes. Ejaculation is guaranteed at least once with both of these options, and there is the potential for more than once on the 'homerun course'. A customer chooses a woman based on her online profile, which consists of racy pictures and a detailed questionnaire about what kind of sexual play she offers. In line with the laws surrounding prostitution, vaginal intercourse is off-limits, but this aside, the customer can request what they like, within reason. As Shinohara-san told me, 'If customers respect the rules, we treat them like gods. If they break them, we respond seriously'.

In the hierarchy of legal sex work and establishments, Deadball is at the very bottom in terms of glamour and earning potential. I was told that other legal agencies providing sexual services require that women be young, beautiful and sexy; however, there are no such standards necessary in order to be hired at Deadball.[1] The owner is happy to have anyone on his books

---

1 Though people of all genders sell sex in Japan, by definition the vast majority of the legal industry consists of heterosexual services for male clients. McLelland (2005) and Mitsuhashi (2006) have touched upon transgender women and sex work and there is an unknown number of services catering to homosexual men (Gilhooly 2017).

PROFESSIONAL AMATEURS

Figure 4.1: A screenshot of Deadball's homepage for the Uguisudani branch, 23 August 2019. It displays deals for sessions and links through to information about available women, rules, terminology and even a careers page. The top right tagline reads… 'To you who want to quit [using] the sex industry… if you play, your relationship [with your wife] will be harmonious! Her gratitude will double!' The word 'play' here is a euphemism for using sexual services. Visible just beneath this is a link to the Sakura Research and Screening Facility, which is used by Deadball for routine sexual health screening. **Colour**, p. 219.

who is interested in working there, though of course their earnings depend on client bookings. The company markets itself as specialising in *busu* women, and their slogan is 'The lowest level Japan ['s sex industry] has to offer'.[2] Though *busu* translates literally as 'ugly', I found it was used rather like the word 'plain' in English, in the sense that it was used relative to those who were considered attractive.[3] In the legal sex industry, to be 'cute' or *kawaii* means you are young, thin, with good teeth and ample breasts. Women are therefore deemed to be *busu* if they do not meet all of those conventional standards for a replace with 'girl' in the sex industry (*fūzokujō*), rather than because they look 'ugly'. That said, customers cannot see the faces of the

---

2   The original Japanese is *reberu no hikusa nihon ichi no fūzoku*. Deadball also has a sister company specialising in more attractive, but also 'motherly', types.
3   All translations are my own, unless otherwise specified.

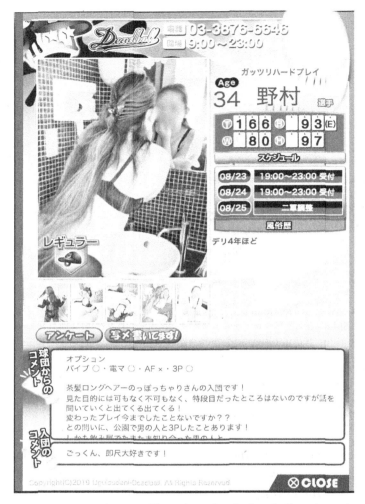

Figure 4.2: A worker's profile in the style of a baseball card, 23rd August 2019. She is a 'regular' level player, which denotes her price. The profile contains basic information such as height and weight, how long she has been in the delivery health industry, as well as detailed descriptions of what kind of 'play' she offers. Her tagline reads: 'I love to give head and swallow!'. **Colour**, p. 220.

workers until the session itself, which is why Deadball is referred to as a 'landmine service' (*jirai no omise*).

At this point it is worth briefly discussing the scope of legal sex work in Japan and how it differs from illegal sex work. Under pressure from the occupying US forces after WWII, the Japanese government implemented the Prostitution Prevention Law in 1958, forbidding 'sexual intercourse with an unspecified party for compensation or for promise of compensation'.[4] To this day, 'sexual intercourse' has never been strictly defined, but the courts have interpreted it to mean coitus: the insertion of a male penis into a female vagina (West 2011; Kuninobu et al. 1998). The narrow definition of prostitution as vaginal intercourse has led to a growing number of sex establishments specialising in other forms of sexual pleasure and the so-called 'ejaculation business' (*shasei sangyō*) is worth 2.37 trillion yen, or approximately 24 billion US dollars (Hoffman 2007; Kadokura 2002). According to the 1948 Entertainment Law, sexual services are defined in a rather vague and heteronormative manner as 'services in response to the sexual curiosity of a customer of the opposite sex'.[5] This ambiguity serves today as a loophole that allows any sexual act other than vaginal intercourse to be sold legally. This distinction between sexual entertainment and 'prostitution', coupled with recent anti-trafficking measures, has led to a huge rise in 'delivery health agencies' such as Deadball, which provide sexual services off-site (McLelland 2005; Koch 2016). According to a 2019 police white paper, there were 20,152 delivery health businesses registered legally across the country compared with 1,222 'soaplands' (Turkish baths that serve as brothels), 770 'fashion health' clubs (erotic massage parlours) and 100 strip clubs (Keisatsuchō 2019).[6] This makes delivery health the most common type of legal sex work by far.

Methodology used in Fieldwork

Deadball's founder, Shinohara-san, is a vocal advocate of legal sex work as a means for women to raise themselves out of poverty (Sueyoshi 2015). He is also an astute businessman and my guess is that he agreed to let me conduct

---

4 *Baishun Bōshihō* (The Prostitution Prevention Law)1956, Chapter 1: Article 2, 'Definitions'. The word for sexual intercourse used in the law is *seikō*. The key wording of the law remains unchanged to this day.

5 The phrase used to describe sexual encounters is '*isei no kyaku no seiteki kōkishin ni ōjite sono kyaku ni sesshoku suru ekimu*'.

6 The Prostitution Prevention Law defines prostitution as 'sexual intercourse with an unspecified party for compensation or for promise of compensation', however this is liberally interpreted in the case of the 'soaplands'. The client and worker both pay a nominal fee to enter the bathhouse, where they 'meet' and spontaneously decide to have sex, therefore turning the 'unspecified parties' into 'specified' acquaintances (West 2011). The authorities recognise soaplands as legal establishments in which vaginal sex is sold.

interviews at his company in order to promote his brand. Shinohara-san was not paid, nor did he expect anything in particular from this research, not even to read my results, it appeared. I advised him that endorsement was not my goal and that all interviews would be private between me and my interlocutors. After an initial interview, we agreed that I could wait in a café around the corner from the office in Uguisudani, where many of the women spend time waiting for clients. If someone wanted to talk to me, they could approach me there. Between April and May 2019, I interviewed 11 current Deadball employees and one former worker. Interviews ranged from 45 to 90 minutes and were conducted by me in Japanese, accompanied by two Japanese friends of mine (only one at any given time).[7] I told them that the content of the interviews would not be relayed to their boss or colleagues. Interestingly, three women asked if their boss could be present at the interviews. I had the sense that they felt more comfortable with him there, especially at the beginning of the interview when they were wary of me. Overall, it was clear that the women liked and respected Shinohara-san and most cited him directly as the reason why they worked at the company. All of my interlocutors signed consent forms and interviews were recorded. The majority of interlocutors were in their 40s and 50s, which reflected the broad demographics of employees I saw during my time around the office. However, on the website there are many more women in their 30s, who might have been busier with clients and/or other aspects of life. Therefore, even within this niche agency, I was likely speaking with a subsection of women, who attracted a certain kind of clientele.

The women I spoke to said that they generally felt safe at work and Deadball's reputation for safety was raised numerous times when we were discussing why they worked there despite the low pay of around at 4,000 ¥ ($35) per hour.[8] After a woman has met her client in his hotel room, she rings the agency to signal the start of play and she rings again at the end of

---

[7] Two friends of mine had offered to attend the interviews with me after I told them that I was concerned about establishing trust. Sex work can be a delicate topic, and I was an outsider (and also someone who was a lot younger than the participants). The presence of my friends (both in their late thirties) lent legitimacy, which was clear from the fact that many of the women initially directed their answers at my companions even though I did the majority of the talking. This changed during the course of the interview; but I sensed that not many had spoken with a foreign researcher before.

[8] See Aoyama (2013; 2014) for common risks women working in the industry face, especially migrant workers.

the session. If they desire, workers can request a buzzer that alerts the office and a private security company directly. Such protocols are part of a wider attempt by the industry to appear safe and to tackle stigma in order to attract new workers (Koch 2020). The women I spoke to mentioned occasional instances when clients had made them feel uncomfortable, but these seemed to be rare. Shinohara-san told me that the company had an internal blacklist of customers who had misbehaved, and that he was not afraid to forward reports to the police. However, this is not to say that the Japanese legal system is necessarily progressive in relation to sex work: women who are suspected of working by themselves (and not through an agency) are dealt with severely. One woman who had been working in the industry for 15 years said that she had been arrested multiple times for allegedly streetwalking during periods when she was homeless.

Different agencies attract different segments of the labour market, and the workers at Deadball tended to be older women who had not worked in the traditional labour market for a long time. Most of the women I spoke to seemed to be lower middle class, judging by the fact that many had gone to university and were or had been married to white-collar salarymen. They had generally entered the sex industry because they wanted flexible and relatively high-paying work. Typically, they wanted to provide extra income to their family. Many had divorced late in life and found employment options lacking or had accumulated large personal debts that they wanted to pay off quickly. Though nearly all the workers said that they disliked the job, they also said that sex work was preferable to the other mediocre labour options available to them. This throws a critical light on the position of older women within Japan's labour market, where the minimum wage is ¥874 an hour (just under $8). Pay from infrequent sex work would still average out at about the same as contracted part-time work, and those over 50 told me that fewer hours doing sex work was preferable to long regular shifts in the service industry. Furthermore, with many working at Deadball as a second or even third job, the ability to choose their own hours was crucial. Yet I was surprised to hear that the women only take home 50% of what the customer pays. This is the industry standard, according to Koch (2014), and yet it does raise some interesting questions about the legalisation of sex work (as opposed to decriminalisation) and whom it actually serves, as the women themselves do not get to set their own prices. However, workers are able to decide what kind of sexual services they provide and all of them said that they wanted more customers. In short, all the women I spoke with chose the work freely and without coercion – as several of them told me, they could easily get another job. Working at Deadball was not a last resort, but rather the best out of a disappointing pool of options.

Reflections on the Process

Choice of topic is no accident, and, as Kato (2007) astutely notes, the Japanese sex industry attracts a certain kind of researcher: usually a white, middle class, Western woman raised in Judeo-Catholic households – criteria which all apply to me. I grew up with British media that views Japan and its sex industry through an orientalist lens, one through which men are portrayed as 'hypersexual virgins' (Alexy 2019: 113) and women as sexually passive and infantile. When I began asking around trying to find women working in the industry, many people reacted somewhat wearily to the request, coming from yet another young, white, female academic.

Eventually I met a broadcaster who had worked on a television documentary about Deadball. She kindly offered to attend the first few interviews in order to break the ice with the women working there, some of whom she knew. In her previous work, this broadcaster had focused on women who had been driven to sex work through poverty and who disliked the job. This is a common depiction of the industry in Japan and a sex worker activist told me that the media almost exclusively deals with the topic through a victim/trauma lens. I was wary of perpetuating this narrative, which the journalist soon noticed. After my second interview, she asked why I was not delving more into their backgrounds, their families and negative aspects of the work specifically (instead I asked about their feelings about the work). I told her that it was not my goal to mine for trauma and that if those things came up naturally as part of the conversation then I would pay attention to them. She seemed genuinely confused that my focus was not the intersection of trauma and sex work specifically.

In fact, in the beginning I tried to keep my scope as wide as possible and let the interviews lead the theme. As Agustín (2002a) notes, the majority of sex work research is funded because it is framed around the notion of trauma – sex workers as victims or as inherently vulnerable populations. My funding carried no such conditions, but on a personal level I believe in the deregulation of borders and tentatively support a decriminalised model of prostitution as favoured by many sex worker activists in the UK and the US. Of course, there is the danger of glorifying sex work to the point where injustices and risks are minimised or erased and I was mindful not to slip into this other extreme. Initially I thought I could withhold my personal views in order not to inject myself into the data, but I quickly realised that by remaining silent on the for/against sex work issue, the women I spoke to automatically assumed I would be anti-sex work. This is a fair assumption to make and, as Smith and Mac (2018) note, there are many researchers looking to marginalise sex work. When interviewing historically marginalised people, we must reflect on our own positionality and methods in order to interrogate our own motivations (Agustín 2002b).

More than is the case in other areas of study, sex work researchers must contend with their outsider status and the power imbalance that this creates (Agustín 2002a: 627). I am an outsider on several levels: I am white, foreign and I have not had experience with sex work. This can obviously hinder research in many ways: as a Westerner my openness and direct manner of speaking sometimes crossed a cultural line, especially regarding topics related to sex, where much is implied or tacitly understood. For example, many of the women I interviewed were reluctant to discuss specific acts, instead referring to the fact that such information was in their online profiles. Though in general there is a social taboo concerning the open discussion of female sexuality, I wrongly assumed that this would not apply to sex workers. At other times, however, I believe that my status as a foreigner was a useful excuse for those I was interviewing to open up. Many of the women I spoke to had not told their friends and family about their line of work, sometimes not even their husbands. The fact that I was both young and not Japanese meant that my reactions and potential judgement were not as valuable or meaningful as the reactions of a Japanese person. My outsider status in this context was useful in that respect. Several of the women I spoke to said it was fun to have a conversation about their work with a foreigner and they were curious to see which points I found surprising or interesting.

It is worth mentioning here that my interview style was quite informal, though I had not always intended this to be the case. In the first few interviews I barely spoke myself. My notebook was open in front of me with questions that had been re-written to perfection by Japanese native speakers. I was careful to not inject my own opinions into the conversation, but this meant I often was not able to really engage or establish a relationship. Meeting these women for the first time during our interviews, I realised I needed to connect more with my interviewees. I decided to put my notebook away, instead having certain questions in mind but allowing the flow to develop naturally, whilst being more present myself in the conversation. Free-flowing conversation plays to my personal strengths as an ethnographer, but at the same time it meant my opinions now became part of the data. It is important to be explicit about this, as fieldwork is intricately linked with the personality, values and experiences of the ethnographer (Coffey 1999). As I mentioned above, I did not openly state my own pro-sex work views for fear of appearing biased. However, it soon became clear that the women were wary of me, assuming that I was anti-sex work and that I would judge them for their choice of profession. On the other hand, I then had to make sure I was not giving the impression that I thought all sex work was liberating and unproblematic. When asked for feedback on my questions, an interviewee challenged my question of 'Why do you do this work?' She said that it is 'not easy to give an immediate answer to the question of why someone does this work. At least that's what I think, because as far as I know, I don't think there is anyone who does this job because they enjoy it'. I had chosen that question in the beginning because I wanted to allow room for subjectivity. However, as someone who was not a sex worker, I had to respect the limits of my understanding and the fact that even a seemingly neutral question had the potential to offend. As Agustín (2002b) argues, we must rethink direct questioning when subjects are stigmatised and subjugated.

Interviewing in the Japanese Context

Another issue I encountered was that short, simple, open-ended questions tended to elicit short, simple, narrow replies. My intention had been to use open-ended questions as a springboard for longer answers, as I had been taught to do during my training as an anthropologist; but when I used questions like this, the women seemed confused as to what shape and length their response should be, as I myself did not provide enough cues regarding my expectations. The women were not comfortable just to offer up their personal opinions without knowing me, but even if they had known me better, I suspect their answers would still have been short. I believe this is a feature of Japanese communication in general, that people are less likely to extrapolate freely based on a single prompt, as it can be considered rude, arrogant or perhaps off-topic. To counter this, at the beginning of interviews, I began explicitly stating that there were no right or wrong answers that I wanted to hear, and that interviewees could bring in topics or details that I had not mentioned. This still did not elicit in-depth answers, which is why at a certain point I began to shift my method and began to engage with the interviews more as conversations. In these conversations, I tended to make general statements about sex work in the UK, which served to provide a comparison with sex work in Japan. Of course, being neither a sex worker nor an expert on UK sex work, I had no basis on which to make such generalisations. However, seeing more of my personality in these conversations and hearing my views, the women seemed more willing to trust me. The answers I received as a result were more meaningful.

Using this more informal, conversational method of carrying out an ethnographic interview meant that I was injecting my own self, personality and opinions into the data. Some anthropologists might argue that this is problematic and that it skews the results. Any detailed discussion of the pros and cons of different methods is beyond the scope of this chapter; but I would argue that it was the most appropriate method of establishing a deeper and more meaningful connection with my interlocutors.

A difference I noticed between Japanese and English-language conversations is that in Japanese a good deal of interjection, affirmation and paraphrasing is necessary in order to show that one is listening respectfully. This affected the course of my interviews. Take this example of when I was discussing the low rates paid by Deadball with Aiko, a 24-year-old former employee:

Me: So, did you never consider working at a different shop?

Aiko: I thought about that, but if I did [move to a different shop with higher pay], I would start to think of it as an easy way to get money.

Me: Oh?

Aiko: I was earning 4000/5000 yen [per hour] – barely saving anything. I really learnt how to save [what I could] at Deadball. But if I had worked for a shop with higher rates, in difficult times I would have just thought, 'Oh it's fine, I'll just go into the sex industry again'. [And because of that] I would never have been able to leave [the industry].

Me: Ah I see, I see. You wouldn't have been able to quit because you'd be earning a higher wage. That's interesting – so because you received an average wage from Deadball, you could easily quit.

Aiko: Right, and because it was daytime work it was easier to have another job outside of the sex industry.

In English, rephrasing someone's words back to them might be considered too leading, but in Japanese it felt like an important sign of respect and presence in the conversation. Therefore, throughout this study, I have included the surrounding conversation when I provide quotes that emerged from a quick-fire exchange like this.

Vaginal Sex as 'The Real Deal'

What makes Japan's legal system unique is the fact the sale of vaginal sex is defined as 'prostitution', but other sexual acts are not. This highlights how body parts and sexual acts are inscribed with different cultural meanings and that sex is created through discursive practices rather than discovered (Foucault 1990). This is evident in censorship practices in Japan. Allison (1996) argues that censorship of adult genitalia in Japanese media has created opportunities for a broad and imaginative sexscape. According to Article 175 of the Penal Code, the penis, vagina and pubic hair are 'obscene objects', and images of them are regarded as inciting sexual desire and they invoke a sense of shame. However, depictions of sadomasochism, paedophilia, rape and scatological pornography are not considered obscene. Aside from creating and fostering certain sexual preferences (say for Lolita imagery), Allison argues that, by hiding sexual organs, the state is encouraging a 'sexual economy' of a certain kind; a hierarchy of body parts, sexual acts and sexuality. The penis and vagina as sex organs come to represent vaginal intercourse in general, signifying a reproductive heterosexuality. The message is that reproductive sex is private and for the domestic context, whilst other kinds of sex are for entertainment. Whether or not everything neatly lines up on either side of the border in reality, Allison argues, is irrelevant. Rather, the distinction itself is enough to suggest that the vagina and penis (and their reproductive capabilities) are sacred, and their use in cheap entertainment is therefore obscene.

We can apply similar logic to the way in which the Prostitution Prevention Law and Entertainment Law have divided sexual acts. In general conversation and within the industry, the term *honban* literally means 'performance' or 'take', but in the sex industry this term refers to vaginal sex. A better translation of *honban* might be 'the real deal'. Of course, if vaginal sex is 'the real deal', it implies that other sexual acts are somehow less serious or valid. In a survey from the newspaper *Nagai Taimizu*, 79.5% of respondents said they believed that a partner was not unfaithful if he used legal sex and 81% of sex workers believed that it was not cheating to either use or work in the sex industry (Kaname and Mizushima 2006: 65). During the conversations I had with sex workers at Deadball, it became clear that they saw a distinction between vaginal sex and the sale of other acts. Although it would be very easy to engage in *honban* on the side and earn a little extra, because clients are often keen for more, 10 out of 11 women I spoke with explicitly stated that they would never sell *honban* because it was something intimate to be saved for loving couples, as Yumi, 55, explained:

> Yumi: It's not just that I'm married, though – it's that I wouldn't want to. I think *honban* is for people you actually like. I'm married, so for me, that's with my husband.

Generally, the women were very judgmental of those who would sell vaginal sex. For example, Naoko[9] told me that even though she worked in this industry partly to 'get back at' her cheating husband, she would never sell vaginal sex: 'I can tell the ones that sell *honban*, you know. I can see it on their faces just by looking at them. At my age and, well, after two years of working in this world, I can just tell.' Another woman told me that those who sold vaginal sex were only making things harder for those who did not want to cross that personal and legal line. If there is one worker who is willing to sell vaginal sex, then she will take away business from others. But as I mentioned above, the line is one that relates to more than simple legal boundaries. When I asked how they would feel if the scope of legal sex work was expanded to include vaginal sex (outside of de facto legal soaplands), most women opposed the idea. They believed that the current Prostitution Prevention Law protects them:

> Yuki (57): The rates and the type of customer are different at the shops that sell *honban*. So depending on the shop there are many things to consider. At my current workplace [Deadball] they are quite clear that *honban* is a no-go and so I feel safe in my job. When a customer asks for it, I can use the law as a shield and threaten to make a complaint. [...] If *honban* became legal, I would have to reconsider this job.

---

9   Naoko avoided answering my question when I asked her age, but she told me that 25 years before, when she was in her thirties, it was much easier to make money in the sex industry, and based on this, I judge her to be in her fifties/early sixties.

Only 24-year-old Aiko, a former Deadball employee, said she was in favour of full decriminalisation:

> I think it would be good. It would mean freedom – the choice of whether to [sell vaginal sex] or not. If you had the law [to legitimise it], *honban* wouldn't necessarily be viewed in such a bad light. There are people who prefer to have vaginal sex, perhaps because they want to earn more or even because they find that more comfortable. Also, even if you didn't want to have vaginal sex, you would be able to work within your comfort zone. It would be a choice.

As many women sell vaginal sex anyway, legalisation would perhaps remove the stigma and shame surrounding the sale of vaginal sex. However, for the majority of women I spoke to, full legalisation meant the removal of all boundaries. This would either draw coveted customers away towards those that are willing to have vaginal sex, or they would be pressured into doing it themselves. It was clear throughout my conversations that there was a huge divide between vaginal sex and other acts, one born presumably out of the legal context but one that has led to the growth of a market for (relatively) acceptable sex work compared to sex work that is shameful.

Being a Professional Amateur

The difference between vaginal sex and other acts is one way in which the women at Deadball distinguish their labour from other sex work, but they also think of themselves as being less 'professional'. As I mentioned previously, the company markets itself as specialising in *busu* ('ugly') women. This 'ugliness' is relative, determined more by the context in relation to other sex workers rather than with by how the women actually look. The women's faces are blurred out completely on their profiles, so unless the client has met with a particular woman before, he has no idea what she looks like. This helps in terms of mitigating expectations. Kazue, who has been in the industry for 25 years, explained:

> Kazue: At other agencies, the girls are scolded if the customer has any kind of complaint. But this is a 'landmine' shop (*jirai no omise*), meaning you have no idea what kind of girl you'll get – that's the appeal. The customers expect the worst kind [of woman].
>
> Me: Oh, really?

Kazue: Yeah, I think so. The customer expects the worst but then the woman arrives and they are relieved when, to his surprise, she looks quite normal.

I asked the women why they thought customers came to Deadball in particular and they replied that it was because of the 'amateur' nature of the services. The low prices at Deadball engender a very different service from that which is sold at other sexual establishments, as 24-year-old Aiko explained:

A lot of what I hear from the customers at Deadball is that the girls at other shops don't really talk. They don't make conversation, and so it's not as engaging. [At other places] it's all about making you ejaculate and that's it. The women don't do anything else, so the men don't get a sense of their kindness.

Whilst women in more mainstream establishments are hired for their beauty, youth and 'cuteness', those very attributes also create a distance between them and the customers, who are often middle-aged office workers. Aiko believes that customers coming to Deadball are looking for someone with whom they can connect, rather than a 'professional' sex worker who seems perfect and polished: 'The Deadball customers are empathetic, so for them the face doesn't matter. Well, it's not that it doesn't matter, but personality is more important'.

It pays, then, to appear humble in terms of skill when carrying out sex work in this context. As Hoang (2011) has noted with reference to Bourdieu (1986), different forms of capital are as important in sex work, as they are in any other form of labour: sex workers deploy various economic, cultural and bodily resources in the pursuit of customers. Normally we envisage this on the elite end of the scale, with sex workers spending money on their bodily appearance: primping, pampering, diets, exercise, surgery, expensive clothes; perfecting their technique in order to attract the top-paying clients. At Deadball, however, it is the *lack* of those attributes that makes them desirable to the customer. They might have a plain face, be a bit older and a little chubbier and their style of sexual play may be less impressive and less technical. However, these are still forms of capital in that they mark them as 'normal' women in contrast to 'professional' sex workers. This does not mean that all women at Deadball avoid makeup or attractive clothes, but rather that they are trying to entice the customer with a certain look – as a woman who is sexy but, at the end of the day, 'normal' and attainable. This contrasts with women who work at more expensive shops:

> Aiko: Because they're pros, they're not very girly (*onna no ko-ppokunai*). You don't get a sense of their lives. Whereas I'm a real woman: someone you might come across in everyday life.
>
> Me: Right, right. So [you're saying that] maybe because you're not a professional, the customer...
>
> Aiko: [*jumping in*] You're closer to them. You're on the same level (*kokoro no kyori ga chikai*). Because no one [at Deadball] is very confident, they seem more human. They're just like the customer – an equal. The customers are ugly like us and so we're the same. We can understand their feelings.
>
> Me: So, because these pros are stunning, there's a big difference between them and an 'ugly' customer?
>
> Aiko: Right, there's an imbalance. They [the pros] are on another level [to the customer].

Yet surely the women at Deadball are professional in the sense that they acquire skills over time and receive money for the service of sexual and emotional labour? This is true, but in order to succeed with customers, it is very important that the women hide this skill and maintain the appearance of being 'amateurs' (*shirōto*). This allows them to connect in a genuine way with the customer.

> Kazue: It's the opposite to professional, right? Of course, ability and technique are important, but you can't treat the customers in the same manner that a pro would [...] I think it's more natural to chat like this [referring to our conversation], kind of bouncing off each other.

These comments strongly echo what Koch found in her ethnography of sex workers in Tokyo, in that sex workers must hide their skill behind 'performances of naturalized femininity', which then marginalizes their own labour (Koch 2020:100). The women at Deadball should appear competent, but not mechanical or overly skilful. It would be inappropriate to put on a condom using only her mouth, for example (a common technique used in soaplands), because this would highlight her refined skills and therefore mark her as a 'professional'. One must become skilled at sex, but not so skilled as to make the session feel fake or constructed. The goal is to create a pleasurable experience that retains some of the feel of genuine connection and practical reality that comes about between two average people having sex, rather than a high-level sex worker/average client imbalance. The client must be able to imagine coming across this person and having sex with them, outside of a paid context – even though, crucially, that is not what is actually happening. In other words, women at Deadball are professional at being 'amateurs'.

Sex Work and Authenticity

Many think of sex work as the sale of fantasy, but in the context of this agency it would appear that workers are selling authenticity – 'normal' women having sex with 'normal' men. I believe that this serves as an example of what Bernstein calls 'bounded authenticity' – sex work that contains an 'authentic emotional and physical connection' within a clearly delineated timeframe (2007a: 103). In short, it is not only the sex that clients are searching for. Crucially, she argues, they are looking for connection that is authentic (or at least feels so to the customer), but that does not come with the strings attached of complex social relations. In this context, payment empowers connection, rather than being detrimental to it. This mirrors a wider shift in late capitalism from the messy diffused nature of non-market exchange towards neatly-bounded commodities (Bernstein 2001:409). Take, for example, the rise of 'the girlfriend experience' in the West, in which intimacy and connection is explicitly advertised and sought in sex work interactions (Bernstein 2007b). I believe the emphasis on workers as *busu shirōto* (plain amateurs) is part of how a sense of authenticity is constructed in order to achieve intimacy.

However, unlike the girlfriend experience, which tends to be vague in its definition, the services at Deadball have been carefully separated into different acts. At Deadball there is no menu, but every woman's online profile gives an insight into what they provide.[10] As well as general information such as age and days available for work, the women comment as to whether and how they would do the following:

French kissing
Intercrural sex (sexual stimulation of the inner thighs)
Ejaculation into the mouth

---

10 It is common in Japan for establishments selling sexual or intimacy services to provide actual lists of acts with corresponding prices.

Masturbation using breasts
Anal licking
Prostate massage
Oral sex maintaining eye contact
Normal oral sex [without eye contact]
Licking of testes
Manual stimulation of the penis
Semen swallowing
Use of a normal vibrator
Use of a magic wand vibrator (*denma*)

At the end of this list, extra information is given about sexual preferences such as whether they would be happy with anal sex (which costs an additional 5,000 yen, approximately 45 USD).

The order and content of the list is telling, especially the fact that it begins with 'French kissing'. Kissing may be considered a basic and obvious part of foreplay, but some sex workers choose to draw a personal line here in order to maintain a sense of privacy (Brewis and Linstead 2000; Oerton and Phoenix 2001; Sanders 2005). The kiss is valued precisely because of its aura of authentic affection, something that is 'now offered back to the client in denaturalised and explicitly commodified form' (Bernstein 2007a: 127). With many customers looking for an authentic experience with a more amateur woman at Deadball, the question of whether or not to kiss is of particular importance.

A further point to be noted is that a list that so concretely lays out specific private acts of sex and intimacy (such as the explicit distinction between oral sex made with and without eye contact) supports Bernstein's (2007b) argument that modern marketing in sex work has moved from *implicit* to *explicit* commodification. This in turn means that once intimate acts have been named, they can be requested, and the worker can market herself in a way that avoids conflict or uncomfortable negotiations with clients. The client can express specific desires to be fulfilled during sessions and the worker can lay out her terms and boundaries and prepare for the sessions accordingly. The inner workings of intimacy are therefore revealed and quantified.

However, at Deadball the client's wishes are not negotiated with the worker directly. Instead, a client discusses the contents of the 'course' with a member of staff on the administration team who is familiar with the worker's personality, style of play and personal boundaries. This member of staff will then relay the result of the conversation to her. This removes the awkwardness of negotiation for the woman whilst allowing her to maintain boundaries. She feels less like a 'professional', but he still gets to convey what he wants. If she is unable to perform certain acts on a specific day, she can let the staff member know. As the negotiation takes place beforehand, the woman has an idea of the customer's requests before she enters the room. Outsourcing the discussion of the session furthermore serves to obscure the professionalised nature of the service, in that the women do not have to discuss those details with the client directly. Sessions maintain the appearance of spontaneity and natural chemistry, even though the sexual contents are often carefully planned beforehand. I sensed that the women would rather not discuss such specifics because it is somewhat distasteful, perhaps bringing them too close to the realm of 'professional sex worker'. By outsourcing the negotiation to other staff members, the clients can avoid embarrassment about asking for things directly in the moment and the women can avoid feeling too much like a professional.

Sex Work as Healing

At 59 years old, my oldest interlocutor, Satoko, spoke quite poetically of her work, and out of everyone I met, she seemed to get the greatest joy and pride from helping others:

> I think of the sex industry as a kind of sexual counselling. [Like] for feelings, you know? That's why I don't have any complaints. I even met my current husband through this [work], so he's very understanding about what I do.

Later in the conversation I asked why she thought customers used this service and she replied, 'Of course there are sexual reasons, but in the end it's for healing (*iyashi*), right?'

The term *iyashi* was mentioned frequently in relation to why clients came to Deadball. Translated as 'healing', Koch has focused extensively on *iyashi* in sex work in Japan, which she describes 'as a form of deep psychological or mental relief' (2020: 108) and 'touch, attentiveness, indulgence and maternally inflected erotic care' (2016: 706). I would add that it is also hyper-individualised care, encapsulated by a sense of being able to relax in someone's company. 37-year-old Emi describes it as:

[It's] that "ahhh…" moment. It's a fuzzy feeling, like a kind of absent-mindedness. For example, a guy has spent all day frustrated with his colleagues and boss, but then he sees my face and he just relaxes – like when you drink some nice Japanese tea. All those pent-up feelings are released.

Ways of achieving the 'healing' include making small talk with the customer about his day or work, reassuring touch, massage and general attentive listening: attributes that are considered 'feminine' and assumed to come more naturally to older workers who may have had more life experience (Koch 2020). However, as Satoko explained to me, true healing is highly individualised. It is different depending on who needs the healing and who is providing it, and therefore whilst she could identify some patterns of behaviour, it mainly involved adapting to that person in that specific moment, in one's own personal style. Most of the women therefore keep detailed notes about customers, jotting down mundane details about the customer's life as well as sexual preferences and details regarding the way they wanted to be touched, in addition to instructions passed on by the office. One woman joked that with so many middle-aged salarymen as clients, it can be easy to mistake one for another based only on appearance. However, it is vital that the women do not lose face and reveal their careful efforts to write down memorable details. It is essential that they show that they remember each individual client. To be healed means to be seen and remembered, and such efforts point to the intersection of sex work and care work.

When I asked why this kind of healing does not take place in customer's married lives, many remarked that customers lived in sexless marriages and so could not be healed in this way. Furthermore, there are often obligations and tension in a family context that means the unmitigated care needed for healing cannot be provided. Here is how 57-year-old Kanae described it to me:

> Kanae: The customers are… well… Most of the customers are sexless in their home lives. Of course, some have sex at home but they come [to Deadball] anyway. I find that in my case a lot of people come wanting to be healed [*iyasaretai*]. People say that they want to communicate with someone. I would say that about 80 per cent of customers come for that; they want to know what a woman is thinking, or they want someone to listen. It's different according to the person, of course. But really there are very few people here for the sex stuff [*echi-na koto*].
>
> Me: Oh, really?

Kanae: Obviously, sex is a relevant part of the service, but really most people come for the company [lit: *komyunikēshon*]. They have issues such as not feeling like a real man at home or being pushed around at work. There's no place that really feels like 'home' and so they are chasing that feeling. At first, I thought of the sex industry as an outlet for men's sexual desires. I had this idea that men were just using women as tools. But when I started this work, I realised it was different. I realised that men suffer at the hands of society too.[11] Under immense pressure, they go out into society and do their jobs and in order to remain balanced, they come here. And that might be receiving sexual acts, or wanting to be cheered up a little bit or something.

By coming to the sex industry, customers are guaranteed that their needs will be indulged, without having to think of those of others. This kind of healing and indulgence is an interesting contrast to the fawning over customers that Allison (1994) witnessed in hostess clubs in the 90s. At Deadball, it seems that the goal is not to make him 'feel like a man', as Allison concluded happens at hostess clubs. It is, rather, the opposite: the goal is to make him forget all that is expected of him in Japanese society.

It would seem that this is more easily achieved in the sex industry than within the mesh of social relationships and obligations of the domestic private sphere. Aside from paying and adhering to the rules, nothing is expected of the customer. The sex industry is an easier place to seek respite, I was told, precisely because it is clearly defined and demarcated through payment. This was expressed by Emi when she explained that customers are drawn to the ephemeral nature of the encounter, which she sees as an integral part of relaxation:

Emi: You don't know where this person comes from, you don't know their real name, or where they live.

Me: [*in affirmation*] You don't know, no.

Emi: We meet here and then it's, 'that was fun, bye'! It means [the customer] can really relax.

Some customers seek out sex work because of what it can offer as a discreet experience with clear boundaries. Though explicitly created for economic purposes, instances of bounded authenticity are experienced as authentic

---

11 Koch (2020) explores the fact that sex work is considered a vital element of Japan's gendered labour force.

and real by the client and, in some cases, by the sex worker herself, even if only fleetingly (Bernstein 2007a: 103). However, unlike relationships in their private/domestic lives, the boundaries and rules governing this interaction are clearly defined and the relationship does not exist outside of the paid service. Therefore sex work can engender real emotions in the client in a context in which there are clear rules and expectations, unlike within social settings (Bernstein 2001). In the case of the emotional work happening in Deadball, healing can be achieved only if it does not entail further social obligations such as reciprocity. Therefore, in the instance of paid sex, healing is possible precisely *because* it is paid, not in spite of it.

It seemed to me that healing as a concept appeared to be aligned with gender, age and ethnicity. The woman providing healing is normally of a similar age to the customer and she is ethnically Japanese (or at least 'passes' as Japanese).[12] Though she acts maternally, it is important that she should not feel like an actual mother or daughter. Instead, it is the meeting of two parties who *should* be equals in the hierarchy, but with one person acting as a caregiver, indulging the needs of the other. In short, the customer is there to be spoiled. Takeo Doi (1981) has famously argued that this one-way dependency (*amae*) is a form of emotional labour specific to Japanese communication; and I would say that we see elements of this Japanese dynamic in certain sex work.[13] During playtime, the customer displays *enryo*, which Doi defines as a 'nonverbal empathic orientation, [...] ambiguity and hesitancy of self-expression' (1973: 75, cited in Takita 2012). The idea is that you and your needs are understood, without the need to demand them explicitly. In this context, the client does not expect to go through the effort of discussing his needs with the sex worker directly (as he has done this already with the middleman); rather, his needs should be understood without the need for words. On the part of the worker, she is expected to read non-verbal signs and empathise accordingly, a skill known in Japanese as *sasshi*. In reality, of course, it does not quite happen like this, as the two may not know each other very well, although, as discussed earlier in this chapter,

---

12 Race and ethnicity certainly play an important role in sex work in Japan and I regret not having delved more into this during my fieldwork. Everyone I spoke with was native Japanese, except one woman who was half Filipina. My guess is that migrant workers might aim for somewhere with higher pay or would not choose somewhere as high profile as Deadball if they did not have a legal right to work.

13 Another translation might be 'permissive love' (Kumagai and Kumagai 1986, cited in Miike 2003).

prior negotiation allows her to appear relatively knowledgeable and familiar with the customer. Getting the atmosphere just right to suit the individual customer is very important, as Satoko explained:

> Each person is unique. For example, what me and Kayo-san would do would be totally different. There are people who chat a lot and then people who get straight down to it. Healing might take place through chatting or performing a certain kind of action – I couldn't give you a specific definition because it's about adapting to the other person. *That's* healing.

It is a careful dance between feeling close and intimate enough to see the ways in which a person can be uplifted and healed, but at the same time maintaining distance in terms of the wider set of social obligations that exist outside of the paid session. The women at Deadball must act as if they know the clients intimately and yet not expect anything of them in that moment; instead, they must focus on indulging their clients' needs (*amayakasu*). The temporary and paid nature of the session seems paramount for healing in this context, echoing former sex-worker and blogger Dr Brooke Magnanti's famous words, 'essentially they haven't paid you to have sex with them, they've paid you to go away' (Magnanti 2014). As Kanae told me, sessions must be a chance to connect and care for the client:

> Sometimes they just want you to listen to their troubles, or they want life advice from you. That stuff is why this job is not just about sexual acts between a man and woman. When I started, I realised that it was much deeper than that, because it's not just the sexual side. It's not just about basic sexual instincts, it's a place of communication. It was surprising at first, but I really feel that now.

A few women at Deadball (notably my oldest interlocutors) told me that healing is not always one-way and when they allowed themselves to be fully present in the moment, they felt the benefits of 'healing' themselves:

> Kanae (57): Everyone thinks of this as something you're doing for someone else, but that's not the case. By engaging in that time, you enter into what we call a *hadaka no otsukiai* [a relationship that is raw and totally honest] with the customer.[14] Moments like that can only happen if you have total trust in each other. Even in a short time, you can build that trust and it can be healing both for the man and the woman. To think

---

14 *Hadaka no otsukiai* literally means 'a naked relationship'.

that *you* have only healed *them* is, well, a little arrogant. You're present during that time, and it heals you a little too; it's a shared process. You're feeling what your partner is feeling.

In other words, the women are trying to *actually* feel what they are pretending to feel in order to align with the client emotionally and sexually. We might say that this is an example of 'deep acting', the attempt to summon and express the desired emotions that the moment calls for (Hochschild 2012). Satoko told me that, for her, being able to share moments of real intimacy is what helps her deal with the negative aspects of the job:

> But that's why I say you can't only do it for the money. Meeting with clients is also a form of healing for me. And if the person properly gives back, it's good for me.

It is important to recognise the potential healing benefits of sex work for the workers themselves, because often the discourse is centred around the possible negative consequences of such work and whether or not they are occurring. Sex work is work, but sex work is also sex, which has the potential to harm and heal in equal measure (Smith and Mac 2018). Including a wider variety of narratives is crucial for deepening our understanding of sex work in terms of providing vital care in the community.

Conclusion

My research was conducted in a short space of time and only shows a small slice of what happens in one form of sex work through a very niche agency, within a huge spectrum of call-girl services in Japan. My methodology worked well because I had cooperative participants who were more likely to approach a foreign researcher and had time to chat with me (mainly women in their 50s).

The fact that my informants considered themselves to be selling an authentic healing experience may be closely tied with their age. Younger workers in other parts of the sex industry in Japan, for example, may be less likely to engage in this kind of seemingly homely and wholesome sex work, with sessions more explicitly sexual or based on fantasy situations relating to various power dynamics. Therefore, as Shaver (2005) suggests, it is useful to examine what factors are key in making the kind of sex work provided through Deadball attractive. Is the form of sex work at this particular agency distinctive, or is something more generalised across the industry, dependent on variables such as age, ethnicity or class of the worker? It would be illuminating to interview customers on the other side of this interaction in order to find out how they understand the services they purchase.

The intimacy, connection and authentic connection sold at Deadball seems quite at odds with its image as an agency specialising in unattractive *busu* women. Acts of intimacy are explicitly codified and negotiated via the agency, allowing the women to feel relatively distant from the mechanics of their labour. They focus on presenting themselves as amateurs in order to better connect with their 'average-joe' customers. Whilst they strive to make the interaction as authentic as possible, it is also bounded: clearly delineated through payment and with clear expectations between worker and client. This does not detract from the service, but rather frees the clients from social obligations so that they can truly be 'healed'.

By indulging their clients, the women are performing a vital form of emotional labour that is frequently overlooked in favour of seedy and sensationalised aspects of the job. Even though there is a long history of the sex industry being regarded as vital for the mental and physical health of the nation, the women providing that service are still too often considered dirty and expendable (Frühstück 2003). Likewise, it appears that there is discord amongst workers themselves in Japan as to how sex work should be viewed. Most of my interlocutors relied on a narrative of 'us' amateur women selling sexual acts, versus 'them', the 'professional' sex workers also selling vaginal sex. The women at Deadball did not seem keen for their labour to be recognised as real work, for that would bring the stigma of being a 'real' sex worker, and all the societal shame that brings. The legal distinction between vaginal intercourse and other sexual acts has created a hierarchy, with those selling vaginal sex (*honban*) as the most shameful of all, even amongst women within the industry.

From an activist perspective, it might be easy to judge the women I spoke to for rejecting the identity of 'sex worker', but revealing their employment risks serious consequences: housing rejection, employment dismissal or estrangement from family members. A number of women lived in fear of being discovered and the shame that would bring, despite the fact that they were not doing anything illegal. One interlocutor had been seen in the Uguisudani area by a female colleague from her day job who then reported her. She was swiftly fired. Many said that they would never tell their family or friends and, in some cases, not even their own husbands, even though they knew their husbands frequented the sex industry. As Yumi told me wistfully, 'When you say you sell your body for money, people put you at arm's length'.

As Koch (2016, 2020) has argued, it is deeply ironic that the insecure circumstances of women working in shops like Deadball helps maintain psychological balance and mental stability for white collar men in Japan. The sex industry is regarded as a vital outlet for stressed workers and it is often believed that it prevents sexual crimes in wider society (Koch 2014). People expect men to use the sex industry but severely judge the women who work within it. Furthermore, in this legalised and highly competitive market it is the managers who determine the price and value of sexual labour and not the workers themselves. The recent coronavirus pandemic has brutally exposed the cracks in this system and it is clear that social recognition and workplace benefits are desperately needed for sex workers in Japan (Ogura et al. 2020). However, it is difficult to imagine a revolution led by women like those at Deadball. They are just trying to live their lives, teetering on the edge of economic precarity.[15]

References

Agustín, Laura M. 2002a. New research directions: The cultural study of commercial sex. *Sexualities* 8(5): 618–631.

———. 2002b. The (crying) need for different kinds of research. *Research for Sex Work* 5: 30–32.

Alexy, Allison. 2019. Introduction: The stakes of intimacy in contemporary Japan. *In* Allison Alexy and Emma E. Cook (eds), *Intimate Japan: Ethnographies of Closeness and Conflict*. Honolulu: University of Hawai'i Press,: 1–34.

Allison, Anne. 1994. *Nightwork: Sexuality, Pleasure and Corporate Masculinity in a Tokyo Hostess Club*. Chicago: University of Chicago Press.

Allison, Anne. 1996. *Permitted and Prohibited Desires: Mothers, Comics, and Censorship in Japan*. Boulder: Westview Press.

---

15 I would like to extend my greatest appreciation to the Daiwa Anglo-Japanese Foundation, which has supported my postgraduate degree – this fieldwork would not have been possible without their help. Thank you to Dr William Kelly, Imoto Yuki, Mochimaru Akiko and Kimoto Kayo for believing in the project and introducing new and exciting opportunities during my stay in Japan, and to the editors of this volume for their insightful comments. Finally, I would like to thank all the women who spoke to me for this research. They were exceedingly forthcoming in response to my questions about the industry and their work, not to mention kind, patient and open.

Aoyama Kaoru. 2013. Moving from Modernization to Globalization: Migrant Sex Workers in Japan. In Kaoru Aoyama and Emiko Ochiai (eds), *Asian Women and Intimate Work*. Leiden: Brill: 263–288.

———. 2014. The sex industry in Japan: The danger of invisibility. *In* Mark J. McLelland and Vera Mackie (eds), *The Routledge Handbook of Sexuality Studies in East Asia*. Abingdon: Routledge: 281–293. Available from: www.routledgehandbooks.com/doi/10.4324/9781315774879 [Accessed July 28, 2019].

Baishun Bōshihō (trans. The Prostitution Prevention Law). 1956. Available from: elaws.egov.go.jp/search/elawsSearch/elaws_search/lsg0500/detail?lawId=331AC0000000118 [Accessed 1 September 2019].

Bernstein, Elizabeth. 2001. The meaning of the purchase: Desire, demand and the commerce of sex. *Ethnography* 2 (6): 239–420.

———. 2007a. *Temporarily Yours: Intimacy, Authenticity and the Commerce of Sex*. Chicago: University of Chicago Press.

———. 2007b. Buying and selling the 'girlfriend experience': The social and subjective contours of market intimacy. *In* Mark B. Padilla, Jennifer S. Hirsch, Miguel Muñoz-Laboy, Robert Sember and Richard G. Parker (eds), *Love and Globalization: Transformations of Intimacy in the Contemporary World*. New York: Nashville: Vanderbilt University Press: 186–202. Available from: muse.jhu.edu/book/10339 [Accessed July 28, 2019].

Bourdieu, Pierre. 1986. The forms of capital. *In* John G. Richardson (ed.), *Handbook of Theory and Research for the Sociology of Education*. New York: Greenwood Press, 241–258.

Brewis, Joanna and Stephen Linstead. 2000. 'The worst thing is screwing': Consumption and the management of identity in sex work. *Gender, Work & Organization* 7(2): 84–97.

Coffey, Amanda. 1999. *The Ethnographic Self: Fieldwork and the Representation of Identity*. London: SAGE. Available from: methods.sagepub.com/book/the-ethnographic-self [Accessed September 13, 2019].

Doi Takeo. 1981. *The Anatomy of Independence*. Tokyo: Kodansha International.

Foucault, Michel. 1990. *The History of Sexuality: An Introduction*. Vintage Books.

Frühstück, Sabine. 2003. *Colonizing Sex: Sexology and Social Control in Modern Japan*. Berkeley: University of California Press.

Gilhooly, Rob. 2017. 'Boys' for rent in Tokyo: Sex, lies and vulnerable young lives [online]. *The Japan Times*, 23 November. Available from: www.japantimes.co.jp/news/2017/11/23/national/social-issues/boys-rent-tokyo-sex-lies-vulnerable-young-lives/ [Accessed 12 September 2019].

Hoang, Kimberly K. 2011. 'She's not a low-class dirty girl!': Sex work in Ho Chi Minh city, Vietnam. *Journal of Contemporary Ethnography* 40(4): 367–396.

Hochschild, Arlie R. 2012. *The Managed Heart: Commercialization of Human Feeling.* Berkeley: University of California Press. Available from: ebookcentral.proquest.com/lib/soas-ebooks/detail.action?docID=870020 [September 6, 2019].

Hoffman, Michael. 2007. Japan's love affair with sex. *The Japan Times*, 29 April. Available from: www.japantimes.co.jp/life/2007/04/29/to-be-sorted/japans-love-affairs-with-sex/ [Accessed 22 May 2020].

Kadokura Takashi. 2002. *Nihon 'Chika Keizai' Hakusho: 23.2–Chō En! Kyōi No Angura Manē* (trans. *Japan's 'Underground Economy' White Paper: 2.33 Billion Yen! Amazing Underground Money*). Tokyo: Shodensha.

Kaname, Yukiko, and Nozomi Mizushima. 2005. *Fūzokujō Ishiki Chōsa: 126nin No Shokugyō Ishiki* [*A Survey of Sex Workers: The Attitudes of 126 Sex Workers Toward Their Work*]. Tokyo: Potto Shuppan.

Kato Estuko. 2007. The sad marriage of anthropology, neo-colonialism and feminism: Or why Japanese sexual behaviour is always intriguing. *Asian Anthropology* 6(1): 81–103.

Keisatsuchō. 2019. *Fūzoku Kankei Jihan* (trans. *Statistics on Crimes Related to the Sex Industry*). Available from: www.npa.go.jp/publications/statistics/safetylife/fuuzoku.html [Accessed 21 August 2019].

Koch, Gabriele. 2014. *The Libidinal Economy of the Japanese Sex Industry: Sexual Politics and Female Labour.* Ann Arbor: University of Michigan Department of Anthropology.

———. 2016. Producing '*iyashi*': Healing and labour in Tokyo's sex industry. *American Ethnologist* 43 (4): 704–716.

———. 2020. *Healing Labor: Japanese sex work in the gendered economy.* Stanford: Stanford University Press.

Kuninobu, Junko, Rie Okamura, Natsumi Takeuchi, et al. 1998. Prostitution, Stigma and The Law in Japan: A Feminist Roundtable Discussion. *In* Kamala Kempadoo and Jo Doezema (eds), *Global Sex Workers: Rights, Resistance, and Redefinition.* London: Routledge: 87–98.

Magnanti, Brooke. 2014. Sex with married men. *The Oxford Union*, 22 January. Video available from: www.youtube.com/watch?v=1Nb5IRnfMeg [Accessed 19 August 2019].

McLelland, Mark J. 2005. *Queer Japan: From the Pacific War to the Internet Age.* Lanham, Maryland: Rowman & Littlefield.

Miike Yoshitaka. 2003. Japanese *enryo-sasshi* communication and the psychology of *amae*: Reconsideration and reconceptualization. *Keio Communication Review* 25: 93–115.

Mitsuhashi Junko. 2006. The transgender world in contemporary Japan: The male to female cross-dressers' community in Shinjuku. *Inter-Asia Cultural Studies* 7 (2): 202–227.

Oerton, Sarah and Joanna Pheonix. 2001. Sex/bodywork: Discourses and practices. *Sexualities* 4 (4): 387–412.

Ogura Junko, Jessie Yueng and Will Ripley. 2020. Japan is offering sex workers financial aid to survive the pandemic. *CNN*, 20 April. Available from: www.cnn.com/2020/04/19/asia/japan-sex-workers-coronavirus-intl-hnk/index.html [Accessed 27 May 2020].

Sanders, Teela. 2005. 'It's just acting': Sex workers' strategies for capitalizing on sexuality. *Gender, Work & Organization* 12(4): 319–342.

Shaver, Frances M. 2005. Sex work research: Methodological and ethical challenges. *Journal of Interpersonal Violence* 20 (3): 296–319.

Smith, Molly and Juno Mac. 2018. *Revolting Prostitutes: The Fight for Sex Workers' Rights*. London: Verso. Kindle version.

Sueyoshi Yōko. 2015. Sekkusu wāku ha hinken josei wo sukueru-ka "jirai senmon" fūzokuten no daihyō ga kataru jitsujō (trans. Can sex work save women? Owner of a 'landmine' sex shop gives his opinion). *Wotopi*, 11 November. Available from: wotopi.jp/archives/29889 [Accessed 19 July 2020].

Takita Fuyuko. 2012. *Reconsidering the Concept of Negative Politeness 'Enryo' in Japan*. Hiroshima: Institute for Foreign Language Research and Education, Hiroshima University.

West, Mark D. 2011. *Lovesick Japan: Sex, Marriage, Romance, Law*. Ithaca: Cornell University Press.

CHAPTER 5

The Coin-Operated Boyfriend

Recognition and Intimacy as Commodities in a Japanese *Josei-Muke* Adult Video Fan Community

Maiko Kodaka

> *Coin-operated boy*
> *With a pretty coin-operated voice*
> *Sayin' that he loves me*
> *That he is thinkin' of me*
> *Straight-up to the point*
> *That is what I want*
>
> The Dresden Dolls (2003)

Introduction

'I really enjoy when the *eromen* I support do well,' Yuri said, confidently flicking her hair, 'it gives me a sense of femininity'. We were sitting on a sofa, sipping *eromen*-themed cocktails while waiting for the main event to start. The occasion was a fan meeting, organised by the female-targeting porn label SILK LABO. Rather than just providing an aid for masturbation, as is the case for pornography made predominantly for men, pornography aimed at women is geared towards thematising female sexual desire (Hambleton 2016). One of the main attractions of this genre is that fans can engage with the male actors, called *eromen* or *lovemen* in the 'real world'. In addition to their performances in pornographic media, the *eromen* regularly appear at fan events: some of these are group-based meetings, others are private 'dates' during which female fans can enjoy temporary intimacy with them, for instance talking on the phone or enjoying karaoke privately. The event we were attending was a talk show-style performance, where the audience could purchase drinks and food from their table while four *eromen* were present on stage, acting out an erotic comedy. Spending was highly encouraged through the fact that each fan would receive lottery tickets from her second order onwards; the more they spent, the more tickets they received and the higher the probability of winning a gift from their favourite *eromen*. The highlight of the event, the final lottery, was a chance to win diverse personal items, including handwritten notes used by *eromen* during the talk show, underwear worn during the shooting of a film, instax photos with *eromen*, and a lottery bag with *eromen* signatures. Winners of the lottery were also given a few moments to interact with the *eromen* when collecting their gift. This interaction made almost all the women blush, but some, including Yuri, were confidently chatting with the *eromen*. From the confidence and familiarity they exuded, I could clearly see the intimacy and emotional attachment fans felt towards their favourite male porn actor.

My informant, Yuri, as I learned later that night, had studied massage therapy at college, but now used her skills as a female escort. She considered herself to be a professional rather than somebody who works in the business to make ends meet. Earning more than a typical female office worker of her age (mid 20s), Yuri spent most of her income on *eromen* and male escorts and justified it to me like this:

> My work is highly stressful and physically demanding – that is why I need to relax by spending money on my favourite men. We [herself, *eromen* and male escorts] work in a very similar environment, where we satisfy our clients' emotional needs. It is an extreme form of service business, so we can share our stresses and concerns because we have a lot in common.

Hearing this comment, I was reminded of emotional labour as discussed by Arlie Hochschild; that is, 'labour [that] requires one to induce or suppress feeling in order to sustain the outward countenance that produces the proper state of mind in others' (1983:7). Especially in the heteronormative conditions that Yuri works under, women are expected to perform emotional labour and therefore need stress relief. To understand Yuri's consumption of *eromen* and male escorts in the context of her desire to relax and to gain a sense of femininity, I employ Axel Honneth's definition of 'recognition' (1995). Recognition in this context means reciprocal affirmation of self that is crucial to achieve self-realisation in an intersubjective society. As Honneth argues, recognition is fundamentally mutual and 'occurs via emotional bonds, the granting of rights, or a shared orientation to values' (1995: 94). However, in this particular heterosexual milieu – the fan community of *eromen* – recognition, as I will show, becomes a way for female fans to purchase self-realisation and a sense of femininity (as Yuri phrased it while we were sipping cocktails), whilst *eromen* attain fame and money through the same process.

This sense of recognition and the way in which it is commodified in contemporary pornographic media and related events aimed at women are the subject of this chapter. Against current sociological theories that conceptualise recognition as a mutual relationship, I argue that sex and fandom industries turn the act of being recognised – as female, as attractive, as a sexual being, as someone with needs and desires and an internal life of one's own – into a commodity that is bought and exchanged. Yuri, who herself works in the industry, was the exception, and this drew my attention towards the idea of recognition. She was well aware of the stakes involved and this kept her from having long-term expectations. Contrary to Honneth's theory, recognition in this context can only be purchased, and cannot be a mutual exchange. Yuri could enjoy the attention of *eromen* both as a consumer (enjoying the service they offered) and as a professional (understanding what resources of erotic capital and emotional labour went into what they do).

For the majority of fans with whom I engaged, however, the recognition they felt in the liminal spaces of fan events was authentic and they developed emotional attachment to their favourite *eromen* or *lovemen*. Employing the term 'bounded authenticity' in Elizabeth Bernstein's sense as 'the sale and purchase of authentic emotional and physical connection' (2007: 103), my aim is to show how fans' interactions with *eromen* and *lovemen* are paradoxically both authentic and commodified; mediated by a certain set of fantasies that the production companies provide. I use fantasy here with Natalie Purcell's definition in mind: 'fantasy is a material – a social – phenomenon that is real in its own way' (2012: 36), which relies on and derives much of its power 'from shared meanings and expectations about sex, gender, race, and other vectors of social division.' (ibid: 29). In other words, fantasy is where our psychological and social needs meet. In this sense, each fan's fantasy is shaped both by their consumption of pornographic products and by their active participation in fan communities.

This specific fan community functions as a liminal space where fans both experience 'bounded authenticity' and compete for the attention of *eromen* and *lovemen*. Female fans do become objects of desire, albeit elusive ones. Fans spend considerable resources pursuing their favourite *eromen* and *lovemen*, helping them build their careers, often to their own financial detriment. I would argue that the female fans' experiences and interaction with male porn actors are both real and at the same time contained in this simulation (Baudrillard 1994), because of the difference between the simulation and the everyday, and the blurring of female fans' understanding of intimacy and romantic relationships, which tends to be premised on unconditional love. What attracts female customers to such fan events? And how can such an engineered interaction with *eromen* and *lovemen* be experienced as authentic?

This chapter is based on the ethnography of an *eromen* event I attended in December 2018 as part of my doctoral research. It draws on conversations with female fans in order to elucidate the expectations fans have regarding their interactions with male porn actors, and how this fan community influences their understanding of love, intimacy and romantic relationships. The first part of the chapter provides an analysis of Japanese pornography aimed at women, which is followed by a deeper exploration of the concepts of *eromen* and *lovemen*. Ethnographic descriptions of one fan event are interspersed throughout the chapter to illustrate the theoretical arguments. Ultimately, my aim is to contribute to a wider discussion of gender and work in relation to commodified recognition and simulated intimacy.

Adult Videos for Women (*Josei-Muke*)

The fan event I attended during my fieldwork was organised by SILK LABO, a female-targeting pornography label of Soft On Demand (SOD), one of the monopolistic porn production companies in Japan. Japanese pornography, known as AV (short for 'Adult Videos') takes its name from the popularity of the home-use VHS video decks that came on the market towards the end of the 1970s. Since the late 1980s, the AV industry dominated the pornographic media industry in Japan, until it faced a downturn with the rise of free online streaming websites around the 2000s. As a result of this shift, SOD decided to expand its market to include potential female audiences by establishing a production line called *josei-muke*, which literally means 'for women'; SILK LABO launched in 2009 and GIRL'S CH in 2012. Note that 'women' here signifies exclusively heterosexual women, in the same way that the 'mainstream' AV are designed for heterosexual men.[1]

The idea of launching an AV line for women came from a young female employee at SOD, Makino Eri, who joined the company straight after studying media production at university. She noticed a female demand for AV during a marketing collaboration project with a sex toy company which later asked her to undertake market research and investigate what female audiences wanted to see. Makino visited sex shops and collected women's comments on existing pornography, which was mostly produced for male, heterosexual audiences. The opinions she collected fell into two groups: one requesting more romantic/intimate narrative-based stories, the other complaining about ugly and stereotypically masculine male actors. Under Makino's leadership, approximately ten female SOD employees discussed what would be suitable for *josei-muke* AV. In the early stage of SILK LABO, Makino and her fellow staff often received unpleasant comments from male colleagues working in other sections of SOD, who would say things like *Omaera hentai ga atsumatteru* ('In your section the perverts are gathered')[2] (Makino, in Iijima 2015: 46), and their brainstorm meetings therefore generally took place outside normal working hours. Hegemonic ideas stipulating that women are not supposed to talk openly about sex are still strong in Japan, even in porn production companies.

'I still feel a bit embarrassed when talking about sex in a public place,' said Yoshiko, an informant who accompanied me to the *eromen* talk-show event, with a nervous laugh. She also told me she had never imagined coming to these AV-related events and that she had never previously enjoyed watching AV alone. While she had watched pornography a few times with her ex-boyfriends, when they had tried to imitate the techniques displayed, it was not something she enjoyed. However, when Yoshiko coincidentally discovered *josei-muke* AV– as a DVD-formatted supplement in the weekly women's lifestyle magazine *An An* – she immediately became interested and soon started watching *josei-muke* AV two or three hours a day before bedtime. As she told me, she was currently on a journey to explore her own

---

1   This does not imply that the Japanese AV industry is exclusively catering to heterosexual desires. There are many different production companies specialising in different sexual orientations and fetishisms.
2   Unless otherwise stated, all translations in this chapter are the author's.

sexual desires and preferences. Coming to the events organised by SOD was therefore a part of that journey.

While *josei-muke* signifies a genre 'for women', Makino acknowledged that *josei-muke* AV are not a general indicator of what women want. Rather, they are better understood as an introduction to the genre of AV. *Josei-muke* AV deliberately target women who are not familiar with watching AV. One of the first products of its kind, *Girl's Pleasure,* was released as a supplement to *An An* on July 29th, 2009. After the success of *Girl's Pleasure,* SILK LABO then released its very first title, *Body Talk Lesson,* in 2009. The content of this video included educational instructions for 'comfortable' sex, such as vaginal exercises and how to give pleasurable oral sex to your male partner. According to a survey Makino conducted, many women in Japan experience difficulties having orgasms and feel uneasy during sex with their male partners, and the term 'comfortable' should be understood in this context. Vaginal exercises known as *chitsu-tore* are featured in many SILK LABO videos. They claim to promote better sexual experiences for women based on the notion that muscle strength around the vagina stimulates a G-spot orgasm. The second title, *Faindā no Mukou ni Kimi ga Ita* ('It was You Behind the Viewfinder') directed in 2009 by Tsunoda Maiko and Miyazaki Rieko, features a woman who has never had an orgasm with her boyfriend, but then discovers sexual pleasure through an affair with a mysterious camera man. In this 120 minute long film, sex scenes are designed in a step-by-step manner, allowing viewers to learn sexual techniques (Hambleton 2016). It is important to point out that SILK LABO does not omit the 'putting-on/of-the-condom scene', which is often described as a 'turn off' by male viewers. Awkward moments and long foreplay, usually missing in pornography aimed at men, are featured prominently in these materials. These additional scenes provide viewers with storylines that explains how the couple build up their emotional and physical connection before engaging in sexual activity. Unlike mainstream pornography designed for male audiences, SILK LABO emphasises a cinematic atmosphere by employing detail-oriented props on set, romantic background music and warm lightning, as Makino explains:

> [f]or most women, sex comes with intimate and romantic relationships. While pornography for men gets rid of all these aspects of human interactions, *josei-muke* AV focuses on each step towards climax.
>
> (Quoted in Iijima 2015: 45)

Whereas AV for men focus primarily on the sex act itself, SILK LABO depicts the narratives leading up to sex; how-they-end-up-making-love is the focus. According to an employee at SOD whom I interviewed, it is important to create cinematic environments to appeal to a female audience. AV for men generally apply pixelization to pre-existing props such as magazines or bottled water due to copyright issues, rather than preparing special props, because men are used to watch pixelisation on genitals. In Japan, it is illegal to produce, distribute or exhibit pornography without genital pixelisation due to the prohibition of commercial sexual intercourse (Watanabe 2017). Besides, pixelisation is considered a 'turn off' for women as it reminds them of AV for men. What is needed in *josei-muke* is a narrative-oriented and cinematographic feel, which requires more cinematic effort in terms of performance, props and scenarios.

Following the increasing popularity of SILK LABO, in 2012 SOD launched GIRL'S CH, an online streaming site with pornography aimed at female viewers. The content was initially cuts and edits from SOD's pre-existing pornography that were considered suitable for a female audience. GIRL'S CH soon became successful with one million users accessing the website each month, and within the last couple of years, Taguchi Momoko has started to produce for female consumers who seek to watch more explicit versions of SILK LABO, such as BDSM (bondage, domination, sadomasochism) scenes. The main contribution of GIRL'S CH was to establish a new genre of 'submissive men', in which boy-band lookalikes are treated as sexual objects for female pleasure. While SILK LABO emphasises intimate romantic sex, Taguchi argues that sex does not necessarily come with intimacy. In GIRL'S CH films, Taguchi focuses on the importance of depicting both male and female bodily expressions, as opposed to most mainstream AV, which only focus on female bodies. The main point here is that this diversity in *josei-muke* AV– romantic narratives-based SILK LABO and GIRL'S CH's depiction of physical pleasure-oriented sex – has enriched the possibility of what *josei-muke* can offer in the current male desire-centred mainstream AV industry in Japan.

Female Fantasies of Belonging to Men

Yoshiko, in her mid-30s, has worked as an office worker in a medical company since graduating from university. With a stable job that earns her more than enough to make ends meet, her current main concern is her lack of a boyfriend and thus of the prospect of marriage. 'I think at my age, women should be married; otherwise people will see you as if you had problems even if you are doing well at work', Yoshiko said sadly, looking down at the table. 'It's getting more difficult to find the right one. I go to many *kon-katsu* (marriage hunting, or speed dating) parties but none of the men appeals to me', she continued. I asked her how she managed to deal with the internal and external pressure to get married and this prompted her to bring up her consumption of porn: 'Coming back from work and watching *josei-muke* AV is very relaxing. Also, coming to these events and meeting *eromen* really cheers me up. I know it is a fantasy, but I wish I could have a relationship like those I see in the SILK LABO videos', she said, putting her hands on her cheeks. Yoshiko's fantasy is to fall in everlasting love with an *eromen*-like male, a type of man she describes as 'definitely handsome but also attentive, caring and someone who knows how to deal with the female body, so that I can have sexual pleasure in a comfortable manner'.

What then characterizes the ideological 'fantasy' which SOD provides via *josei-muke* AV? Taking an exploratory look at the content of *josei-muke* AV, Hambleton analyses SILK LABO films as a porn category aimed at women and argues that such films ultimately end up 'reinforcing ideas of normative female desires and sexual behaviour' (2016: 439), because female sexual desire and behaviour are defined in a heterosexual matrix. Parallel to Hambleton's argument, Wong and Yau (2018), who have examined the history of the Japanese AV industry, argue that Japanese AV embody a 'salvage ideology': 'women cannot save themselves but have to rely on men sexually. Men therefore are women's saviours.' (Wong and Yau 2018: 5). This creates a particular cultural code: a lack of agency in women's sexual pleasure and a justification of male domination over female bodies. Although Wong and Yau exclusively discuss mainstream male desire-centered AV, salvage ideology can also be identified in many of the *josei-muke* AV.

A typical SILK LABO film begins with a female protagonist who has certain problems in her life – overwork, bodily injury or boyfriend-related issues – as for example seen in films such as *Arinomama Dakishimete* (Embrace Me As I Am; 2019) and *Rihabiri no Sensei* (The Physiotherapist; 2018). The female protagonist resolves her personal problems with help from a male character. For instance, *Rihabiri no Sensei* depicts a female patient with broken legs from a traffic accident and her rehabilitation instructor who, coincidentally, was her high school crush. Through mental and physical support, they develop an intimate relationship and make love after her discharge. In contrast to Wong and Yau's definition of salvage ideology, the female protagonist's initial problems are not always about her physical ability to obtain orgasm; rather the problems tend to be emotional issues often associated with loneliness, stressful daily lives, anxiety about romantic relationships and secret desires for more intense sexual intercourse. It is also important to point out that GIRL'S CH initial films tend to build on narrative conventions that we do not see in conventional AV aimed at male audiences. For example, a single female protagonist is typically approached by multiple good-looking men, not the other way round. Confused by her own popularity, the protagonist then has sex with men who represent different social types: the cute little brother/junior,[3] the mature, serious older brother/boss/senior figure, the wild rebellious adventurer and the boy-next-door type who will stand by her no matter what. Common to SILK LABO and GIRL'S CH films, then, is that female protagonists are always the centre of male attention, both romantically and physically.

The assumption that women's identity must be based on male attention is also a staple in Japanese pop culture, especially in products designed for heterosexual women. In her study of *shōjo manga*, a mainstream *manga* genre designed for teenage girls, Fujimoto Yukari argues, 'what most *shōjo manga* have in common is the constant self-questioning of "where/whom do I belong to?" and the desire to be accepted or embraced as she is' (2008: 143). In *shōjo manga*, the social identity of female protagonists thus depends on others (including family and friends, but mostly men); it is through recognition by others that these young females fulfil their self-esteem. The typical storylines in these media, however, suggests that the relationship between men and women is not equal, since the women generally 'belong' to someone in a patriarchal manner – for examples as daughters or wives – a relationship that in effect objectifies them. This echoes Yoshiko's difficulties as a single woman. Her words, 'unless you have a boyfriend or are married, people think there must be something wrong with you', underscore the way in which female subjectivity depends on male presence. Male subjectivity, on the other hand, is realised by male homosocial recognition, as feminist scholar Ueno Chizuko (2010) points out. Drawing on Eve Sedgwick's cultural analysis of men's same-sex

---

3 When siblings appear in pornographic content, it is mainly as non-blood related kin, such as step brother and sister. While pornographic content that depicts incest does exist, it is a minor fetish genre.

bonds (1985), Ueno argues that male subjectivity depends on misogynistic discrimination and the ability to control women. The creation of heterosexual male/female subjectivity is based on 'othering' its counterpart; to be female is to belong to men, and to be male is to exclude women. Recognising this gendered system of subjectivity allows us to see how female selves are created as reflections of male counterparts in a heterosexual milieu such as pornography, and thus why women such as Yoshiko respond to storylines in the porn industry that contribute to her fantasy of having a boyfriend.

Eromen and *Lovemen*

The 'other' in the context of *josei-muke* AV is the male actors, *eromen* and *lovemen*. Their role in *josei-muke* AV is to embrace the female protagonists as if they were Prince Charming, so that female protagonists can restore their self-confidence and realise their female subjectivity.[4] This idea extends to fan meetings of *eromen* and *lovemen*.

'Who is your favourite *eroman*?' Yuri asked me with curious but speculative eyes. I replied that Azuma was my favourite as he was the most handsome man, in my opinion. She nodded and said, 'It's a pity that he doesn't hold private fan meeting events as much as other *eromen*, such as Mukai-kun and Uehara-kun. I go to every event of Uehara-kun's so he remembers me. It makes me feel so good.' She then showed me her instax pictures with Uehara, saying 'Don't we look like a couple?'. It was quite impressive to see dozens of her instax pictures with *eromen*, which obviously indicated her passionate engagement in this fan practice. Yoshiko, who was sitting next to me, also took a photo album from her bag and said, 'Here is mine!' The file was full of instax pictures of her and *eromen*. I asked how much they paid per picture and Yoshiko said, 'It's 2000 yen per picture; I normally get more than five pictures per event.' The event was meant to promote *josei-muke* AV, but the main purpose for Yuri, Yoshiko and probably a majority of the audience was to see the *eromen* in person. Who are they, I came to wonder, and what is their job, apart from performing in *josei-muke* AV?

While the word *eromen* is a combination of 'erotic' and 'men', *lovemen* is a contraction of 'love' and 'men'. This distinguishes them from male actors

---

[4] GIRL's CH produces exceptional titles which features men becoming dominated by and submissive to female dominatrixes. Taguchi stated that her inspiration for this came explicitly from Japanese gay pornography.

Figure 5.1: Oikawa, Mukai, Uehara and Azuma (from left to right) at SILK Fest, November 2018. Photo: Maiko Kodaka. **Colour**, p. 221

in mainstream pornography known as AV *danyū* (male porn actors): a generally hyper-masculine figure with a muscular body and large penis who can maintain an erection for a long time. The *danyū* archetype is consonant with Akagawa Manabu's 'society that problematizes male impotency' (1996: 173): that is, one's masculinity is defined by having a hard erection, and the ejaculation of dense semen. Contrary to this, *eromen* and *lovemen* are required to 'maintain a non-threatening, sexually innocent image inspired by the aesthetics of Japanese pop idols' and have an 'approachable "everyman" aesthetic that is central to Japan's boy-band industry' (Hambleton 2016:432). In addition to that, they should be handsome and able to act in front of the camera, which is particularly important because *josei-muke* AV contain a good deal of dramatic dialogue. The only difference between *eromen* and *lovemen* is that the former belongs to SILK LABO, the latter to GIRLS' CH; however, some male actors perform for both studios and may therefore be both *eromen* and *lovemen*.

Since 2008, SOD has actively recruited *eromen* and *lovemen*. Suzuki Ittetsu (1979–), who started his career with the inauguration of SILK LABO, has become the iconic face of *josei-muke* AV and plays an important role as spokesman for sex education. Suzuki Ittetsu, Tsukino Taito (1979–) and Mūtan (1983–) are described as 'the three musketeers of *eromen*' (Cyzowomen 2010) due to their popularity. Suzuki Ittetsu became the first male AV actor to have an exclusive contract with a studio in 2012. This was a significant moment for the wider industry since most male AV actors work as freelancers. It is estimated that while there are more than 10,000 active female AV actors, there are only about 70 male AV actors who work freelance (see *The Other Side of Sex*, a documentary film by Enoki and Takahara, 2012). Suzuki's exclusive contract with SOD signifies that within *josei-muke* AV it is male actors who are objects of desire rather than female bodies that are objects of the male gaze. This is corroborated by the custom that female fans use *kun* rather than the general honorific *san* when speaking to and about specific men working in the industry. While the non-gender-specific *san* suggests mutual respect between adults, *kun* signifies a strong sense of affection and familiarity – especially that directed by adults towards male children. Whereas it shows respect to use *san* to and about a stranger, the fact that female fans call male adults *kun*, by contrast, indicates that they are cutifying them as small boys.[5] Through language, then, female fans demasculinise *eromen* and *lovemen* while demonstrating their own power to objectify men.

When the 'three musketeers' completed their contracts in 2017 in order to expand their career paths,[6] they were replaced by the second generation of *eromen*: Mukai Riku, Uehara Chiaki, Azuma Sōsuke, and Oikawa Daichi. These younger *eromen*, born between 1988–1992, have contributed to attracting a wider fan base, expanding from women in their 30s and 40s to now also including women in their 20s.

The marketing system for *eromen* and *lovemen* is similar to that in other idol cultures in Japan. In the same way that idols are professionally-created popular figures (Galbraith and Karlin 2012), *eromen* and *lovemen* appear both on cross-media platforms to promote the genre of *josei-muke* AV and at physical fan meeting events. This carefully calculated marketing strategy is partly a reaction to the significantly increasing popularity of user-generated tube sites such as *xvideos*, *Pornhub*, and *xHamster*, so-called 'Porn 2.0' (Jenkins 2017), which offer non-membership streaming. In order to survive in this new environment, existing AV studio companies such as SOD decided to

---

5   The honorific *kun* is often used in professional circumstances, for instance workplaces and medical fields, in general from male senior to male junior. When females address male juniors using *kun*, it indicates either familiarity and affection or that the addressee occupies an inferior status.

6   Mūtan was not in an exclusive contract with SILK LABO.

turn their male and female AV actors into idols, with the intention of creating stronger emotional bonds with their customers. As Nakamura Atsuhiko (2015) points out, showcasing good-looking AV actors or adding a rich fetish feel is no longer enough. Companies have to cater to fans' feelings in order to compete with Porn 2.0. It can thus be argued that the AV industry has become a service industry. Nakamura (2015) also argues that the AV industry has two ways to survive: either to cultivate international markets by promoting AV as Japanese culture, or to cultivate female consumers by making AV aimed at women. *Josei-muke* AV emerged from this sense of desperation, which explains how turning male AV actors, *eromen* and *lovemen*, into idols has now become the main business model.

Eromen and *lovemen* often perform at events, where fans can interact with them by shaking hands, taking photographs or hugging. SILK LABO organises, for example, bimonthly events at which four popular *eromen* perform an erotic comedy on stage, and monthly DVD signing sessions at the biggest nationwide chain of video/DVD rental shops and bookstores, TSUTAYA in Shibuya. Events are always carefully planned to maximise potential income. At signing sessions, fans receive, for instance, one ticket per DVD purchased, a marketing strategy that causes some fans to buy multiple DVDs in order to meet their favourite *eromen* as many times as possible. GIRL'S CH plans similar events, conducting monthly events with an entrance fee at the SOD office in Shin-Nakano, where they provide fans with the opportunity to take instax photos with *lovemen* for 2000 JPY per shot. From my observations, it appears that most women buy more than two photos per event, suggesting that this transaction is also very worthwhile for the company. For this event *lovemen* appear at the SOD office *shain bar* (corporate member bar), where male and female AV actors serve visitors as bartenders. A visit to the *shain bar* costs 2980 JPY for 50 minutes and includes a selected DVD of the AV actors/actresses on duty as a souvenir.

In addition to these major coordinated events, individual *eromen* and *lovemen* also often have their own private fan meetings at which they provide a 'boyfriend experience' (Hambleton 2016: 432). These types of events are either open to groups of fans or exclusive to one fan who has won the lottery for a 'dating experience'. In this way fans of *eromen* and *lovemen* are presented with a significant number of opportunities to engage directly with the men they desire. More mediated ways of experiencing intimacy with *eromen* and *lovemen* include, for instance, telephone dates – which cost 5000 JPY per

20 minutes – which give fans the opportunity to have casual conversations that may simulate a temporally-bounded pseudo-relationship. In 2018 dating experiences were developed further when GIRL'S CH began to recruit male escorts working within the *josei-muke fūzoku* industry, a collection of brothels offering women erotic massages or other sexual treatments – apart from penile-genital penetration, which is illegal to sell. This means that female fans can now enjoy temporary intimate moments with an actor and thereby a chance to experience an embodied version of the fantasy sold in *josei-muke* AV. With the price set at 25,000 JPN for 70 minutes (the minimum rate), both Yuri and Yoshiko informed me that they enjoy going to these *josei-muke fūzoku* because it provided them with the fantasy of being princesses. For my informants, the excitement of going to *josei-muke fūzoku* is therefore not only about obtaining sexual pleasure, but also very much about boosting their sense of femininity. Thus, audiences are able to involve themselves to different degrees: a female fan can not only watch performances on the screen, but also meet her favourite star in person and even have sex with him.[7] As Yuri said, there are several ways fans can become known to *eromen* and *lovemen* (depending on how much they take up what is on offer) and this is how fans develop a feeling of commitment to their own favourites, by continuing to purchase merchandise associated with them and attending events. The way in which *eromen* and *lovemen* are marketed can be understood as a form of commodification of intimacy. The business model is straightforward. The popularity of *eromen* and *lovemen* depends on their performative ability to embody and convey the fantasies of the fans who repeatedly come to the events.

However, how should we understand the fantasy embodied in this transaction? In her work on the pornographic imagination, Purcell (2012) neither assumes that sexual fantasies lead to the 'acting-out' of the sexual fantasy in real life, nor does she maintain that they are 'just fantasies' and therefore of no consequence. Instead, she shows how fantasies are carefully imbricated in everyday life, often modulating mundane experience by adding elements of escapism and wish-fulfilment. Thus, fans come to events to temporarily become part of the fantasy and with the expectation that they will fulfil their psychological and social needs. The work of *eromen* and *lovemen* is to aid and abet this collective boyfriend fantasy. They are, in other words, performing

---

7   Note that I am not defining 'sex' as penile-genital penetration. I here define it as an intimate communication, the forms of which vary, including touching, kissing and stimulating genitals and other parts of the body in order to induce physical and emotional pleasure.

emotional labour. *Eromen* and *lovemen* collectively present their masculinity in a way that renders it consumable by individual fans. This includes the often-stylised behaviour that is assumed to make women feel appreciated: individual attention, eye contact, paying fans compliments and so forth. This kind of emotional work shares elements with Japanese host clubs, to which we can refer here as a point of comparison.

Takeyama Akiko's ethnographic study (2010) of Japanese host clubs, a specific space in which male hosts provide intimate companionship for women, demonstrates the complexity of gender dynamics. In this environment male hosts use their erotic capital and emotional labour to fulfil female clients' desires in a context of hyper-neoliberal competition, hosts depend financially on their own performances in the club. In host clubs, first-time customers meet several hosts for a reduced price (typically starting at 3000 JPY per hour including all-you-can-drink). This first-time special allows female customers a chance to meet various hosts and indicate who they are interested in being hosted by during future visits, and this 'in-store' relationship conditions the development of intimacy between host and client. Within the club, hosts are ordered into a hierarchical pyramid; top hosts with many clients cost the most while low level hosts cost much less (Takeyama 2010).

Traditions from the host club are brought into the fan culture of *josei-muke* AV. During the talk show event I attended, I noticed how *eromen* received store-bought drinks and foods from the audience. For example, at the end of the first part a member of the audience presented a bottle of Moët & Chandon champagne to Mukai, a former host club worker. This act prompted him to respond with a typical host club 'champagne call', a tradition within host clubs where hosts burst into song in appreciation of a customer buying an expensive champagne. Entertained and confused at the same time, Yoshiko flushed and whispered to me: 'You know, that champagne is not actually for the benefit of the *eromen* at all.' Yoshiko was referring to the business model according to which the event is planned. With the purchase of drinks and food, buyers receive lottery tickets – one ticket per 500 JPY spent; and as the rules stipulate, although Mukai may have been the receiver of the champagne, the woman who bought it would have received 40 lottery tickets (a bottle of Moët & Chandon champagne is generously priced at 20,000 JPY). On the one hand, when fans treat their favourite to drinks and foods this is a performance of affection and support that makes these emotions public; but on the other hand it is also an act that increases competition among fans. While any purchase directly relates to individual men's success at a host club (Takeyama 2016), the purchase of a bottle of Moët & Chandon champagne is in effect more of a financial benefit for the bar where the event takes place; and a chance to increase her own luck in the lottery for the female spender herself.

The Vicious Circle of Performing and Consuming Recognition

The *eromen/lovemen* business model is premised on the idea that female fans can enjoy the fantasy of being desired in a safe milieu. I would here like to return to the question of subjectivity and to consider why the presence of 'others', in this context of males, is important. The idea of centring one's subjectivity on others, often known as 'theory of recognition', is discussed by two of the most significant contemporary philosophers, Axel Honneth and Charles Taylor. Both Honneth and Taylor emphasise the importance of recognition as a condition for a fully achieved subjectivity, as social life is intersubjective. Taylor asserted that recognition 'is a vital human need' (1994: 26) and that misrecognition 'can inflict a grievous wound, saddling its victims with a crippling self-hatred' (ibid). Honneth argued, in a similar vein, that social struggle is experienced through 'disrespect'; that is, being denied the conditions of self-formation. As crucial components of recognition, in order to attain self-realisation, Honneth (1995) enumerated love, rights and solidarity in intersubjective relations. Of those three components, love is the most fundamental, and is required to develop self-respect and self-confidence. Lack of love, on the other hand, leads to a pathological mentality. While the concept of love per se is difficult to define, it is possible to argue that the power of language functions as an index for social recognition. Taylor pointed out 'the genesis of human mind is [...] not monological, not something each person accomplishes on his or her own, but dialogical' (1994:32). In other words, everyday dialogue with 'significant others', according to Taylor, functions to shape self-realisation. The philosopher Washida Kiyokazu's discussion of *kao* (face) speaks in a similar way of the creation of identity as a reciprocal process:

> 'Face' is constituted in exchange. It does not belong exclusively to anyone in a way that can signify a specific persona. 'Face' is not beyond reciprocity; rather it appears and vanishes, is attained, and stolen in reciprocity.

It is therefore accurate to say 'self' comes into 'face' or 'face' appears in one's face.

(1998: 196)

This means that one's everyday identity is constituted in sometimes precarious dialogue with others. One's identity is acknowledged only when it is seen or recognised by others. Washida therefore speaks of this idea of 'face' as an interface of mutual recognition between the self and the other.

Self-realisation is not, however, only attained through the power of language. While language is crucial, it must be consolidated with nonverbal messages in dialogical communication. While Butler spoke exclusively of gender, she asserted that 'the self is not only irretrievably "outside", constituted in social discourse, but the ascription of interiority is itself a publicly regulated and sanctioned form of essence fabrication' (Butler 1988: 528).

The idea of performativity is thus undergirded by a hegemonic social discourse that is acted out by the participants, while the idea of self-realisation is conditioned by a particular social discourse. The problem of recognition theory is that neither Honneth nor Taylor define what the 'good life', which accompanies fully attained self-subjectivity, consists of (Fraser 2001). In the particular context of *josei-muke* media, I would suggest that the 'good life' for women is to achieve male attention and to have men become agents of their physical or emotional pleasure and satisfaction. Furthermore, the significant point here is that the particular discourse that appears in *josei-muke* media is a staged 'performance'. *Contra* Honneth, Taylor and Washida, who conceive of recognition as a macro-phenomenon that pervades society and takes place only as a reciprocal phenomenon, this suggests that performative recognition can take place, as it does here, along a power differential.

Yoshiko and Yuri would often go to private events organised by *eromen* Uehara and Mukai. The aim of such private gatherings is for *eromen* to get to know their fans better, and it was clear to me that Yoshiko and Yuri were proud that the porn actors knew their names, taking this as evidence that they had a personal relationship with their favourite stars. 'I let them touch my breasts and I'm sure they like it', giggled Yuri confidentially (her breasts are bigger than the average Japanese women's and it was obvious that she was proud to show them off). Yoshiko suggested that I should have applied for these private events as well: 'You can only spend a lot of time with them if you are willing to invest. For me, seeing them or talking to them on the phone is a means to relax. I normally complain about my work, but they always cheer me up.' For *eromen*, giving recognition to someone like Yuri and Yoshiko is part of the emotional labour they are paid to do. This is why I put emphasis on 'performing and consuming recognition': the exchange of recognition between fans and *eromen* appears reciprocal, but the motivation for giving and receiving recognition is different for the two sides. For fans, it is to enjoy their fantasy and fulfil self-realisation, while for *eromen* it is about earning money and fame. The interesting point about Yuri is that she herself also provides emotional and physical services to her male clients, and she gains money and fame in return. She then seeks the company of *eromen* and other male escorts to receive emotional and physical services, rather than having an actual boyfriend based on an idea of 'love for free' (which I use here to literally mean 'free of charge'). Nonetheless, it is crucial to acknowledge that fans' experience of recognition is real and not the result of what might be termed 'false consciousness'; that is, an ideological blindness to their own social positionalities and interests.

I would suggest that fans' authentic feeling of recognition is a result of 'bounded authenticity', in Elizabeth Bernstein's definition – 'the sale and purchase of authentic emotional and physical connection' (2007:103). In her analysis of sex workers, Bernstein argues that sex workers at the American sex workers' rights organisation, COYOTE (Call Off Your Old Tired Ethics), described their work as prroviding an authentic experience achieved by a 'single self'; they did not see themselves as having a 'double self' that consisted of a 'front' and a 'backstage'. As she notes, this stands in contrast to the view of the majority of streetwalkers, who explain how they distinguish their emotional engagement in sex work from their private sex lives, through having 'double selves'. Bernstein argues that commodified intimacy is intimacy that is part of people's authentic experience, and is different from having a 'double self', which involves drawing a distinction between 'private' and 'commodified' intimacy. The distinction lies in a binary opposition between the authentic and the artificial, between single and double, and between private and commodified. Bernstein's bases her argument on the fact that almost every COYOTE sex worker identifies as polyamorous, non-binary and non-monogamist; therefore, sexual interaction with multiple people does not divide the perception of self – not professionally and not privately. However, in the Japanese context at least (and perhaps elsewhere) it is important to bear in mind that the perception of 'self' is very much relational; this means that the perception of 'self' is constantly – and often quite consciously – in the process of being reshaped in different social settings (Kondo 1990; Rosenberger 1992; Lebra 2004; Kimura 2005). Returning to recognition theory, it could be argued that different 'selves' appears in various settings, depending on the sociocultural environment. Thus, in a sense the point is not whether fantasy is pitched against reality, or private against public. The point is that society – in Japan, and, in fact, everywhere – is built upon an assemblage of different social settings, to which we all constantly adjust and adapt according to different motivations and values. Therefore, the question is, in fact, what female fans actually do in different settings – rather than what 'bounded authenticity' means to them.

The Ritual of Simulation

After watching the *eromen* talk show, the final part of the event was upon us: lottery time. Yoshiko and Yuri were excited to see the results. They each had more than five tickets stubs; I only had two. The woman who had ordered champagne had more than 40, which clearly seemed to annoy Yuri, since, as she had pointed out to me, that purchase of an expensive bottle of champagne would support the bar and the woman herself more than it supported the *eromen*. Following the usual procedure, each number was called out by an *eromen*, which then prompted the winner to blush and walk to the stage to receive her prize directly from her favourite. All of a sudden, my number was called out by Azuma. I was shocked and suddenly felt giddy. Yuri and Yoshiko both said 'Congrats! Go to the stage!'. Although I was not a fan, I found myself drawn into the situation, and I felt nervous that I had suddenly become the focus of attention, warmly applauded by others. I walked to the stage, where Azuma approached me, saying, '*Uchi de taisetsu ni tsukatte ne* (Please make the most of this when you get home).' Smiling, he handed me a pair of neatly folded boxer underpants in a ziplock bag. This was clearly not just any pair of boxers; the common understanding – and indeed what gave this pair value – was that they had, presumably, been worn by Azuma. My prize was thus not only of a sexual and intimate nature; it signified a highly personalised bond between myself and Azuma. This is a gift concept designed to make fans feel lucky, enhancing their attachment to their favourite star. And yet a clear distance between us was maintained. Whereas underwear worn by female porn stars is auctioned unwashed (with an emphasis on the total number of hours it has been worn) in the porn industry aimed at men, the plastic-wrapped boxers I was holding in my hands had – as customary within the *josei-muke* industry – been washed since they had covered Azuma's hips, penis and anus. All evidence of his body (i.e., sweat, drops of urine and semen or skid marks) had been removed, and what I was left with was an object that might encourage me to fantasise about his body, but which did not insist that I face the full bodily reality. This suggests another gendered dichotomy within the porn industry: while male porn fans are expected to want to fantasise about women and sex not only through images but also via stains and smells, it is expected that female fans would find this 'dirty' and unattractive. This gendered dichotomy seems to link up well with the overall aim of the event – to allow women to explore and fantasise about men and sexuality in a safe 'clean' place.

As I walked back to my seat, Yuri was called out by Uehara. Unlike me, she confidently chatted with him as she too received a pair of his underpants. When Yuri joined us again, she raised her hand to do a small high-five with me, and, as I followed suit, Yoshiko seemed happy for us. The event finished soon after this, and as the three of us walked to the bar to pay for our food and drinks, information about upcoming *eromen* AV releases and future events was announced. We then made our way to the exit, where the *eromen* were lined up to say goodbye with a handshake – an indication of intimacy, rather than of formality, as it would have been in an American or European context. Waiting our turn, Azuma recognised me and said with a wink '*Boku no shitagi tanoshinde ne. Kyō no fuku, ii ne. Sugoku eroi.* (Please enjoy my underwear. I like your outfit, it's really hot)'. I nodded awkwardly and moved forward. I was surprised to notice that my heart was beating fast and that I still felt excitement from the interaction with him earlier. I was not even a fan – how come these encounters with the men affected me so much, I was left to wonder. Perhaps it was the whole communal atmosphere of the fan community set up by the organiser, SOD, the *eromen* and all the female fans that surrounded me to which I was somehow responding. The entire event was, after all, planned and highly choreographed to instil very specific emotions in female viewers. Before we left the event venue, Yoshiko and Yuri chatted with Uehara and Mukai for a short while. In total, three and a half hours had passed when we headed back to the station.

Observing Yoshiko and Yuri and other fans having lengthy chats with *eromen*, I saw that there clearly is an emotional attachment to the porn actors among fans. Although I was there as a researcher, even I experienced a feeling of excitement and was flattered by my short conversation with Azuma. It seems clear that these kinds of events are planned and structured in order to cultivate in women a certain emotional involvement with their favourite *eromen*. The question here is why these women continue to commit, invest in and support the porn stars although they know that they are never going to be their girlfriend. What struck me is that women often used the term *ōen-suru* ('to support'), when describing their activities as fans. As at host clubs, female fans at *eromen* events are not looking for a specific boyfriend but for a place where they can feel at ease. What has brought these women together is the affection and the curiosity that they feel towards the *eromen* on the one hand; but also a desire to feel a sense of belonging in the fan community that has emerged out of their sexual fantasy. Even though at a certain level I could see that there was competition, and perhaps even jealousy, amongst the women, the strong sense of community I felt at the event – for example when the other fans shared their enthusiasm on my behalf as I went on stage to receive my gift – was much more prominent. In fact, an important part of the experience for these women seems to be the possibility of sharing moments of excitement with other female fans. This suggests that fans not only develop a certain attachment to their favourite *eromen*, but also to the community as a whole – a point that has also been observed in other female fan communities such as the Takarazuka theatre troupe (Robertson 1998). The sexually open atmosphere of the event seemed surreal to me, especially in Japan, where women who speak about sex in public are often stigmatised. In this context, the community set up by SOD provides a sanctuary in which women can engage in conversations about sex without fearing that they will be judged.

Given the fact that an event like this is a highly choreographed space in which both the men who perform and the female fans who consume have clear roles to play – even down to detail such as blushing on the part of the women – the fan community of *eromen* and *lovemen* is best understood as a ritualistic place that is separated from the norms of social life in Japan. This is what Bruce Kapferer describes as 'virtuality'. Not to be confused with cyber space, which has a literal reference, 'the virtual of ritual is a thoroughgoing reality on its own, neither a simulacrum of realities external to ritual nor alternative reality. It bears a connection to ordinary, lived realities as depth to surface.' (Kapferer 2004: 37) In defining the concept of virtuality, Kapferer referred to Victor Turner's concept of liminality. In his classic anthropological study of ritual, Victor Turner (2017 [1969]) defined the ambiguous and indeterminate characteristics of persons in initiation rituals as 'liminal', in the sense that 'liminal entities are neither here nor there; they are betwixt and between the positions assigned and arrayed by law, custom, convention, and ceremonial' (ibid.: 95). Liminal space does not exist independently from so-called 'reality'; rather, the two are mutually constituted. Therefore, the 'virtuality' to which Kapferer is referring is to be understood as a kind of social bubble which is part of a wider social ecology in which people display different aspects of their selves. Although Turner's primary focus was religious rituals, I feel that the idea of the liminal, as well as Kapferer's idea of 'virtuality', are relevant to the context on which I focus here, which eliminates certain pre-existing social norms, rules and discourse by artificially creating unique social settings.

People join liminal spaces to overcome a certain fear of reality or to avoid the problems that they face; they are seeking a 'liminoid' moment. Turner (2011 [1974]) uses the term 'liminoid' to refer to a liminal phase that does not necessarily relate to the resolution of personal crisis; it is one that is a form of play and an escape from reality. The liminoid space provides a level of ambiguity as well as a safe space; there is a promise that anything that happens in the liminal space stays there. The theoretical premise is that those who have entered liminal space return to social reality with a sense of resolution or at least with a certain emotional or physical development. This process is applicable to the fans of *eromen* and *lovemen*. Yuri's and Yoshiko's experiences indicate that female fans' support for *eromen* results from a desire to have a safe place in which they feel flattered, and to gain recognition for their femininity in exchange for (financial) support. They enter a liminoid space in which fans can play and, for a while, forget the problems they have outside the fantasy world; and in which they can feel excitement and fulfilment in a place that is separated from ordinary reality. It should be kept in mind, however, that this does not mean that what the women feel is not real.

The marketisation of intimacy has an impact on female fans' perception of ideal romantic relationships, marriage and love. This was, for example, suggested by Yoshiko when she stated: 'I wish my husband were an *eromen*, because single men my age don't understand how to deal with women!' Thus their ideal male romantic and sexual partner becomes, for fans, a production of the fantasy created by SOD. Despite the fact that fans are aware of the fantasy nature of the relationships, the commodification of intimacy and romance seems to affect these women, who increasingly have difficulty in finding 'the right one'. For someone like Yuri, who is a female escort herself and who therefore knows the nature of the 'game', as it were, her interaction with *eromen* works to relieve stress. Rather than spending time with men free of charge, Yuri spends large amounts of money on *eromen* and other male escorts. This is, on the one hand, because the intimate feeling she receives from this exchange feels authentic to her; but on the other hand, and perhaps more importantly, it is because the fantasy that *eromen* and *lovemen* provide never fails to give her what she craves, without the risk of rejection – a risk everyone faces in the realm of 'love for free'. Put differently, in non-commodified relationships commitments and compromises are required in the name of love, but in this system of exchange recognition is guaranteed.

Through these events, which offer both a fan community and a chance to have intimate moments with *eromen* and *lovemen*, women can experience intimacy and romance in a safe liminal space in which there is no risk of rejection. While recognition theory is based on reciprocal and autonomous recognition between individuals, the communication with *eromen* and *lovemen* provides fans with social recognition in a hierarchical, paid context. The 'bounded authenticity' that they experience allows them to overcome their own fears – even though it is necessarily time-limited and commodified. The level of 'bounded authentic' intimacy a fan achieves depends, of course, on how often they buy experiences – how often they go to events and venues and how often they pay for exclusive dates with *eromen* and *lovemen*. However, as long as they are willing to pay extra, fans can achieve as much heterosexual attention as they wish, in the shape of *eromen* and *lovemen* – good looking men who shower them with compliments and recognition. Through this, fans are able to achieve self-realisation.

However, a significant aspect of this fandom is that fans rarely leave this liminal/liminoid space. Instead, as suggested by the frequency with which Yuri and Yoshiko attend these events, female fans are likely to invest more and more money as they commit to fandom, because of the satisfying feelings they receive from *eromen* and *lovemen*. It is a well-thought-out business model. For these women there is a huge gap between their own social reality and their ritualistic interaction with *eromen* and *lovemen*. This means that it is increasingly difficult for them to adjust to the reality of intimacy in Japan, where women often feel a strong pressure to hold standardised views of marriage, love and romantic relationships.

Conclusion: Fantasies of the Coin-Operated Boyfriend

This chapter has looked at the fan culture surrounding male porn actors, *eromen* and *lovemen*. Through this lens, I have asked how fantasy in *josei-muke* AV and the consumption of recognition affects fans' gendered understanding of intimacy in contemporary Japan. Like female AV actors, boyband lookalike porn actors – *eromen* and *lovemen* – are idolised through their performances in films, at fan events and through mediated ways of delivering intimacy to a female audience.

Considering this in the context of what Wong and Yau (2018) call 'salvage ideology' in mainstream AV oriented towards male desire (through sexual acts, males provide females with salvation), it is clear that *josei-muke* AV – porn aimed at women – serves a similar 'salvage ideology'. This is evident in the dominant storyline, in which female protagonists' emotional or physical problems are resolved by male figures. Previous studies on gender representation in mass media designed for women, with both nonfictional and fictional content, have demonstrated how dominant storylines advocate that women should fulfil their self-esteem through recognition and validation by others. The idea is that the 'self' is continuously built upon recognition from others – not only through language but also through nonverbal messages in dialogical communication. A fully attained self is based on performativity; thus, it is a hegemonic discourse on social norms that we continuously reproduce by our behaviours. In the specific context of *jsei-muke* AV, a certain archetype of gender performance is provided: women achieve male attention while men become the agents of their physical or emotional pleasure and satisfaction. This is the performance structure of SOD's fantasy products. This chapter has looked at how performing and consuming recognition in this context functions within the fan community.

Through multiple opportunities to interact with *eromen* and *lovemen*, each fan is also encouraged to develop a certain intimacy and sense of attachment to the fan community itself, which, developed by SOD, provides a positive mode of fantasy production where women can depart from everyday routine and feel at ease. Although female fans are fully aware of the fact that what they are being given is a set of SOD products, they are nevertheless deeply affected by the nature of the fantasy relationships they experience, and this causes them to experience difficulties in pursuing romantic relationships based on mutual and autonomous recognition between individuals. Yoshiko, for example, who is actively looking for a relationship, has not found a partner yet, despite attending a series of match-making events. As her ideal man is produced by SOD as a fantasy performed by individual *eromen*, there is a gap between what she is hoping to find and the average Japanese man. Yuri, by contrast, rejects the idea of seeing someone 'free of charge', as she puts it, because she feels that spending large amounts of money on *eromen* empowers her femininity, since there is no risk of rejection.

Despite the potential problems associated with becoming a fan, brief experiences of this fantasy, in which self-esteem can be fulfilled, are not necessarily negative, but can be seen as a safe place to restore recognition from others. Interactions with *eromen* and *lovemen* are commodified, but it is precisely because of their commodification that female fans can feel relief, in ways they might not be able to in 'love for free' relationships. 'Love for free' requires constant mutual exchange between the two parties, while through these commodified relationships women can 'pay as you go', as it were. It can at least seem to them that they are always in full control of what they wish to give and take. However, while the commodification of intimacy frees women from undertaking the unpaid emotional labour often required in 'love for free' relationships, it also embeds their emotional and physical satisfaction within a potentially exploitative economic system.

The song *Coin-Operated Boy* by the Dresden Dolls (2003) tells the story of a woman who bears the scars of a traumatic experience from a past relationship and is now enjoying a fantasy with a plastic toy boy. The toy only tells her sweet things, as that is what he is programmed to do. There is no drama, no responsibility and no childcare pressure. The irony here is that her relationship with the plastic boy only lasts while she is feeding him coins. In other words, the investment is equivalent to the recognition she receives. In this, I see a crucial similarity with the way in which female fans interact with *eromen* and *lovemen*.

The liminal/liminoid space that SOD provides is no more than a fan meeting service. Financial and emotional investment on the part of fans will always vary in degree, depending on the extent to which fans get invested in the service provided. The fact that women do engage at all is likely to be a result of the gendered structure of contemporary Japanese society, in which women are generally objectified and under pressure to belong to someone. The interaction of *eromen* and *lovemen* with female fans and the attention they bestow on women validates female fans' self-recognition, something that is often difficult to achieve in 'reality'. I have pointed to the existence of a vicious circle of performing and consuming recognition within *josei-muke* AV fan culture, and I would argue that this circle affects understandings of intimacy, love and romantic relationships on the part of women who become fans.

Although my findings relate to a specific group, a fan community, my argument in relation to intimacy marketisation contributes, I would suggest, to our understanding of commodified intimacy in Japan more broadly, including in the context of the ever-popular maid cafes, services providing boyfriends/girlfriends for rent and *soi-ne* (cuddling) services. The problem of (or the lack of) recognition is a central key to explaining structural elements of gender inequality and sexuality within wider Japanese society.

References

Akagawa Manabu. 1996. *Sei He No Jiyū/Sei Kara No Jiyū: Porngraphy No Rekishi Shakai-gaku* (trans. *Freedom for and from Sexuality: A Historical Sociology of Pornography*). Tokyo: Seikyu-sha.

Baudrillard, Jean. 1994. *Simulacra and Simulation*. Ann Arbor: University of Michigan Press.

Bernstein, Elizabeth. 2007. *Temporarily Yours: Intimacy, Authenticity and the Commerce of sex*. Chicago: University of Chicago Press.

Butler, Judith. 1988. Performative acts and gender constitution: An essay in phenomenology and feminist theory. *Theatre Journal* 40(4) (Dec. 1988): 519–531.

Cyzowomen. 2010. *Onnadarake no AV Danyū Ibento Kaisai* (trans. *Male AV Actors Event Full of Women*). 15 September. Available from: www.cyzowoman.com/2010/09/post_2385_1.html [Accessed 10th Feb 2020].

Fraser, Nancy. 2001. Recognition without ethics? *Theory, Culture & Society* Vol. 18(2–3): 21–42. Available from: doi.org/10.1177/02632760122051760 [Accessed 10th Feb 2020].

Fujimoto Yukari. 2008. *Watashi no Ibasho ha Doko ni Aruno? Shōjo Manga ga Utsusu Kokoro no Katachi* (trans. *Where Do I Belong? The Nature of the Heart as Reflected by Shōjo Manga*). Tokyo: Asahi Shinbun Shuppan.

Galbraith, Patrick W. and Jason G. Karlin. 2012. *Idols and Celebrity in Japanese Media Culture*. Houndmills, Basingstoke, Hampshire, UK and New York: Palgrave Macmillan.

Hambleton, Alexandra. 2016. When women watch: the subversive potential of female-friendly pornography in Japan. *Porn Studies* 3(4): 427–442.

Hochschild, Arlie R. 1983. *The Managed Heart: Commercialization of Human Feeling*. Berkeley: University of California Press.

Honneth, Axel. 1995. *The Struggle for Recognition: The Moral Grammar of Social Conflicts*. Cambridge: Polity Press.

Iijima Tomoko. 2015. *Tayō ka Suru Sexuality no Shōhi Keitai – Josei-Muke Sexuality Sangyō no Chousa Yori* (trans. *Diverse Consumption Patterns of Sexuality – Survey of the Sex Industry for Women*). The Bulletin of Jissen Women's Junior College, Tokyo: Jissen Women's College Press.

Jenkins, Henry. 2017. 'Porn 2.0'. *Confessions of Aca-Fan*. 14 October. Available at: henryjenkins.org/blog/2007/10/porn_20.html [Accessed 10th Feb 2020].

Kapferer, Bruce. 2004. Ritual dynamics and virtual practice: Beyond representation and meaning. *Social Analysis: The International Journal of Anthropology* 48(2) (Summer 2004): 35–54. Special Issue on 'Ritual in Its Own Right: Exploring the Dynamics of Transformation'. Available from: www.jstor.org/stable/23178856 [Accessed 10th Feb 2020].

Kimura Bin. 2005. *Aida (In-Between)*. Tokyo: Chikuma Shobō.

Kondo, Dorinne. 1990. *Crafting Selves: Power, Gender and Discourses of Identity in a Japanese Workplace*. Chicago: University of Chicago Press.

Lebra, Takie Sugiyama. 2004. *The Japanese Self in Cultural Logic*. Honolulu: University of Hawai'i Press.

Nakamura Atsuhiko. 2015. *AV Bijinesu no Shōgeki* (trans. *The Impact of AV Business*). Tokyo: Shogaku-kan Shinsho.

Purcell, Natalie J. 2012. *Violence and the Pornographic Imaginary: the Politics of Sex, Gender, and Aggression in Hardcore Pornography*. New York: Routledge.

Robertson, Jennifer. 1998. *Takarazuka: Sexual Politics and Popular Culture in Modern Japan*. Berkeley: University of California Press.

Rosenberger, Nancy R. 1992. *Japanese Sense of Self*. Cambridge, Cambridge University Press.

Sedgwick, Eve K. 1985. *Between Men: English Literature and Male Homosocial Desire*. New York: Columbia University Press.

Takeyama Akiko. 2010. Intimacy for sale: Masculinity, entrepreneurship, and commodity self in Japan's neoliberal situation. *Japanese Studies* 30 (2): 231–246. Available from: dx.doi.org/10.1080/10371397.2010.497579 [Accessed 10th Feb 2020].

———. 2016. *Staged Seduction: Selling Dreams in a Tokyo Host Club*. Berkeley: Stanford University Press.

Taylor, Charles. 1994. *Multiculturalism and the Politics of Recognition: An Essay*. Princeton, Princeton University Press.

Turner, Victor. 2011(1974). Liminal to liminoid, in play, flow, and ritual: An essay in comparative symbology. Rice Institute Pamphlet – Rice University Studies 60 no. 3. Available from: hdl.handle.net/1911/63159 [Accessed 10th Feb 2020].

———. 2017 (1969). *The Ritual Process: Structure and Anti-Structure*. Oxford: Routledge.

Ueno Chizuko. 2010. *Onna Girai-Nippon no Misoginī* (trans. *Hating Women; Japanese Misogyny*). Tokyo: Kinokuniya Shoten.

Watanabe Takuya. 2017. *Waisetsu jōhō to waisetsu zai no kouiyoutai/sairon* (trans. Consideration of the system of obscenity and its law). *Tsukuba Law Journal* (22): 181–205. Available from: www.lawschool.tsukuba.ac.jp/wp/wp-content/uploads/2017/08/704768ee3f2e0cea109f3521b5f7f788.pdf [Accessed 10th Feb 2020].

Washida Kiyokazu. 1998. *Kao no Genshō-gaku; Mirareru koto no Kenri* (trans. *Phenomenology of Face: The Right to be Seen*). Tokyo: Kōdansha.

Wong Heung-Wah and Yau Hoi-yan. 2018. *The Japanese Adult Video Industry*. Oxford: Routledge.

Filmography

Arinomama Dakishimete (trans. *Embrace me as I Am*). 2019. [File purchased online]. Directed by KINO. Tokyo: SILK LABO.

Body Talk Lesson. 2009. [DVD] Directed by M. Tsunoda. Tokyo: SILK LABO.

Girl's Pleasure. 2009. [DVD] Directed by KINO. Tokyo: Magazinehouse and SILK LABO.

Finder No Mukou Ni Kimi Gai Ta (trans. *It Was You Behind the Viewfinder*). 2009. [DVD] Directed by Tsunoda Maiko and Miyazaki Rieko. Tokyo: SILK LABO.

Rihabiri no Sensei (trans. *Instructor of Rehabilitation*) 2018. [File purchased online] Directed by KINO. Tokyo: SILK LABO.

Sex no Mukou Gawa (trans. *The Other Side of Sex*). 2013. [DVD] Directed by Yujiro Enoki. Tokyo: Makuzamu.

Music

Palmer, A. 2003. *Coin Operated Boy* by The Dresden Dolls, track 6. New York: 8ft. Records.

CHAPTER 6

Intimacies of Exposure

Public Space, Gendered Presence and Performance at a Tokyo Train Station

R. J. Simpkins

On a humid summer's evening in 2013 I approached a female musician as she performed outside Kōenji Station. She sat on a narrow kerb in front of the shuttered shop entrances, singing confidently and strumming a large acoustic guitar, which looked all the larger because of her relatively short stature. I was at the beginning of my research on musicians in the western Tokyo neighbourhood of Kōenji; I was green, nervous and unsure of myself.

The woman eyed me with suspicion from under her straight black fringe when I smiled and crouched down in front of her. Nervously I mustered the Japanese I had learned since moving to Japan and blurted out a succession of quickfire questions. She did not look impressed and avoided eye contact with me, looking instead down along the beige-lit passageway of shuttered shop fronts and up to where it intersected with a station walkway. Crowds passed on their way to the ticket gates or towards the tumult of tightly interwoven shopping streets and backstreets. She answered just one of my questions, in a few words. I shuffled uncomfortably, feeling the palpable tension in the air and resisting my rising urge to apologise and leave. The formal questions were not working, so I attempted some small talk. This appeared to set off a peal of alarm bells in her head. She picked up her guitar again and wedged it between her chest and knees; a move that felt like the imposition of an acoustic barrier. Another terse reply. I felt that I should stop talking, but I was afraid of missing out on the perspectives and stories of a regular performer at Kōenji Station. The harder I tried, the more uncomfortable she appeared.

Her expression betrayed her doubt about my claim to be doing research about amateur music practices. An awkward silence. Sensing her discomfort rising up again, I stood up, apologised for the interruption and left. 'A shame', I thought. She was the first female musician I had met on the street.

'Wouldn't you say it is uncomfortable to be around a frightening person?' another female musician called Sayaka said to me one afternoon at a local Kōenji coffee shop near the station. I reflected upon the rhetorical tone of Sayaka's comment as the sounds of background chatter filled the air, and recalled that first meeting with a female street musician, which I described above. Over a year had passed since then, I had met other female musicians with whom I felt myself to have developed a good relationship. Had I been one of those frightening people for her, I wondered. Sayaka spoke again: 'So it is about a sensitivity to the atmosphere and surroundings.' She began talking about the importance of putting the general public at ease around her when attempting to gather an audience. I had to reorder my thoughts when she suggested that the frightening person she was referring to was in this case the musician playing in public. I wondered why Sayaka was so attuned to the comfort of strangers around her. As my research continued, the more time I spent conducting research with female musicians at Kōenji Station the more the concepts of comfort and discomfort appeared in conversations with them; these seemed to pervade their experiences of music performance. But what does 'uncomfortable' mean in the context of music performances at a train station, and how is it 'sensed' as Sayaka suggested, as an atmosphere? Was it the claustrophobic air I sensed when I approached that woman back in 2013, cutting through the tumult of the underpass and enveloping us both in its own microspace? That discomfort ultimately compelled me to leave, fearing that otherwise she would leave before me, and to the detriment of her attempts to perform. The question 'Wouldn't you say it is uncomfortable to be around a frightening person?' is one that I return to throughout, in order to bring us back to a space of reflection and to a sensitivity to the emerging atmosphere of the chapter.

Who can enter, loiter in and be transgressive in a space like Kōenji Station? Emerging from hours spent in the company of male and female performers, this question is at the heart of my investigation of gendered presence and performance in public space, which is presented in this chapter. As such, the chapter also offers a comparison of male and female experiences of making music on the street. I will gradually develop an increasing focus upon the women's perspective as this highlights the gendering of 'atmospheres' created in performance at the station, and of hospitality as a complex strategy emerging from the interplay of public space and social expectation. Throughout my research with musicians in the western Tokyo neighbourhood of Kōenji, conducted during a number of research periods between 2013 and 2020, I worked mostly with men, who outnumbered women at the station by seven to one. They performed what they called *rojō raibu* or 'street lives' – a double meaning referring both to 'live' music and to 'living' on the street, which became more significant as I accumulated hours and months and seasons spent in their company. The gendered perspective in what they were doing arose first as one of presence: who was present, where and at what times. The men generally spent much more time just hanging out, which made it significantly easier for me to talk to them. It was more difficult to gather ethnographic material about the women because of their comparative absence. The sustained presence of male musicians became a gendered landscape of music performance that shaped my daily experiences of doing fieldwork, and from a gender perspective this landscape cries out for further analysis.

    I will begin by setting the framework for station music performance, one shared to a certain extent by the men and women who choose to play in Kōenji. The central role of the station space in producing and sustaining relationships between the musicians and their audience creates an environment in which exposure facilitates connection to strangers, to the public who are at the station. In this context it is perhaps easier to understand why I chose to begin this chapter with a recollection of my first meeting with a female musician. Performing in the station space, she is exposed; she is in a space of movement in which she can be approached by all and sundry. As a musician looking for an audience, this exposure is ideal, creating a space of connection through music. Unfiltered, however, it can also act as a vector for either a remaking or an appropriation of space, which I suggest I sensed as a claustrophobic atmosphere when I made my awkward attempt to include her in my research. Exposure through performing music in the public space of a train station can bring both benefits and costs. I hope to show that the manipulation of this exposure to generate atmospheres that engender more comfortable ways of relating to people in different parts of the station becomes a way for musicians to manage their presence and their experiences of performing.

Kōenji Station is a type of urban space that influences the practice of music performance quite significantly. It is a space with which my interlocutors needed to engage just as much as did their audiences. As a transport node it is a transient, interstitial space, a point in between the steel and electric veins of the railway system and the neighbourhoods, workplaces and entertainment districts of the city. Its architecture, daily rhythms and its own particular atmosphere of space influence the ability of individuals to move and behave as they please around the station. I would suggest that ability of the musicians to do what they do when they play music is directly influenced by the kind of space the station represents, socially and historically, and this also influences the way in which ideas about presence and behaviour circulate within it. It is a distinctive space. While I do see parallels between station spaces and other open and accessible 'public' parts of the urban environment, I hesitate to claim that the station fully represents public space or the public realm in daily life in Japan. Stations represent a distinctive fabric of space in the interweaving of different fabrics of space that make up everyday life in the metropolis.

As a stage, Kōenji Station is an exposed space that provides access to a lot of people, some of whom are unknown potential new fans, supporters and friends for the musicians. But the musicians cannot afford just to play wherever, whenever and however they please. Sayaka told me that playing at the station 'takes time to learn' and contrasted it with performing at the many live venues hidden from view along back alleys and in basements in the neighbourhood. Spatially and interactionally, some musicians have learned over time to build an atmosphere of private space within the public walkways, junctions and underpasses. The process might begin with selecting a performance pitch, perhaps within an underpass rather than a major walkway; or it might begin through choosing a certain way of playing music, of posturing towards passersby. Some musicians make a direct invitation to the public to stop and listen, to sit and spend time together. I aim to demonstrate here that, for men and women alike, constructing a stage at the station involves a process of drawing people in and of creating a kind of intimacy from a position of exposure. It is within this process that I begin to locate some gendered aspects of presence and performance at the station, particularly where intimacy is revealed as a threshold of interaction. While the threshold is one that male musicians generally feel able to cross and to have crossed by others, it represents a more complicated and sensitive boundary for the women.

While I use intimacy as a lens through which to analyse both male and female experience, it also operates as an affective relationship that differentiates men and women experientially and strategically; it acts as a lens that reveals the differences in their experiences. In discussing this, I draw upon participant observation conducted with men and women who played music at Kōenji Station during my fieldwork. I will begin by introducing two male musicians, Fuji and Tsuntsun, and I will then move on to focus on three female musicians, Sayaka, Reina and Hitomi. All the musicians are between the ages of 20 and 35. All moved to Tokyo from other prefectures in Japan, except Reina, who only visited Tokyo to perform, while I was in Japan, but who lives in Nagano city in Aichi prefecture. The musicians all worked in part-time jobs outside of the music industry to ensure that rent and food were paid. Their working lives were marked by change; most of them switched jobs at least once while I was in Japan. Fuji's performances had to fit into his nightwork schedule, but he usually managed to play at least four times each week. Tsuntsun was in Kōenji every night, and at the station at some point on most days. Sayaka played at Kōenji Station on average four times a week. Reina visited Kōenji Station twice, as far as I know, on what she claimed to be a 'music pilgrimage' of Japan. Kōenji was her final and most anticipated part of the tour, as a friend from her hometown had told her of its popularity. Hitomi played less often than Sayaka, but I usually met her two to three times a week. The when and where of these performers' presence at the station was, I would argue, itself a significant element in their experience and also in their manipulation of exposure and intimacy in the context of performing music.

By digging into the complexities around desire and discomfort in the production of intimacy, as part of musical performance, I will highlight its gendered construction. In doing this I will be building upon recent attempts in anthropology to investigate the ways in which intimacy is involved in social relationships beyond the boundaries of intimate love, and what forms it takes beyond the private realm. I aim to contribute a new perspective, one that considers how space is used in the manipulation of intimacy in social life.

Boundaries of bodily space, thresholds of familiarity and strangeness and exchanges of attention are key elements of what may be called 'railway sociality' in Japanese cities (Tanaka 2008; Freedman 2011). I will sketch the gendered terrain of social life within the railway infrastructure of Japan, with a particular focus upon its spatiality and on the use and manipulation of the gaze in the production of uncomfortable intimacies. In doing this, I will draw a connection between female performance at Kōenji Station and the railway system in Tokyo; a system producing gendered behaviour and ordering gendered space. The rail network as a totality is a dynamic ensemble that facilitates collective life in Tokyo (Fisch 2018: 45), and to enter the station grounds as a female musician is to enter the kind of space described by Judith Butler (1993) – one in which the incessant work of gender is performed and improvised within a web of others composing their own relational sense of a public self.

The final section of this chapter, and its longest, is given over to an exploration of the 'intimate strategies' of female musicians during performances. This term, coined by Derek Layder and referred to by Emma Cook in her study of intimacy and power relations in the context of shifting gender roles, is used to explain how benign forms of power are used to get what one needs (Cook 2019: 140). I aim to reveal that despite the unequal and gendered power relations behind the answer to the question 'who can be seen in and be transgressive within public space in the city?', an analysis taking into account 'intimate strategies' provides a perspective on these relationships as nevertheless open to manipulation. I take this discussion further by suggesting that a consideration not just of intimate relations but of intimate spaces reveals how the navigation of encounters at the station involves the production of intimate atmospheres: a sense of intimacy that must be controlled by women to prevent it from becoming real and unwanted. Intimate atmospheres, much like the performances of station musicians, exist in the context of an awkward balance between busy publicness and private encounters, between hospitality and hostility, and for the women they are both a necessary concession and a strategy they use to enjoy their musicianship on their own terms.

The Stakes Involved in Making Music at the Station

People often asked me why musicians would choose a train station as a space for performance – an understandable question, given the fact that there are likely to be easier or more obvious places to choose. So I will begin here by discussing the stakes involved in playing at the station, for the musicians I worked with. In doing this, I emphasise the importance of the way they play, as well as the kinds of relationships they create with their audiences. Discussing these things will set the scene, within which I can then explain the role of intimacy in station music. The station is not just a backdrop for what the musicians are doing when they play, but another actor in the relationships I describe. Its influence is sought out and it affects performances. Playing music at the station requires being and staying at the station, and this requires both an understanding of the space, as Sayaka told me, and an ability to engage with it.

Female musicians made up ten of the 77 musicians with whom I have been working. This low figure is interesting because women account for approximately 50 percent of musicians participating in a local Kōenji indie (*indīzu*) scene that is ongoing in the many 'live houses' (*raibu hausu*) in the neighbourhood. Both male and female musicians noted that playing at a live house felt significantly different from playing at the station, because there are clear rules and expectations in live house performances, which determine aspects of behaviour and relationships with others inside the venue. However, quite a few of my female interlocutors performed at the station in a way that replicated certain aspects of live house performances, including formal introductions of themselves and their songs or limiting their performances to a time slot.

The men generally spent much more time simply 'hanging out' during and after their music performances, and this made it much easier for me to spend time with them. They were there more often, and had more spare time when they were. The women tended not to loiter in their preferred parts of the station late into the evening because, Hitomi told me, the later hours are times when more music is shut down by local police, and when the revellers and drunks emerge. Why some musicians might be more sensitive to the possibility of being shut down than others is, I suggest, a gendered issue related to the mobility of different individuals within the negotiated space of the station, as well as being related to who can be seen and where, a point which I focus on more later in this chapter.

The way in which gender affects mobility within the station was relevant to my own position, as a white male researcher. My gender influenced my own ability, as well as that of the people with whom I was working, to move freely within station space. The discomfort of my first conversation with a female street musician can almost certainly be attributed to the fact that I am male, which was not only significant in itself but is likely to have influenced my behaviour and the questions I asked. Confusion was not an uncommon feature of initial conversations with musicians, and almost all of my interlocutors wondered why I would be interested in talking to them as a researcher. To a (female) individual who was also on the lookout for her own personal safety, aware of the possibility of harmful or frightening encounters at the station, my presence as a male was an additional, gendered, factor affecting her response to me.

Regardless of gender, the backstories of the musicians followed a similar general pattern. Many had arrived in Tokyo from other prefectures, most in their early twenties, with a desire to perform music for a living and for this to define them in their relationships with others. Almost without exception they found part time work, such as in restaurants and bars, which supported their music performances. For some, the work was there to buy them time to be 'scouted' (*sukauto sareru*) or discovered by a music industry employee walking by the station, for others it gave them an opportunity to build a fanbase from which they could make money through regular live house performances. The musicians were buying time, immersing themselves in a music-oriented lifestyle. For some of them this was equivalent to recognising themselves as meaningful, creative individuals. For the majority, however, the imagined progression they had hoped for has not been reflected in the actual circumstances of their music practices. As I continued to speak to the musicians I noticed that their initial hopes were being reconciled to an everyday reality of life maintained by irregular work interspersed with music performances. Their affective attachment (Berlant 2011) to music performance as a source of income or professionalism has given way to new relationships with their music as well as alternative understandings of its role in their lives. The station has played a role in reordering their social and spatial conceptualisations of what it means for them to have a life in music.

Musicians often pointed out to me that the station is a space in which performing costs them nothing, which is a significant consideration for financially insecure performers in Japan, as there are hefty costs associated with playing at live house venues, where a musician must pay the proprietor in order to gain access to a stage and associated gear such as amplifiers, microphones and drum kits (see Hadfield 2013; Martin 2016). By focusing on the station, musicians have learned to manage multiple groups of supporters, each of which offers different levels of fandom, assistance and friendship, and they have developed approaches that attract and maintain connection with strangers – the ever-changing public at the train station. Their original notions about progression within the music industry, about contracts and organised performance schedules have been replaced. Their stakes in relation to music, for these station musicians, have changed and diversified. The relationships they have developed through their music practice at the station have become a way to engage with and live a life as a musician, to nurture wellbeing, to live reflexively with financial insecurity. Spending time at the station has come to be about local conviviality and overcoming loneliness, finding a physical place where they belong, and finding an alignment with the creative people and places of the Kōenji neighbourhood.

The Emergence of Intimacy

In the context of the adaptations that musicians make, in performing at a train station, and in the context of the new perspectives they develop regarding the position of music performance in their lives, intimacy has emerged as a framework for connection and for overcoming the tumult and transitory flow of the station. A focus upon relationships defined by shared time and conversation, or by friend-like fandom, has reframed the social distance at which musicianship takes place; at the station, this occurs not through industry contracts but through local ties and shared time.

The experience of intimacy in station music is not, however, the same for all musicians. It is different for men and for women. The gendered nature of intimacy is revealed through different sensations of comfort and discomfort, mobility and immobility, security and threat. Intimacy emerges as something that is felt differently by men and women, and male and female musicians' ability to do what they visit the station to do, to loiter, to play and to transgress, is different. It is, as I will argue here, shaped by the station, which is a gendered environment. In discussing the emergence of intimacy in my research with the musicians, I turn now to Fuji, a male musician who moved to Tokyo from Osaka in 2014.

Fuji talked to me a lot about his sense of disconnection from everyday life in Tokyo, which he felt especially keenly because of his estrangement from his family in Osaka, his uncomfortable night working hours, and the loneliness that he experienced at his flat in neighbouring Asagaya. For Fuji, the station remains today a place where his music connects him to a world he feels separated from, and to people with whom he can enjoy the shared attention and conviviality of music and conversation. He told me, 'I depend upon the walkways of the station to provide me with opportunities to pass time with others based upon their appreciation of the music I create.' These are 'real connections', he told me, in contrast to the ones he felt obliged to form in his part-time work. These

Figure 6.1: On the south side of the station, a passerby mistakes Fuji for a popular musician. Photo: R. J. Simpkins. **Colour**, p. 221.

were intimate moments for Fuji, often experienced as one-to-one conversations in the darker station underpasses and walkways where privacy and separation from the main flow are easiest to produce. Yet they were also a managed, limited kind of intimacy formed with strangers, distinguishable from the close family relationships that had caused him emotional pain. Family presented a source of discomfort in his life, but affective relationships with strangers at the station could, by contrast, offer a comfortable sense of connection that he could control. Comfort and discomfort both appeared to be linked to intimacy in social relationships, for Fuji. Returning to Sayaka's statement, 'Wouldn't you say it is uncomfortable to be around a frightening person?', it seems that for Fuji fear was not found in station architecture among strangers, but in the familiar setting of the family home.

To speak of intimacy as something sought out and produced in a place like Kōenji Station is against a general grain of thought, which aligns intimacy with romantic closeness, with those human relationships based primarily upon love and trust (Giddens 1992; Jankowiak 2008). Yet it is a powerful alignment for musicians at Kōenji like Fuji. In highlighting this alignment here and exploring its gendered composition, this chapter contributes to recent attempts in anthropology to investigate the ways in which intimacy is involved in social relationships beyond the boundaries of intimate love, or what forms it takes beyond the private realm. Allison Alexy suggests that relationships based upon or affected by intimacy are not just about who has control, who wins or loses, but what kinds of intimacies 'create relationships that are good for people involved in them' (Alexy 2019: 4), and, even more so, 'to whom and in what contexts' intimacy matters (ibid.: 17). Releasing intimacy from a state of emotional involvement and looking at it as a strategy, Alexy and Cook demonstrate in their edited volume (2019) how people construct and manipulate it in different ways. I build upon Alexy and Cook's work here, which stops short of exploring how intimacy operates in the context of busy urban spaces.

In her article 'Giving an account of oneself'(2001), Butler recognises exposure to others as an inescapable and essential part of knowing and understanding oneself. Butler illustrates a point that has become popular in contemporary feminist theory – that gender identity is an assemblage in continual flux (Coffey 2019; Coleman 2009; Currier 2003). It is useful in my investigation of presence and performance at Kōenji Station because it helps me to explore not only how an individual's exposure to others in public parts of the city produces responses that are in flux between intimacy and anonymity, but that anonymity itself may engender particular kinds of intimacies that recognition and knowing cannot. Formed from an anonymous public, intimacy can build a sense of community, and in so doing can generate a known sense of self.

For Tsuntsun, a very poetic soul and well-liked male musician in Kōenji, the station was an environment where he claimed the ability to 'expose his weakness'. This self-exposure, a self-professed expression of vulnerability was something he performed unashamedly as messy music with mistakes and loose vagabond behaviour that he associated with his hero, the Los Angeles poet of poor American street life, Charles Bukowski. This was, Tsuntsun claimed, an invitation to others to connect with him on a basic and stripped-down human level devoid of the formal structures that made everyday life in Tokyo one of complete drudgery. For him, letting his guard down in public was a cathartic exposure, producing a more intimate framework for performance and performer-audience relationships based upon a trust that his exposure would be seen as an authentic expression of 'real life'.

Tsuntsun feared the inauthentic as he understood it, the humdrum of an office job or the façade of mass middle class life. As a microcosm of city life, he saw the station as an authentic stage on which he could connect with people, somewhere a performance could break into a conversation and a shared drink or two with those who stopped to listen or respond to his presence. He felt unrestricted in his use of space as well; he could play along a busy walkway, or in one of the two station public squares (*hiroba*), and later move to a quieter sheltered area under the tracks. He felt able to position himself and refer to himself as a *makegumi* (loser) in his approach to performing at the station, and he felt that this was something he could do in front of other people without fear of their response. In performing this position, he believed that his music would afford him the self-assurance of authentic musicianship and, like Fuji, real human connection, via an intimacy produced through willing exposure to strangers.

For both Fuji and Tsuntsun, the positive affective elements of performance involved intimacies of exposure, an exposure that was desirable in order to produce connection, achieved by letting their guard down and/or inviting conversation and shared space. Neither talked about experiencing discomfort or having encounters that were harmful or frightening to them. Nor do I recall any of the men making comments like Sayaka's, which spoke of a concern for the comfort of other people using the station, a sympathetic contemplation derived from personal experience. I do not mean to suggest here that male musicians were unrestricted in their performances at the station, or that women like Sayaka were fearful of performing, but rather I aim to illustrate a sensitivity to an atmosphere of discomfort and threat that is gendered, in the context of station music, and one that can also be read as representative of female experience in public space. I am talking about a perception of the environment as sensed even while it remains unproblematic during a performance. Not everyone responded to Tsuntsun and Fuji's attempts to elicit particular reactions and moments with their audiences, but in general they did not suffer setbacks from failing to do so. The most significant factor that endangered their ability to play as they wished in the station and develop relationships with their audiences was the authorities – the station authorities, the local police and the railway staff, who would move them on for 'disruption', for selling CDs (a commercial activity that was not permitted) or citing complaints by locals. This happened to both male and female performers, but was experienced as relatively benign by male musicians. This enabled Fuji, Tsuntsun and other male musicians to dwell in station space for what could be hours at a time, and to go about and perform in whatever way best suited their goals and desires. Building intimacy with their audience through an evening at Kōenji Station created relationships that were good for these male musicians.

A point to draw out in relation to Fuji and Tsuntsun is that their connections with other people around the station, their production of intimacy, involved transgressive behaviour. Tsuntsun would drink alcohol on the walkways, and framed this positively as exposure, as revealing the authentic commonality of human vulnerability. However, transgressions of this kind, even high octane transgressions, did not significantly affect Tsuntsun, Fuji or any of the other men I spoke to. Nor did they appear to care very much about how they might affect those around them in a negative way: their perception of their behaviour in station space was one framed by possibility, authenticity and positivity. Looking back to my first meeting with a female musician, again, the claustrophobic atmosphere and her extremely cautious response to my approach stands in contrast to the mobility and unreservedness of these male musicians.

'Wouldn't you say it is uncomfortable to be around a frightening person?' is a question that simply through being spoken points to a whole other perspective on music performance at Kōenji Station. This is a perspective that complicates and tinges the threshold of intimacy as a strategy in performance with an atmosphere of discomfort and uncertainty. The busy public quality of station space and the private, intimate relationships engendered within performances seemed to be navigated in the context of gendered styles of intimacy. The men would establish performer–audience relationships that were about a private conviviality. They often enjoyed interactions that were instantly friendly, dissolving into relaxed conversation. As I spent more and more time with them, the way they performed began to emerge as being tied up with what affordances the station presented to them (see Gibson 1979; Knappett 2004). They could be punk, or they could be messy and disorganised. They could be 'real' and experience 'real connection'. The atmosphere of their intimacy could be aggressive, engaging people by reaching out to them, by approaching, making the move and moving themselves.

I too, as a male, was able to view the station as a place that provided me with affordances. This chapter discusses the connections between affect, atmosphere and gendered experiences of presence in urban space; and my own experiences and sense of security resonate much more closely with the male than with the female musicians. With one or two exceptions, my interactions with female musicians were more guarded on both sides, with limitations placed upon both the amount of time we could spent together and where this would happen. Almost all of my time with the men was spent at the station; with the women, by contrast, extended or deeper conversations often occurred at one of the coffee shops surrounding the station. My interactions with male musicians, and with the public, echoed those I describe above – there was the possibility that they might dissolve easily into relaxed conversation, loitering or metamorphose into spontaneous events over an evening. As I gained experience, I felt quite capable of building and occupying intimate moments and experiences as a part of my daily life as a fieldworker. I enjoyed the privilege of spending hours at the station each evening, up until and after the last trains had departed. I never once felt restricted or felt any sense of threat. Without question my research benefited from the relative ease with which I was able to get to know and spend extended time with male musicians, just as they would do with others at the station.

A fuller discussion of male station music in Kōenji is available elsewhere (Simpkins 2018). I now move on, however, to question and problematise the process of producing intimate interactions in station music as enjoyed by men like Fuji and Tsuntsun. I return to the question Sayaka posed, and recount the event that led to her asking it.

A Space for Intimacy?

Fuji and Tsuntsun both spoke about what they were hoping to get out of music performances at Kōenji Station with a language that suggested that this was something they could do comfortably because the station afforded them the opportunity to do it. Exposure and intimacy, as two contrasting but connected elements of music performances, create relationships that are good for Fuji and Tsuntsun, because the process Butler describes as an exposure to others in order to know the self has produced community for them and a sense of the self they desired to craft at the station.

Female musicians usually spoke in a different way about their performances at the station. They expressed a desire to build similar supportive relationships with locals and regular audience members, to advertise their music, distribute flyers and sell CDs, to enjoy meeting new people and making friends. The female musicians I worked with emphasised how their performances were part of a plan, of progression and professionalism, even though they understood as well as the men did how unlikely such a scenario was. However, while the reality of amateur music practice led to a desire for authenticity, wellbeing, street camaraderie and more affective relationships with their audiences among the men, the same did not seem to be the case with women like Sayaka. They did not use language that described what they were doing as exposure of some part of their selves, of some kind of deeper character or soul. Neither did they make statements that suggest the station afforded them possibilities to connect with others in a way that was personally rewarding for performer and audience alike. Did the women not desire the same things as men through station music, or did they feel unable to express these things or to make them happen in the same way?

By giving some examples of events occurring in station spaces in the evenings while women performed their music, I will draw attention to how intimacy and station music performance, as a couplet that creates relationships that are good for male musicians, is a more awkward fit for the female musicians who share this space. Where intimacy does feature in these women's stories, it is often much less positively expressed, and even emerges as something they cannot control or that they experience as something imposed upon them by strangers. I begin with Sayaka, one hot summer evening, as we sat on the faded concrete floor of Kōenji's second railway underpass.

'Robāto-san, I need to give you my new number', Sayaka said and flipped open a battered-looking purple mobile phone with her thumb. 'What happened to your iPhone?', I asked. 'Somebody stole it last week', she responded with a tired sigh. I started adding her new number to my contacts as she began to recount to me her memory of what had happened.

> Last week I was playing at Asagaya Station with a girlfriend of mine. You know that spot by the traffic crossing, on the other side of the road from the station and under the railway line? ['Yeah...'], well, we were playing there. These two guys started watching us. Maybe in their thirties. That wasn't anything unusual necessarily, even as they moved in closer and sat down beside us. Sometimes people want to ask a question or make conversation for a few minutes. Anyway, one of them was really talkative and arrogant. He said 'I used to play street music as well, but these days I'm in the music business' (*Ore mo mukashi rojō yattette, ima ongaku gyōkai ni imasu yo*). I just thought, 'Okay, sure. Maybe.' That was possibly interesting, but I also found him annoying because we both wanted to continue playing. He gradually started to creep me out. He kept asking me questions about where I was from, what I was doing in Tokyo, and both

he and his friend seemed determined not to leave. By the way she was glancing over at me, I could tell that my friend was also uncomfortable.

I needed to go to the bathroom, so I crossed the road towards the station. I looked back and could see the arrogant one had moved in closer to my friend. I wasn't gone for long, but when I returned they both stood up, made their excuses and left. We thought it was just another run-in with guys who were out for the evening to have fun. But when I reached for my phone it had gone, along with my wallet. I had been keeping them hidden from view in between our guitar cases. That's horrible, right!?

Talking to Sayaka in the underpass, I was struck by how her recollection and subsequent comments focused upon the place, more than on the act of theft. She continued:

We both loved that spot. And it was a favourite of mine to perform in, and even more convenient than Kōenji because I live in Asagaya. Ever since last week I just can't play there anymore, it doesn't feel right. It's like it has become dirty now... That's the worst of it.

What began as a local space for Sayaka's performances became, during the course of her evening at Asagaya, a space felt and later understood in a completely different way. In her recollection Sayaka recalls twice how she had felt that their space was being imposed upon, as the men 'moved in closer'. Both she and her friend became 'uncomfortable'. And though she felt frustrated, Sayaka chose not to speak her mind, instead putting up with the extended presence of the men as they continued to talk to her and her playing partner. A sense of claustrophobia builds in Sayaka's recollection until it is released with the departure of the men and the act of theft. Choosing to perform at Kōenji instead of Asagaya from that evening onwards, she expressed her decision using words that described the atmosphere as she now experienced it: it 'doesn't feel right' and 'has become dirty'.

Fuji's and Tsuntsun's felt sense of being at the station grew out of their ability to reach out to others sharing the station space and to feel a positive connection with those who emerged from the public crowds. 'Being at the station' as an affective sense of connection with the space was tied to this sense of the unknown, of excitement infused with the potential for spontaneity, qualities that turned the station into a temporal, interstitial space and a microcosm of everyday life (Kon 1987; Pendleton and Coates 2018; Freedman, 2011). Because the experience of being at the station is largely one of opportunity and positivity for them, the walkways and underpasses places to appropriate, to loiter, the station has the capacity to become a significant place in their lives, one that forms their sense of self and produces wellbeing (Otaya 2012; Allison 2013).

Sayaka's case, however, underlines the fact that stations do not always present these opportunities or their attendant positive emotional experiences to all. The appropriation of a train station is never complete, and the ability of musicians to do this affectively and in a way that gives them a sense of meaningful connection to the station is impacted by the gendered quality of the transport space. Despite enjoying many positive evenings of performance in Asagaya, Sayaka and her friend felt long after the theft itself that they had 'lost' Asagaya Station as a space for music performance because neither felt confident or comfortable to begin performing there again. A place to be in the city had gone, felt particularly keenly by Sayaka because this was also a part of the town in which she rented an apartment. This experience offers a glimpse into how a public space itself may be affected by gendered experiences, through the actions of people within it. Her performance beneath the railway line in Asagaya exposed her to something that is more likely to be experienced by some people (women) than by others (men). Paying attention to the ethnography of the musicians at the station allows us to approach the space not as an efficient architecture of transport, but as one filled with differing tempos, lived affects, sensory knowledge and competing orientations (Stewart 2011: 446).

A central question is: to what extent do women like Sayaka feel able or unable to manipulate more intimate relationships and atmospheres related to music at the station, to limit their production or to use strategies of their own making to deal with what they encounter? It is certainly a difficult balance, for female musicians. I noted this in particular in relation to a woman whom I met one evening at Kōenji Station. I was particularly struck by how difficult it was for her to achieve the right balance between exposure and invitation to interact. For male musicians, it is much easier to achieve the right balance and to produce a smooth, rewarding and intimate experience. Inviting people to take a close interest in them appears to involve a disproportionate sense of risk for female musicians, of interactions tipping over the boundary into unwanted intimacies that affect both their enjoyment of the performance and their ability to perform. When I spent evenings with the women, I saw that the fragile boundary between comfort and discomfort, between security and threat, was clearly exposed in the negotiation of intimacy in performance.

Exposure and the Threshold of Intimacy

Reina was visiting Kōenji Station as her final leg of what she described as a station music tour of Japan. She is from Aichi prefecture, some 300 km west of Tokyo and was looking forward to completing her tour in the capital. Reina had set up in the second railway underpass. She was dressed for the warm summer evening, in jean shorts and black vest, and would have appeared to be simply another station performer if it were not for the leather wrestling mask that she had strapped to her head.

I got talking to her about this mask during a break in her performance. I asked her about it and she replied: 'The mask is a trick I have tried a few times during this tour of mine. It was particularly effective at Hamamatsu Station in Shizuoka. One group of tourists from Taiwan kept taking pictures with me, then they gave me a bundle of money because they were leaving Japan.' She went on to explain that increasing the attention paid to her helped to bring people in to the point where she could talk with them, give them a flyer, talk about her CD and establish a rapport. 'The people I talk to are much more often the people who stay in contact and become fans or supporters', she claimed, handing me a flyer. It appeared to be working at Kōenji as well. As she played her guitar and sang through the faux-leather, people slowed to snap pictures, a couple mused that she might be a famous singer in disguise, and a small gathering amassed opposite her on the other side of the underpass, leaving a space in the middle for commuters and locals to pass through. Questions and answers and light conversation were exchanged between songs. One young man stopped his bike and lent on his handlebars, watching her from a metre away. A little later he was joined by another man, slightly older, who appeared to enjoy this closer position than the one taken up by the other audience members and who began taking photos. Reina acknowledged these two men, and handed them flyers, which only one of them took. She was hospitable to them, thanking them specifically, in addition to thanking the main audience, despite the fact that they did not applaud and did not move.

During a more significant break in her performance, I explained my research and told her that I was interested in her perspective as a visiting musician. 'Is it common to have these gawking men at her performances?' I

Figure 6.2: Reina's mask was effective in drawing attention. Photo: R. J. Simpkins. **Colour**, p. 222.

asked. 'I think that it happens more when I wear this mask,' she said, unfastening the straps, complaining that they were itchy. 'But yes, sometimes I get people who don't seem to respect my space or they stay without interacting with me. It can't be helped, as I stand out more, I suppose.' She said this thoughtfully. Just then she turned and said: 'Actually, can I ask you about something?' 'Sure,' I responded. Reina then described to me how earlier in the evening a man in his forties sporting an Hawaiian shirt, cargo shorts and flip flops had approached her and handed her his business card. He wanted to help her in the music business, he claimed, and said he had connections. He thought they should meet to discuss this later in the evening. Reina told me that because she didn't know what to say, she had agreed to the meeting. She clearly regretted this now, becoming uneasy and asking me for a second opinion: 'Is that a bit suspicious? It could be, couldn't it? I wonder what I should do …'. As we continued to talk she noted with a start that it was nearly 10.30 p.m. (the time she had arranged to meet him) and she asked me to help her gather her things quickly so she could leave before he arrived. We rushed to the station ticket gates and, taking me slightly by surprise, Reina stopped to ask a restaurant tout, who had approached us bearing discounts, if he also thought the offer from the flip-flopped man was suspicious. She asked a final time as we said our goodbyes at the station, and I walked away wondering about this need for confirmation. The obvious discomfort expressed by Reina's suspicions about the man's intentions, and the parallel discomfort felt by other female musicians in this chapter in situations like this, suggest a gendered awareness of vulnerability as women in the station space. The fact that she felt the need to question both the man's intentions and her own evaluation of them also aligns with studies that recognise the ever-present sense of concern women feel and the confusion that this concern can cause – a form of gendered trauma that women, consciously or unconsciously, feel just beneath the surface of everyday life experiences (see Luckhurst 2008; Caruth 2016).

I have since thought that Reina's mask is a good representation of the relationship between exposure and intimacy as experienced by my female interlocutors. The mask represents Reina's presence at the station as she performs. As a gimmick to heighten her visibility, Reina used it to invite and encourage interaction on the part of the public at the stations where she performed during her tour. These were her terms. While some reactions aligned with her desire to build a rapport with people, others were unwelcome and made her feel uncomfortable about staying where she was. Exposure can lead to possibly rewarding intimacies, but it is also an open door to all responses from the public. The flip-flopped man crossed the threshold of intimacy in a way that worked for him; but it was not of her design. Being approached for conversation and a drink is something that Fuji and Tsuntsun regard as ideal. Reina, however, understood the man's unsolicited offer of mentorship and help with her career as one that came with the condition of a private meeting and a drink. The potential for a more intimate relationship brought about through performance at the station was awkward for Reina in a way that it would not have been for Fuji or Tsuntsun. Her exposure came at the cost of her sense of security, and her transgression (standing out by wearing a mask) contributed to her cutting her performance short and leaving early.

It becomes clear from Reina and Sayaka's uncomfortably intimate experiences during their performances that spaces like the train station are spaces in which intimacy can be something imposed on others without any invitation. Intimacy can just as easily entrap or harm as it can facilitate positive affective relationships. For Fuji, familial intimacy was perceived as being the most harmful type of intimacy, while an atmosphere of intimacy at the station was able to produce a sense of connection and comfort, of being at home. Expressions of intimacy, or intimacy itself, are read and experienced by musicians in different ways, and no single musician was the sole architect of the intimacy that they experienced in the company of strangers. Peter Geschiere has shown that far from being a harmonious relationality with others, the often uncanny nature of intimacy can hide dangers and aggressions. His study of witchcraft, intimacy and trust in Cameroon illustrates the fact that intimate relationships may not be trustworthy ones, but may be open to manipulation – in that case in the context of the operation of occult powers – in order to bring about desired events or harm those considered close, even family (2013: 66). Influenced by Sigmund Freud's work *The Uncanny* (2003 [1919]), which tells of a young man's discomfort at seeing somebody who looks as much like a close, old friend of his father's as his father's murderer, Geschiere suggests that intimacy can appear in social relationships in ways that intertwine the familiar or the intimate with insecurity and fear.

The relationship between exposure and intimacy in station music is a complex one, and it is also a highly gendered one. For male musicians like Fuji or Tsuntsun, exposure is a manipulated aspect of performance that resolves into a form of intimacy, crossing a threshold that produces connection with the public. This connection is experienced as meaningful, producing a sense of recognition, of being in and even belonging in a space that they feel able to manipulate, despite it also being part of a transport hub. For Reina at Kōenji Station and Sayaka in Asagaya, on the other hand, exposure through their performance resolved into a form of intimacy experienced as discomfort and threat. In other words, it turned into another, undesired exposure. It is interesting to note that in the face of this, both Reina and Sayaka responded hospitably. They did not immediately react to their discomfort, but rather tolerated it. 'It can't be helped if I stand out more, I suppose', Reina suggested, when talking about the men who made her feel uncomfortable by invading her sense of physical space and snapping photos of her in the underpass.

The process of engaging with strangers and of creating or experiencing shades of intimacy at the station is, I would suggest, tied to the question that I raised earlier about gendered behaviour in a public space – who can inhabit or transgress this. The permeability and malleability of intimacy as a facilitator of relationships comes across as being under much more control on the part of male musicians. While Kōenji train station offers opportunities for musicians to appropriate, its spaces appear unevenly accessible, providing mobility for some and restricting others. Intimacy may slip from the private to the public realm by creating spaces that usurp places meant for other kinds of relation (Berlant 1998: 282). I suggest that this threshold also exists as a construct of the gendered sociality of rail spaces in Tokyo. Presence in a public space like the station, and particularly transgressive presence, is one that, for Reina and Sayaka, may be determined as much by the kind of space they are entering as by who else is sharing the space and what those people feel themselves able to do.

Intimate Alienation

To what degree are the restriction and the intimacy imposed upon Reina and Sayaka connected to what may be the inherently gendered nature of railway spaces? Michael Fisch has shown in his study of Tokyo's commuter railway system that the network is not just a set of railways and buildings that transport bodies, but a dynamic ensemble that facilitates collective life (2018: 45). Collective life as a way of behaving in the city is transported along with the commuters for whom the railways have become an integral part of Japan's contemporary social history. James Fujii, for instance, considers the railways to be a collection of routes for relationships based upon contemporary capitalism in Japan. Its carriages, he suggests, create 'intimate alienation', or an uncanny shared closeness, a 'subjection to a social space defined by the logic of capital' (1999: 108). This is also the logic of post-war urban gendered divisions of labour, which include male commuting and male corporate sociality in the entertainment districts surrounding commuter hubs, long associated with men's working life during the height of Japan's economic growth (Allison 1994; Dasgupta 2011; Fujii 1999; Freedman 2011). Kōenji Station is one of these hubs, and has a strong association with commuting and with entertainment.

As the lifeblood of the city, the railways have been a prime site for the growth and expression of the gendered values of postwar Japan, facilitating the circulation of social expectations of presence and behaviour. These are expectations that impact upon women's experience of inhabiting spaces (Mulvey 1975; Iwabuchi 2002; Kinsella 2013). As a 'dynamic ensemble', what happens in one part influences the totality, and anthropologists have begun to study rail spaces as particular instantiations of gendered relationships. Observation, the exchange of attention and the predominance of male presence are all, for instance, recognised as key parts of railway sociality (Tanaka 2008; Freedman 2011). Brigitte Steger's (2013) investigation of *inemuri* (napping) behaviour in train carriages is an intriguing study of the manipulation of intimacy, through the operation of the male gaze in a confined space – something that is desired by men and experienced negatively by women. I suggest that this type of interaction, observed both by Steger and also by Getreuer-Kargl (2012), emerges from a web of gender-specific expectations and affordances that complicate the use of intimacy as an affective structure for performer-audience relationships at the train station.

In the space of the carriage, unlike in a walkway or an underpass at a station, female commuters are much less able to resort to a physical exit strategy, as my interlocutors did when they were exposed to discomfort. Instead, Steger identifies strategies among women for negotiating a situation in which a threshold of intimacy has been crossed. She describes a strategy called *inemuri* that is used by women to deflect invasive male observation by partially extricating women from the relationship between observer and observed. This strategy involves appearing to be asleep; Steger argues that such a strategy works because a person who appears to be asleep is neither cognisant of their own actions nor capable of being drafted into unequal power or gender relations of looking (2013: no pagination). The ability of female passengers to use strategies like this to address the physical experience of gendered power relations reveals the nuances of agency that complicate the way gendered space is experienced. It also has implications for the way in which gender-determined social relationships operate in rail spaces. What strategies or approaches might musicians like Reina and Sayaka take in order to interrupt the gendered manipulation of intimate space in the environment of Kōenji train station?

Female Intimate Strategies: Negotiating Rail Space as a Stage for Male Intimacies

In thinking about how female musicians at Kōenji Station strategise and develop approaches to negotiating their exposure to a predominantly masculine place-making process during performances, I am inspired by Derek Layder's notion of 'intimate strategies' as a means of getting what is desired in subtle power struggles (Layder 2009: 6). I am also inspired by Cook's more recent discussion of how couples with relationship dynamics that fall outside standardised male breadwinner and female homemaker roles may revert to more stereotypical gender power roles in order to negotiate difficulties that arise from their transgression (Cook 2019: 131). Both Sayaka and Reina showed reactions to discomfort caused by the manipulation of space by audience members with patience, restraint and even hospitality. There are clearly occasions when they have not benefited from this passivity; however, the nuances of the performer–audience relationship crafted in a public space prevent them from reacting with more certainty and conviction. Like the men, they still desire to be present and to appropriate the space. In this final section I aim to bring out the ways in which the female musicians manoeuvre within the expected boundaries circumscribing female presence in station space through the exposure that comes from performing music within it, including the way they navigate the threshold of intimacy, which is, for them, a consistently uncomfortable aspect of performer–audience relationships. I revisit the question that Sayaka raised at the local coffee shop: 'Wouldn't you say it is uncomfortable to be around a frightening person?'; and I suggest that the 'sensitivity to the atmosphere' she claimed was important when performing station music is part of a wider strategy for being present and for appropriating station space. Here I return once again to the coffee shop south of Kōenji Station:

Aikyō ga ii hito desu ne ('It's people with charm, isn't it'), Sayaka said after a pause for thought while spooning another cloud of coffee froth into her mouth. We had begun a conversation about what qualities make a good street musician. *Aikyō*, meaning 'charm' or 'attractiveness' in Japanese, was, in Sayaka's opinion, the capacity to attract others in a specific environment, and to turn the performer's presence into a positively-interpreted element of that space.

Wouldn't you say it is uncomfortable to be around a frightening person? To that extent it [*aikyō*] is also about sensitivity to the atmosphere or to the surroundings. *Aikyō* is not the same thing at a live house and at a street session, because of the context. The live house is a more straightforward performance, and maybe easier to understand. Street music is less determined, it takes time to understand it and to be able to do it. Being approachable, appearing to welcome questions or conversations, are just as important qualities as being a good musician.

I had known Sayaka for a couple of years at this point, and in the early days she had talked about her musical performance in ways that suggested she considered it genuine and without social artifice. Sayaka was keen to be scouted on the street, to 'turn pro' as a musician, when she first moved to Tokyo. Gradually, however, the repetition and accumulation of evenings spent at the station, combined with a pattern of swapping part-time work in one ramen restaurant for another, appeared to cultivate in her a more pronounced relationship with strategy and performance beyond the straightforwardly musical. She began to understand the range of realistic possibilities affecting her life, as an amateur musician unlikely to become professional, and concomitantly those of the station as her principal stage.

Grounded in this understanding – a locality-based conception of musicianship – Sayaka appeared to see her performances as more relational: she was not performing *at* the station but *with* the station, including the space and its public. Her experiences of performance over time have distilled in her an awareness that the norms and rules by which she is attempting to make herself recognizable as a musician at the station are not entirely hers. Her suggestion that station music is 'less determined' is followed by a suggestion that she must be ready for what comes and appear to welcome it, to be hospitable. In other words, she understands that to give an account of herself as a musician is to expose herself to, and to accommodate, a 'publicity that is variably and alternately intimate and anonymous' (Butler 2001: 25). This opaque sense of self is likely to be derived from her circumstances and from her experience as a woman attempting to perform in the public space of the station. This contrasts with the male musicians' exposure, which is a more empowered performance; but it also provides her with an understanding of the relationships ongoing in the space, which allows her to navigate these and even benefit from them. I suggest that the term *aikyō* represents this subtle negotiation, for Sayaka: it stands for a reconciliation of her exposure to a variously intimate and anonymous public, its gendering gaze, and her own attempt to manipulate this, as a strategy developed over time.

In his work on hospitality, Jacques Derrida (2000) suggests that to be hospitable to a stranger is to offer a gift of sorts, a generosity that can turn them into a friend for a limited period. At times, the openness of hospitality, of welcoming in the outsider to a private space, involves accepting them on their terms, but in doing this the potential for new and meaningful relationships also exists – the potential to cross 'thresholds of hope' (O'Gorman 2006: 55). The importance of *aikyō* for Sayaka is, as she describes it, that it provides a strategy for navigating thresholds, including that of intimacy, that men do not fear to cross. Hospitality as a positive lived experience of welcoming in strangers speaks to the cases of Fuji and Tsuntsun, for whom a stranger at the station was also somebody who could easily become a friend in the context of the performer–audience relationship. In the cases of Sayaka and Reina, however, Derrida's attention to the discomfort of relationships developing through hospitality appears more relevant. Sometimes the threshold between oneself and a stranger must be maintained, he claims, through a self-limitation within hospitable acts, because to accept a stranger fully as who they are, and to expose oneself in the process, also invites a closeness, with the potential to harm.

Derrida describes actions that limit hospitality as a kind of hostility, but I suggest that this takes for granted that those providing hospitality are in a position of power. For my female interlocutors, however, hospitality is not a complete choice; it is partly a product of their position in the space of the station. I have shown how understanding intimacy as a threshold that operates in the context of social relationships occurring in physical space creates a frame through which to view female musicians' experience of intimacy as both potentially rewarding and potentially threatening. Hospitality, incorporating *aikyō*, as described by Sayaka, is a strategy that intermingles the gendering of space and social relationships at the station, and manages shifts in the balance of intimacy. Understood in the context of the strategy of hospitality, the notion of intimacy as close emotional and affective relationships between people is released from the need to be 'authentic'. By managing the threshold between oneself and another in a public space, by manipulating intimacy, it becomes possible for Sayaka and others to affect their ability to be present and visible – and also transgressive – in a public space.

Linking *aikyō* to a sensitivity to the atmosphere of the station, Sayaka describes the need to maintain a constant awareness and to adopt a reactive stance towards unknown elements of the train station environment. Just as she describes the importance of 'appearing to welcome', I suggest that she understands that her position is one that requires her to produce an air or atmosphere of intimacy that aligns with her audience's expectations of her but that also allows her to enjoy the benefits of this as a musician. This is a strategy that acknowledges the station as a gendered space in which her presence as a musician is transgressive.

After Sayaka talked to me about *aikyō* in the context of music played at Kōenji Station, I became alert to the term, and I discussed it with other musicians. On one of her regular visits to the station, speaking from her favourite pitch on the main North Exit thoroughfare, Hitomi, who was both a pianist and singer–songwriter, expanded on Sayaka's notion of *aikyō* in relation to the way in which she created an atmosphere during performances. In order to build relationships of 'patronage' (*aiko*) with her audiences, Hitomi suggested that she needed to offset her presence as an interloper in and appropriator of the train station walkway. This was especially important in her case because she preferred the busiest part of the station, which exposed her to the most commuters. She suggested that her exposure in this space could be softened by drawing attention back to the overtly feminine aspects of her performance:

> In the end I am borrowing a public space and performing as I please, so it is something I shouldn't really do… While I know that I shouldn't, I'm doing it anyway. So I try to appeal to the public in every way I can. I have natural advantages, I'm physically small, and short. When I play, the sound I produce is that of a female voice and a piano… They are beautiful, clean sounds that I think most people feel comfortable hearing. When I speak to the public my voice is soft, and I think that a female voice is easier to listen to. Even if you move in closer towards me, I'm not frightening, right (*chikazuitekitemo kowakunai deshō*)? Nobody is afraid to approach me, which is good for me, and sometimes bad. But I give away more flyers, receive more questions and meet more people because I use my physical attributes as a woman.

These comments of Hitomi's highlight her use of hospitality in order to negotiate her place at the station. Hitomi was particularly aware of her presence as an act of transgression, that she should not be doing as she pleases in such a space. As a consequence, she appeared to understand that she must make up for the transgressive act in order to interact with her audience in the most favourable way. Negotiating her place at the station involves righting the perceived wrong that she has done by assuring the public of her qualities as a woman. Hitomi's *aikyō* is an essentialised femininity: a petite body, a soft voice, and the 'clean' sounds of a piano. She is not frightening and so appears approachable. The atmosphere that she creates is both one that she feels obliged to create and one that she desires, because creating it increases her chance of connecting with larger numbers of people, building an audience and gaining support.

People often approached Hitomi at the end of her performances. There was one regular who would stand grinning at Hitomi until she finished playing, holding fast to a plastic bag laden with folders. Hitomi always gave the impression that she was delighted to see him, and she remembered little details of his life to ask about (including the folders), was quick to laugh and was always extremely grateful. She would load him with flyers, voicing her hope that she would see him again next time. There were invariably others like him, and she would repeat the process over and over again with the same gusto. I remarked upon her relationship with these audience members one night at the station, and her response again suggested that she was manipulating her encounters, just as she managed her musical performance, in order to produce an intimate atmosphere within which she could play, be seen and remain in station space.

I try not to be negative in any way when I am at the station, in fact I pretend to be even more positive than I feel. I always try to present an easy-to-understand character (*itsudemo, wakariyasui kyarakutā de iru yōni shitteru*): easy to talk to, and whose songs make people feel better, make them want to return to the countryside (*inaka ni kaeritakunaru*). I want people to think that there is something nostalgic (*natsukashī*) about my music and my personality. I attempt to become somebody around whom people can feel relaxed and secure, whenever they see me (*itsu attemo anshin dekiru*).

Hitomi's hospitality appears to intentionally create an atmosphere that can be enjoyed by the station public, and one that she is capable of managing. In her comments about the man with the folders who regularly comes to listen to her, she claims that she avoids any negativity, suggesting that she offers a positivity that is greater than that which she actually feels. Here Hitomi's comments align with those of Sayaka, for whom appearing to welcome was also a characteristic of a good musician. Hitomi then makes three claims about her intentions that suggest active attempts to exhibit gendered tropes of behaviour between men and women in public: she presents herself as uncomplicated and easy to talk to; as someone who makes her audience desire a return to the countryside in an experience of nostalgia; and as someone who wants her audience to feel secure and relaxed around her, to be put at ease. In the context of railway infrastructure, this idea of awakening a longing for the countryside in her audience through her presence and performances replicates an association of women with natural settings that has been strategically used in Japan Rail advertising campaigns. This association has been explored by Marilyn Ivy in *Discourses of the Vanishing* (1995). Ivy demonstrates how the association between women and nature in Japan Rail marketing posters was designed specifically to increase male professionals' demand for travel to the countryside, through their own gendered notions of country women, activated by such sights as a kimono-wearing girl on a bench in an autumnal landscape (ibid.: 48–54). Hitomi's attempts to be easily understandable, uncomplicated and positive are also a common feature of popular expectations of young women 'who serve' within the public realm (Ichimoto 2004; Allison, 1994).

These performance strategies are also strategies of using space and of managing the nature of one's presence at the station. They appear close to what is described by Edward Casey as 'hospitality on the edge' – a giving up of place and position in order to remake the boundary between an individual and a stranger (2011: 45). Brian Treanor regards a place-giving act of hospitality as one performed by an emplaced person, such as a local in reception of a foreigner or stranger (2011: 50). I suggest that Hitomi's hospitality is, in contrast, the act of a displaced person, and also that it is, in fact, a gendered act operating in reverse. As a displaced person, an interloper in station space, Hitomi offers her feminised hospitality to her audiences in the largely patriarchal space of the station. This strategy is also one that accepts that Hitomi's account of herself in station music is one she must give within the social conditions of the station as a gendered space, and of the train station as a form of gendered architecture in the Tokyo context. There is no station music for her that is not also one that 'conform[s] to norms that govern the humanly recognizable, or that negotiate these terms in some ways, with various risks following from that negotiation.' (Butler, 2001: 26). Hospitality, in the context of performances by musicians like Hitomi, does not come from a position of power or free choice, of being able to offer hospitality and choosing to do so, as Derrida approaches the relationship. Nor is it a place-giving act on the part of an emplaced person, as Treanor suggests. Instead, hospitality on the part of female musicians is here a strategy of intimacy drawn out of a context of gendered differences within the public space of the station. It is a concession to these differences but also a way of tip-toeing between discomfort and comfort, as well as a means of welcoming a stranger, a potentially frightening person, as a fan, a supportive individual and a friend.

Conclusion: Intimate Atmospheres

Perhaps it is all a matter of time and experience. 'It takes time to be able to do it,' Sayaka told me, which is why so much of what musicians like her did at the station was about *becoming* something they were not. 'I try to become somebody around whom people feel relaxed,' Hitomi said. Looking at the appropriation of station space, a requirement in station music due to the limitations on who can do what and when in its environment, has revealed the role of intimacy in actively reaching out to people, or else drawing them in closer. Examining this process has allowed me to return to one of my central questions: who can loiter, who can be transgressive in a public space? As a lens of analysis, intimacy has brought into focus how entering and performing at the station is differentially experienced and manipulated by men and women.

When women step into station space as musicians, they cannot be assured of the same ease of presence that male musicians like Fuji and Tsuntsun have, nor their relatively uncomplicated ability to increase their visibility through what Tsuntsun described as 'exposure' to the surrounding public. Reina's final evening of her station music tour of Japan demonstrated how, when female musicians stand out, they risk the invasion of their personal space and the theft of their ability to define their own experiences of performing. While intimacy that connects performer to audience is desirable to most Kōenji Station musicians, my interlocutors have shown that the fit is more awkward for women. Male performers felt able to use the station to be *more* themselves, and by reaching out to people and inviting shared time and space, they also felt themselves able to perform more authentically. But being authentic is not a choice that women like Hitomi necessarily felt able to make. In sharp contrast with the experience of male musicians, she believed that her attempts to draw an audience required that she relinquish authenticity, by downplaying herself. By emphasising a need to develop 'a sensitivity to the atmosphere' Sayaka made an important point about musicians at the station – she pointed to the fact that, as Butler argued, they must necessarily take into account the desires and intentions of those sharing the space with them, for whom it means something else and has a different set of rules. However, this affects women more than men, and women react, therefore, very differently to the affordances that the station potentially offers.

The way in which men and women react to the potential of exposure is an example of this. Exposure is for men. It is something that they feel has the ability to bring them together with people, because others benefit as much as they do from it. My male musician informants seemed comfortable and confident about deciding when exposing themselves to others would benefit other people. My female musician informants, on the other hand, appeared to believe that what was good for others was not rooted in taking up the opportunity to make 'real connections', to use Fujii's term, but from their reading of the station as patriarchal – as a space with expectations of gendered presence. The women negotiated, they were hospitable; at times they became performers and manipulators of femininity, of the subtle competencies of gender as subject positionality when the stakes are known (Hansen 2016: 31), in order to navigate their transgression into the station space as something more than female commuters.

The act of hospitality itself was one that women could control to a degree, through strategies such as *aikyō*. Hospitable performance drew in an audience by producing an atmosphere of intimacy, 'appearing welcoming' as Sayaka said. I do not consider this to be an act that can be described as inauthentic, however, but to be, rather, one that recognises the position of women like them in the public space. This underpins Sayaka's question 'Wouldn't you say it is uncomfortable to be around a frightening person?' While this could be viewed as a considerable compromise, which trades their authenticity for a space at the station, the reality is a more nuanced picture. Producing an intimate atmosphere in performances, even one that does not spill over into actual intimacy, still assembles the public and involves them in the production of collective affect. And as Ben Anderson writes, an atmosphere can in itself produce new feelings of self and connection with others (2009: 80).

I suggest that to recognise the production of intimate atmospheres in music performances at Kōenji Station is to appreciate the musicians' attunement to the gendering of public space, to relationships constructed in an uneven field of possibility, presence and performance (Stewart 2010: 446; Tan, 2013: 720). Released from its association with romance, physical touch and privacy, intimacy becomes an atmosphere, forming and dissipating, and manipulated as a strategy to enable musicians to enter, remain in or transgress the public spaces of a city.

References

Alexy, A. 2019. Introduction: The stakes of intimacy in contemporary Japan. *In*: Allison Alexy and Emma Cook (eds), *Intimate Japan: Ethnographies of closeness and conflict*, 1–34. Honolulu: University of Hawaii Press.

Alexy, A. and E. Cook (eds). 2019. *Intimate Japan: Ethnographies of closeness and conflict*. Honolulu: University of Hawaii Press.

Allison, Anne. 1994. *Nightwork: Sexuality, Pleasure and Corporate Masculinity in a Tokyo Hostess Club*. Chicago: University of Chicago Press.

―――― 2013. *Precarious Japan*. Durham: Duke University Press.

Anderson, Ben. 2009. Affective atmospheres. *Emotion, Space and Society*, 2: 77–81.

Berlant, Lauren. 1998. Intimacy. *Critical Inquiry*, 24(2): 281–288.

―――― 2011. *Cruel Optimism*. Durham: Duke University Press.

Butler, Judith. 2001. Giving an account of oneself. *Diacritics* 31(4): 22–40.

Caruth, Cathy. 2016. *Unclaimed Experience: Trauma, Narrative and History*. Baltimore: John Hopkins University Press.

Casey, E. S. 2011. Strangers at the edge of hospitality. *In*: Richard Kearney and Kascha Semonovich (eds), *Phenomenologies of the Stranger: Between Hostility and Hospitality*, 39–48. New York: Fordham University Press.

Coffey, Julia. 2019. Creating distance from body issues: Exploring new materialist feminist possibilities for renegotiating gendered embodiment. *Leisure Sciences*, 41(1–2): 72–90.

Coleman, Rebecca. 2009. *The Becoming of Bodies: Girls, Images, Experience*. Manchester: Manchester University Press.

Cook, E. 2019. Power, intimacy and irregular employment in Japan. *In*: Allison Alexy and Emma Cook (eds), *Intimate Japan: Ethnographies of Closeness and Conflict*, 129–147. Honolulu: University of Hawaii Press.

Currier, Dianne. 2003. Feminist technological futures. *Feminist Theory*, 4 (3): 321–338.

Dasgupta, Romit. 2011. Emotional spaces and places of salaryman anxiety in Tokyo Sonata. *Japanese Studies*, 31(3): 373–386.

Derrida, Jacques. 2000. *Of Hospitality. Anne Dufourmantelle Invites Jacques Derrida to Respond*. Stanford: Stanford University Press.

Fisch, Michael. 2018. *An Anthropology of the Machine: Tokyo's Commuter Train Network*. London: University of Chicago Press.

Freedman, Alisa. 2011. *Tokyo in Transit: Japanese Culture on the Rails and Road*. California: Stanford University Press.

Freud, Sigmund. 2003 [1919]. *The Uncanny*. London: Penguin.

Fujii, James A. 1999. Intimate alienation: Japanese urban rail and the commodification of urban subjects. *Differences*, 11(2): 106–133.

Getreuer-Kargl, I. 2012. Gendered modes of appropriating public space. In: Christoph Brumann and Evelyn Schulz (eds), *Urban Spaces in Japan: Cultural and Social Perspectives*, 167–184. New York: Routledge.

Geschiere, P. 2013. Sociality and its dangers: Witchcraft, intimacy and trust. In: Nicholas J. Long and Henrietta L. Moore (eds), *Sociality: New Directions*, 61–82. Oxford: Berghahn Books.

Gibson, James J. (1979) *The Ecological Approach to Visual Perception*. London: LEA.

Giddens, Anthony. 1992. *The Transformation of Intimacy: Sexuality, Love and Eroticism in Modern Societies*. Stanford: Stanford University Press.

Hadfield, James. 2013. The pervasive curse of pay-to-play in Tokyo. *Live Music Exchange*, 19 September. Available from: livemusicexchange.org/blog/the-pervasive-curse-of-pay-to-play-in-tokyo-james-hadfield/ [Accessed 15 September 2021].

Hansen, Gitte Marianne. 2016. *Femininity, Self-Harm and Eating Disorders in Japan*. Oxford: Routledge.

Ichimoto, Takae. 2004. Ambivalent 'selves' in transition: A case study of Japanese women studying in Australian universities. *Journal of Intercultural Studies*, 25(3): 247–269.

Ivy, Marilyn. 1995. *Discourses of the Vanishing: Modernity, Phantasm, Japan*. London: University of Chicago Press.

Iwabuchi, Koichi. 2002. *Recentering Globalisation: Popular Culture and Japanese Transnationalism*. Durham: Duke University Press.

Jankowiak, William R. 2008. *Intimacies of Love and Sex across Cultures*. New York: Columbia University Press.

Kinsella, Sharon. 2013. *Schoolgirls, Money and Rebellion in Japan*. Oxford: Routledge.

Knappett, C. 2004. The affordances of things: A post-Gibsonian perspective on the relationality of mind and matter. In: Elizabeth DeMarrais, Chris Gosden and Colin Renfrew (eds), *Rethinking Materiality: The Engagement of Mind with the Material World*, 43–51. Cambridge: McDonald Institute Monographs.

Kon Wajirō. 1987. *Kōgengaku Nyūmon* (trans. *An Introduction to Modernology*). Tokyo: Chikuma Bunko.

Layder, Derek. 2009. *Intimacy and Power: The Dynamics of Personal Relationships in Modern Society*. Basingstoke: Palgrave Macmillan.

Luckhurst, Roger. 2008. *The Trauma Question*. Oxford: Routledge.

Martin, Ian F. 2016. *Quit your Band: Musical Notes from the Japanese Underground*. Tokyo: Awai Books.

Mulvey, Laura. 1975. Visual pleasure in narrative cinema. *Screen*, 16 (Autumn): 6–18.

O'Gorman, Kevin. 2006. Jacques Derrida's philosophy of hospitality. *The Hospitality Review*, October: 50–57.

Otaya Satoshi. 2012. Kodomo, wakamono wo meguru shakai mondai toshite no 'ibasho no nasa': Shinbunkiji ni okeru 'ibasho' gensetsu no bunseki kara (trans. The lack of 'ibasho' [a place where one feels at home] as a social issue: An analysis of the 'ibasho' discourse in newspaper articles). *Nenpō shakai-gaku ronshū*, 25: 13–24.

Pendleton, Mark and Jamie Coates. 2018. Thinking from the Yamanote: Space, place and mobility in Tokyo's past and present. *Japan Forum* 30 (2): 149–162.

Simpkins, Robert. J. 2018. *Lost in the Dream: Negotiating a Life in Street Music in a Tokyo Neighbourhood*. Ph.D Dissertation. London: School of Oriental and African Studies.

Steger, Brigitte. 2013. Negotiating gendered space on Japanese commuter trains. *EJCJS*, 13 (3): no pagination.

Stewart, Kathleen. 2011. Atmospheric attunements. *Environment and planning D: Society and space*, 29: 445–453.

Tan Qian Hui. 2013. Flirtatious geographies: Clubs as spaces for the performance of affective heterosexualities. *Gender, Place & Culture*, 20 (6): 718–736.

Tanaka Daisuke. 2008. Shanai kūkan to shintai gihō. Senzeki densha kōtsū ni okeru 'waizatsu' to 'kōkyōsei' (trans. Body techniques in a train: Publicity and deviation in urban traffic during the prewar period). *Shakaigaku hyōron*, 58 (1): 40–56.

Treanor, B. 2011. Putting hospitality in its place. *In*: Richard Kearney and Kascha Semonovich (eds), *Phenomenologies of the Stranger: Between Hostility and Hospitality*, 49–66. New York: Fordham University Press.

CHAPTER 7

I Sing the Body Contingent

Transition as Gender-Work in Contemporary Japan

Lyman R. T. Gamberton

> It's true that I am somebody who was born a long time ago as male and who now wants to live as a woman, but I carry both of these identities in this person called 'Hanako'. There are both masculine and feminine aspects to my personality. They're both in this one body. I can't deny one or the other in my life. Both are OK. That's because I've been an engineer throughout my whole life. When I was little, it's true that there were some times and ways where I seemed like a girl, but more than that I loved to handle machines and ride on the train. If I think about it, I wonder if that's changed yet at all. (Interview with 'Hanako-san', 3 April 2019)

'Forgive me for saying so directly, but I think it's very much the same for you, Lyman, isn't it?' The remark came from my Japanese tutor on the heels of my translating the above quotation, which is taken from a semi-structured interview I conducted with one of my transgender respondents. 'You identify as a man, and certainly I can see that in you, but you also always dress very femininely and cutely', my tutor continued, gesturing to the pink pashmina I had thrown on over my T-shirt that day as I left the house. I explained that I'd made the conscious decision, before I came to Japan, to live as female for the duration of my fieldwork. 'It's a nuisance to keep on correcting people every time they call me a woman', I told her. 'Fieldwork is already stressful enough without adding the trouble of trying to pass as a man.

Any blow-by-blow explanation of how a culture *does gender in the everyday* has to encompass a broad analysis of dress, deportment, presumed or actual sexual behaviour, use of gender-separated facilities such as changing rooms and public toilets. In this, the anthropologist's own body and habits offer a prism through which to view one part of the whole. It mattered that I *did* make gender-related decisions based on context in the field, and not all of them conformed to my simplistic explanation that I had chosen to live 'as a woman'. Some parts of the work I did were straightforward enough decisions, primarily around clothing; some other parts required a little forethought and a linguistic 'code switch' when talking to different groups of people. For example, I never used the feminine-specific pronoun *atashi*; I generally compromised with the more gender-neutral, if slightly too polite at times, *watashi*; on some occasions, and only around other LGBTQ people, I used the masculine casual *boku*. The most difficult work involved quite literal public exposure. The name by which my respondents know me, which I have used since 2011, is not the name on my passport. Seeing that name on official paperwork, including my student visa and my Alien Registration Card, was a disorienting experience: none of the details that claimed to be my 'identifying data' (name, gender, nationality) was accurate at all. In bathrooms, on residence permits and health insurance forms, and at the neighbourhood bathhouse (*sentō*), I had to grit my teeth and select the door, the binary column, or the *noren* curtain with the symbol for 'woman' (女) marked on it. In England, I changed in the 'male' changing rooms after *kendō* (fencing) practice; in Japan, I had to change for *iaidō* (sword-work) sessions in the solitary surroundings of the 'female' changing room. Even at the gift and religious supplies shop attached to the Buddhist temple I attended, silk prayer cowls and the long tassels hanging from glass rosaries are divided into colours considered 'female' (purple, pink) or 'male' (mustard, dark red).

All of this – choosing the door with the 'female' symbol on it at bathhouses and in public bathrooms, but using only male pronouns in speech; my participant observation and my own private life; the conscious selection of gendered clothing and the equally-conscious times when trans people let misgendering slide – comprises 'the work of gender' in a trans context. Transition itself has been theorised as a form of labour, most strikingly by the Scottish writer Harry-Josie Giles in their 2019 essay *Wages for Transition*: '[T]he labour that continually gives birth to gender, that produces liveably gendered lives under intolerable conditions.' The concept of 'gender labour' that I use in this chapter draws on both Giles' (2019) and Ward's (2010) work on the affirmative emotional labour undertaken by the cis female partners of transgender men. My definition of trans-related gender labour is: the financial, practical, and affective work demanded by cisgender society of transgender people, in order to render trans people's transitions and identities palatable, legible and non-threatening.

None of the gendered decisions I describe above were undertaken for my own comfort or my own freedom of expression. They were in large part a performance for the benefit of others, so that my resistance to being identified as a woman did not become a flashpoint for contention. As Giles correctly identifies: 'To transition is not to cross from one fixed point to another, nor to become the gender that one always was, but rather to engage with dubious agency and fraught embodiment the ongoing work of being gendered.' These everyday actions gendered me in the eyes of others through my conscious processes of selection: if someone enters the women's side of the bathhouse, or has an F on their passport, or wears a dress for comfort in the muggy Kyoto summertime, that person appears outwardly to be a woman, regardless of their inner reality. If we class gender transition as part of the *work* of gender in Japan, we must ask: On whose behalf is the work undertaken? Who is burdened by it, and who benefits from it?

Methodology

The basis for this chapter is one year of immersive language study and eighteen months of anthropological fieldwork conducted in Kyoto and Osaka from autumn 2017 to summer 2020. The topic of my research is transgender and gender-nonconforming lives, communities and identities in contemporary Japan, with a regional focus on Kansai. I chose Kansai deliberately due to the fact that almost all work published in English on 'Trans Japan' restricts its focus only to Tokyo[1] or speaks in generic terms about southern Honshu (Yonezawa 2003; Ishii 2018; Tsuruta 2009), despite Kansai's rich contributions to trans language and cultures in Japan. I drew on four prominent ethnographic research methods: participant observation, semi-structured interviews, secondary/archival sources, and incidental ethnomethodological experiments in disrupting or contradicting 'standard' expectations of gendered behaviour or presentation, then noting the fallout. A few small examples of the latter form: I did not use an honorific at all where one was not indicated for accommodation bookings in English, or else I wrote down 'Mr.' when a title was required. In cases where I had not indicated my gender,

---

1 For a critique of which, and a fuller analysis of 'LGBTQ Kansai' than space permits here, see Wallace (2020) and Dale (2012).

my hosts uniformly expected me to be a (cisgender) man, with several people remarking on my 'female' appearance. Another frequent context of ethnomethodological experimentation was buying clothes. 'Women's' jeans in Japan are rarely available for purchase in my size: there was more than one occasion when I selected jeans from the men's section of the shop and was not prevented from using the single-occupancy stall marked 'male' [男], as if the tag on the clothing (or the area of the shop in which it could be found) overrode the presumed gender of the wearer.

The participant observation was functionally multi-sited within a small geographical catchment area: that is, I went to different physical venues (coffee shops, rental spaces, cafés, the Yoshida-ryō student hall at Kyoto University, etc) within Kyoto and Osaka. The furthest afield I went for my research was for conferences in Okayama (March 2019) and Tokyo (December 2019). The most basic form this took was going to places where trans people gathered and observing what went on. The field sites for this were eclectic: meet-ups of the LGBTQ group Shinzen no Kai ('Friendship Society') every two weeks; semi-public events such as blossom-viewing parties or grilled sweet potato cookouts in public parks, usually co-ordinated via closed Facebook groups; the annual Kansai and Osaka University Queer Film Festivals; a pop-up brunch club run by and for queer people in Kyoto; LGBTQ community volunteer events, such as litter pickups along the Kamo River; Zoom meetups during the SARS-CoVid-19 crisis; public lectures on LGBTQ civil rights at Kyoto Campus Plaza; and private parties hosted by friends in the city. Outside of my own semi-structured interviews with people in the local community, I drew on the longform interviews and life histories provided by trans people on the Japanese website *LGBTxER*. One or two of the people who were interviewed by LGBTxER were people I met during my fieldwork, and I drew both from my own interviews with them and from their longform published narratives; others were people I had met in person (e.g. at the Kansai Queer Film Festival) but who were unavailable for semi-structured interviews; yet others were strangers.

The central question of my research is: how do transgender and gender-non-conforming people in Kansai conceive of, create and maintain their gender identities and gender presentations in everyday life? The Japanese state's requirements for legally-recognised gender transition are both invasive and predicated on a set of assumptions about what it means to be 'truly transgender'. Many trans people in Japan are unable or unwilling to conform to the demands set by medico-legal gatekeeping in order to change the name and gender listed on their legal paperwork, including health insurance, passports, residence certificates, etc. What do transgender people's lives look like in the gap between legal assertions and everyday enactment? What can cisgender people's reactions to transgender people tell us about the way gender is understood and constructed in Japan? What assumptions, what expectations, what moral panics undergird the structure of gender, and how are they exposed (or made visible) through everyday interactions? My aim in this chapter is to use ethnomethodology as a paradigm for analysing specific examples from my fieldwork that demonstrate moments of what we may term 'ethnomethodological crisis', i.e. where some assumption about gender has been contradicted, or where some aspect of a person's gender/gender expression presents a third party with an unexpected surprise. By analysing the nature of the crisis in each case, we can draw conclusions about the unexamined – indeed, often unconscious – logic, or what ethnomethodology calls the 'natural attitude', of gender in Japan; in particular, how it relates to transgender experience. In this chapter, I will draw on individual examples and case studies from my fieldwork, and will also consider on a broader scale the coercive nature of the relationship between the Japanese state and the individual trans person, as regards the draconian requirements imposed as preconditions for changing the foundational unit of legal personhood (i.e. the family registry or *koseki*).

Research that centres trans people must also take into account the social assumptions, privileges and unconscious biases of the cisgender society around us. 'Cisgender' or 'cis' refers to people who are not transgender. For purposes of this chapter, I define 'transgender' people as 'anyone, regardless of medical intervention or social transition, who does not identify with the sex they were assigned at birth'. This work was undertaken on my part from the lived experience of being a transgender man. Claiming to speak from any 'emic' perspective automatically means situating oneself in a contingent and unstable position: while it is true that I work from authoritative lived experience as a transgender person, I could not expect automatic acceptance from a new (to me) trans community, especially one within a different linguistic and cultural context. Achieving this access was a delicate balance of knowing when to persist and when to refrain from pushing. I gained physical access to the communities in which I did my participant observation by booking a reservation for a Shinzen no Kai meetup one day in April 2018 and showing up at the rental space, where the meetup went on for two hours. My

Japanese language skills at that point were still at a very rudimentary stage, so I observed most of the event in silence with some limited small talk in Japanese as my ability permitted, and some chatting in English. The next week, I was invited to the post-meetup brunch at a nearby café; the week after that, one of my new friends suggested we go together to a different local queer pop-up lunch event; the group's Facebook page advertised a trans-interest film screening in Osaka; and the events I was able to attend snowballed from there. That was the persistence: the refraining period came in waiting almost nine months before I mentioned casually in the group that I was hoping to study 'trans Japan' at all, and nearly a year before I submitted my first formal request for interviews via the group Facebook page. This initial period of observation, and my position as a 'naive' observer insofar as I literally could not understand what people were saying, established my presence as a known quantity in the group and seemed (from feedback I received later from my respondents) to affirm my 'earnestness' and my dedication to 'trying my best'.

This evident sincerity on my part and its importance to my respondents was borne out by the actual process of my acceptance. After the Shinzen no Kai meetups, especially those held in Kyoto rather than Osaka, it is customary for a group of attendees to go for brunch at a nearby Saizeriya restaurant. Not everyone attends the post-meetup brunch. However, there is a core group of five or six people who almost always participate. I had attended this brunch group several times after my fieldwork began, and it was friendly enough, but I still felt like I had no particular insight into what my respondents made of me. Was I a novelty? An eccentric to be humoured? A stranger to whom politeness dictated they be nice, but not really to be taken seriously? One evening in March 2019, about a year after I started attending Shinzen no Kai meetups and a few weeks after I began actively soliciting respondents for my research, I went with my respondent Makoto-san to see the film *A Woman is a Woman* (Hong Kong, 2018, dir. Maisy Goosey Suen) at the 11th Osaka Asian Film Festival. When we were standing on the platform at Osaka Station, waiting for the train back to Kyoto, we were talking (in English) about language and translation. I confessed that I sometimes worried whether or not my Japanese language skills, including my pronunciation, were good enough. 'Oh no, it's fine! You're very easy to understand', Makoto-san told me, 'and what's more, you're very sincere. Your sincerity comes through.'[2] And that's why we all

---

2 Makoto-san and I had an interesting linguistic dynamic throughout my fieldwork: I would talk to them in Japanese and they would reply in English. This quotation is not translated from Japanese.

like you, and we've all decided to help you as much as we can. Everybody has.' Very casually, Makoto-san had given me a glimpse of the backstage proceedings that enabled the 'performance' of my research. Their use of the word 'everybody' indicated that my research and my presence at Shinzen no Kai had been the subject of communal discussion to which I was not privy, as did the fact that, in the weeks preceding this event, my respondents had been proactive in recommending other members of the community as potential interview participants. Had I not been found trustworthy, I would have been politely stonewalled.

In stark contrast to the popular images of both trans lives and Japanese society as alienated and atomised, trans existence in Kansai as I experienced it really is a communal affair. The process of vetting me was collaborative and involved multiple participants. Any semblance of privacy vis-à-vis individual respondents was almost impossible, as people would not only suggest potential respondents but would also check in with me later to see whether or not I had taken them up on their suggestions. Nor was there any sense amongst my respondents that my lack of medical transition was in any way suspicious or unexpected, or that it somehow diminished my professed status as a trans man. I suggest that this is due at least in part to the nature of Japan's requirements for legal change of gender: when medical transition is expensive, difficult to access and mandatorily invasive, everyone with skin in the game understands the potential (and indeed the necessity) for trans identity to work on the honour system. My work was necessarily prone to error, awkwardness and misapprehension. Race and medical transition status, or lack thereof, were the two most prominent faultlines that I identified in my reflections on fieldwork. I was a pre-transition trans man amongst people who, for the most part, were years along in medical transition; and I could only embody white, Western masculinity against the backdrop of culturally-specific, and often culturally-exceptionalist, attitudes to gender. Therefore, I strive in this chapter to both centre the voices, experiences, and lifeways of transgender people in contemporary Kansai and to acknowledge the limitations and complexities of my own participant observation, with reference to 'mainstream' Japanese attitudes to, and conceptions of, gender where necessary.

Autoethnography and Non-Linear Becoming

The multiplicity of overlapping truisms about trans lives and trans identities has the potential to run rings around the ethnographer, producing a sensation rather like using a Venn diagram as a Hula Hoop. The difficulty of trying to write about trans experience as a discrete category is that every assertion about what trans people feel, want or do vis-à-vis our transition journeys throws up counter-examples at every turn.

To elaborate on this: all of the following statements about transgender life are true. It is possible to be transgender without any kind of medical intervention (surgical, hormonal, psychotherapeutic, etc). Some trans people do transition medically, and they may do so to differing degrees (only hormones; hormones and chest reconstruction surgery; chest reconstruction surgery without hormones; genital reconstructive surgery, etc). The process of medical transition is often erroneously conceived of by cisgender people as being a linear process from diagnosis, through the commencement of hormone therapy, ending finally in gender confirmation surgery (GCS). Curiously, this often seems to entail a belief that trans people stop taking hormone replacement therapy (HRT) after we have undergone 'The Surgery': several cisgender acquaintances have been surprised to learn that trans people usually continue taking HRT for the rest of our lives, in the same way as, for example, do cisgender women who have had a bilateral oophorectomy prior to natural menopause.

The dominant narrative of trans identity is that it is a process of 'bodily becoming.' The concept of 'becoming' is one currently enjoying a vogue in autoethnography: Luvaas (2019) uses it as the theoretical peg on which to hang the component parts (physical, sartorial, online, offline, mediated by photography, in-person, up-close) of the *habitus*-ensemble in which he clothed himself to create his ethnography of street fashion bloggers. The non-linear nature of my transition therefore problematised any attempts at delineating an 'autoethnographic *becoming*'. Like Israeli-Nevo (2017), I am 'taking my time' as a transitioning person; also, parallel to her descriptions of transgender temporality, I often experience my positionality as a trans person as being 'out of time':

> [I] would like to argue that as trans subjects in this transphobic world, we are encouraged and forced into a position of not being present. [...] This dissociation throws us into a far future in which we are safe after we have passed and found a bodily and social home. However, this future is imagined and unreachable, resulting in us being out of time.
>
> (ibid.: 2017: 38–9)

How does one create a narrative arc of 'becoming' when they both already have and have not yet 'become'? I came out as transgender in 2011, nearly a decade before my time in Kyoto began, which means that I did not begin my fieldwork as a heterosexual or cisgender person entering queer space as a tourist or a guest, or even as a newly-out trans person still at the beginning of a transition journey. Nor were my participant observation venues especially novel or strange: the language and city were different, but I went to LGBTQ meetups and social events in Oxford and London in much the same way as I attended them in Kyoto and Osaka. In that sense, I had already 'become' trans, and become familiar with trans life in community, before my research began. But I did not medically transition during the fieldwork period, and as such had not yet achieved any discrete markers of medical transition (starting hormones, completing any desired surgical procedures, etc.). Within those temporal limits, especially as friends back home came out, started hormones, posted triumphant post-top-surgery photos on social media and otherwise moved through various transition milestones, I was constantly engaged in auto-reflexive consideration of my own gender and the way it was received by the people around me. In this, I had to determine the fine balance between prioritising my own experiences to the point that they occluded the lives and experiences of my respondents, and retreating completely from the narrative without analysing the ripples of the 'observer effect' that my presence produced.

Transgender Ethnomethodology

'You know, from your name, I expected you to be a man.'

Many meals have been made out of the raw ingredients of supposed 'cultural differences' between England and Japan, but the apparent gender ambiguity of my personal name remains a constant in both languages. At first I was startled, followed in short order by amusement, then resignation, then a desire to turn these frequent blips of 'contact shock' to methodological ends. When both obvious answers to a question are inadvisable (lying and pretending to 'confirm' my supposed womanhood, or saying 'You're not wrong, I am a man'), the ruptures of unexpected gender faultlines between transgender and cisgender people make themselves known. Doing gender-related fieldwork as a trans, disabled, smallish-fat, foreign ethnographer is never just classical anthropological methodology: it is specifically *ethnomethodology*, the practice of understanding social relations and conventions through observing what happens when those conventions are flouted. This is the paradigm of observing the 'natural attitude' to gender advocated by McKenna and Kessler in their 1978 text, which drew on Garfinkel's (1967) foundational work, and has been elaborated upon by West and Zimmerman (1987), West and Fenstermaker (1995) and Stokoe (2006).[3]

I argue that every person with a shareholder's stake in gender, which is to say every person, acts as an ethnomethodologist of gender every day. Gender is something that is real but inchoate, the underlying sense of which is only made visible through error. There is no objective set of rules setting out Gender Standards in black and white, but we often behave as if there were; and we may not know that we have veered too far off-message in our behaviour or clothing choices until the negative feedback from our peers or passers-by indicates our error. Transgender people have been a topic of abiding interest to ethnomethodologists since Garfinkel's research in the 1960s (Garfinkel 1967), a great deal of which involved extensive and invasive interviews with a young transgender woman called Agnes.[4] However, he did not develop a schema of the natural attitude to gender as a specific object of study. That was the brainchild of McKenna and Kessler (1978), who proposed that gender is not a set of empirical observations from which the researcher need only draw inductive conclusions, but rather an attributive process: gender is not something one *has*, but rather something one *does*. Although the natural attitude to gender is itself descriptive and observational, the policing and construction of gender has a

---

3   In ethnomethodological thought, the concept of the 'natural attitude' refers to a shared, 'common-sensical' understanding of the natural and social world. Gender, in this understanding of reality, is not an *action* – not something consciously constructed, performed, or interpreted variously by individuals – but rather a discoverable empirical fact. Crucially, the natural attitude is not a fixed text of 'rules', set apart from the context of everyday life, to which we may refer for guidance; it is something that emerges from individual, interpersonal encounters and that is relative to them.

4   A glaring lacuna in both Garfinkel's original interviews with Agnes and McKenna and Kessler's account of the natural attitude to gender vis-à-vis trans people is their conception of the nature and purposes of *transitioning itself*. That is: there was only one model of 'successful' or 'authentic' gender transition in Anglophone medicine from the 1960s through to the early 2000s (although its hangover manifested in several ways as the author's cohort began transitioning ca. 2011). The only diagnosis available to the transgender people of the time was that of the 'true transsexual', who wanted every possible medical intervention; dressed and behaved in appropriately 'masculine' or 'feminine' ways; was heterosexual; and was willing to go to any lengths to break with their pre-transition life. Viewed from a trans perspective, Garfinkel's Agnes was less a 'methodologist of gender', carefully selecting and discarding gendered behaviours to fit her needs, than someone being systematically punished by the medical establishment.

strong prescriptive element: it is not enough that one 'does gender', one *must* do gender 'properly'. This mandate obtains for both cisgender and transgender people alike. The immediate questions this raises relevant to my research are: what *does* that construction of 'proper gender' look like in practice for trans people in Japan? On whose supposed behalf is it enforced?

The Work of Gender At Home and In The World

This policing and enforcing of 'proper' (binary, complementarian) gender roles is primarily justified as being for the protection of children and the family unit.[5] The idea that children must be shielded from non-normative gender expressions, and that they will be harmed if not provided with suitable gendered role models and gendered socialisation at home and at school represents a classical example of a moral panic. The experiences of my respondent Makoto-san provide a case in point vis-a-vis this moral panic around children's potential exposure to gender nonconformity. Makoto-san was at one point employed as an English teacher at a 'cram school'. They told me during our interview in November 2018 that, although they were the most popular language instructor amongst the students and demand for their classes was highest, the director began to receive calls from perturbed parents:

> When I was working as an English teacher at a cram school, of course I would always introduce myself by saying 'I'm [Miss] Tsuneko Nakamura' and 'Although I have short hair, I am a woman!', stuff like that. The head teacher would also confirm that I was a woman and would give an introduction on my behalf, and that was OK. But... sometimes the parents of the kids at the cram school would come along to observe the classes, and after they saw me, they'd telephone the head teacher. 'There's one teacher who I can't tell if they're a man or a woman. Which one are they? If they're a man, I want to end my daughter's enrolment, since it would be bad for her to have a male teacher. But if the teacher's a lady, that's OK.' When they said this kind of stuff over the phone... you know, it's difficult to explain.

For the (over)protective parents of Makoto-san's students, the demands of cis/heterocentric propriety enabled and empowered them to demand

---

5   Most notoriously by the Supreme Court of Japan in their January 2019 ruling against Usui Takakito, which stated that sterilisation mandates are constitutional 'in order to prevent confusion in the family and society': www.loc.gov/item/global-legal-monitor/2019-04-12/japan-law-requiring-surgery-for-legal-change-of-gender-ruled-constitutional/.

'confirmation' that their child's English teacher conformed to one of two binary genders. Demanding to know the particulars of a stranger's gender (and, by extension, the configuration of their genitals) would ordinarily be seen as *at best* presumptive and – more likely – a breach of the social contract on the part of the asker, in comparison to which the respondent's gender incongruity would pale as a faux pas. Educators in Japan, of whom I counted several amongst my respondents (including a university lecturer, an LGBTQ-related educational outreach lecturer, a freelance language tutor and a career counsellor specialising in LGBTQ clients), independently corroborated the tacit social approval given to otherwise-rude or intrusive questions about gender – as long as the questions were being asked of someone who appeared gender-nonconforming.

> I've had some students just straight-up ask me 'Are you a man or a woman or what?' during our first orientation meetings at the beginning of the academic year. They'd never usually ask a professor such a personal question, you know? There's a certain level of respect that's expected between a professor and their students. But it's like they feel like it's OK if you're trans or if your gender isn't immediately 'obvious'.

This was the experience of Hotaru-san, a transmasculine person born and raised in rural Kansai, who works as adjunct faculty at a small private university in Shiga Prefecture. Nor was their gender seen as an issue of public interest only within the boundaries of a lecture room: it rose, in fact, to within the remit of the unofficial neighbourhood watch. They told me that their neighbours couldn't seem to decide on a satisfactory solution to the riddle of their gender. In a Japanese neighbourhood, the most intimate material culture of the home is regularly exposed to public scrutiny: that is, very few homes have the luxury of a tumble drier, and so underwear is hung out to dry alongside the rest of the laundry to a greater or lesser degree of visibility. Hotaru-san's neighbours, upon first meeting them when they moved to a residential area of southern suburban Kyoto, assumed they were female. However, seeing that the underwear and other clothing drying on Hotaru-san's balcony was strictly 'masculine' (T-shirts, boxer shorts, cargo trousers, etc.), some confusion arose: was Hotaru-san a man, or did they perhaps have a boyfriend whom no-one had ever seen coming or going from the house? Finally, after noticing that Hotaru-san had a female partner and that the underwear on the line had, after some time, become the 'expected' mix of masculine and feminine garments, the neighbours drew the conclusion that they were a man after all. One neighbour went so far as to apologise to Hotaru-san for having initially 'mistaken' their gender, which was the first time they had been privy to this ongoing debate.

Hotaru-san did not seem disgruntled when they relayed this anecdote to me. On the contrary, it was presented as a comic interlude, with the butt of the joke very firmly being their neighbours. They were not afraid of negative social consequences; since the 'mistake' in gendering them was committed by their neighbour across the way, they did not have to apologise, and indeed were not expected to explain or justify themselves. However, they were genuinely annoyed by the lack of respect displayed by their students. Both incidents encapsulate moments of ethnomethodological crisis, where the social contract is threatened or subverted in some way. In the case of the neighbourhood laundry watch, their neighbours' behaviour remained within the boundaries of what was proper to their concern. By contrast, a first-year undergraduate student barrelling past the expectation of respect held by the instructor, in order to ask personal and prurient questions about that instructor's gender, was a breach of the social contract that could not be downplayed. For both Makoto and Hotaru, the emotional and affective work they had to do in response to others' anxieties or challenges around their gender presentation – to remain calm and professional; to 'reassure' their interlocutors by verbal affirmation of their birth sex; to struggle privately in the aftermath with second-guessing their own reactions to gendered harassment – are precisely part of the 'labour of transition' identified by Giles (2019), specifically the element of it concerned with emotional labour (Hochschild 1983): the burden of processing other people's gendered anxieties and responding in ways unthreatening to their challengers is one that their cisgender colleagues do not have to shoulder.

For Hotaru-san's neighbours, their gender was a communal concern. So too with Makoto-san, whose gender performance brushed up against one of the main anxieties expressed in the law that dictates the form gender transition must take in Japan: the idea of a teacher or adult figure disrupting the smooth transmission of 'proper' gender roles to the next generation, thereby sowing confusion and socially disruptive behaviour amongst the youth. Modelling these roles in action is also believed to require the students and teacher to be of the same gender, as we see from the parents threatening to pull their children from Makoto-san's class 'if Miss Nakamura is actually a man'. And yet, if gender roles are so biologically innate or immutable, why do they require so much maintenance and policing by others? The stated reason why transgender parents of minor children are not allowed to update their family registry until their child has reached the age of majority is to 'avoid confusion'. This is presented as a foregone conclusion, the necessity of which is presumed to be self-evident to the reader.

Assumptions of Heterosexuality

This theorised assumption of what trans people are, do and should be extends beyond the bare texts of the law and the physical body into the wider social sphere. Such was the case with Ikuko-san, one of my respondents, who is a fortysomething trans woman; she was previously married to a woman, with whom she had two children. As of our interview in Spring 2019, her younger child was just about to start their first year of undergraduate study. Since the children had not yet reached the age of majority (20 in Japan), she was not yet allowed to change the name and gender listed on her *koseki*. Doing so – living as her true self – also mandated a divorce from her wife, as Japan does not recognise same-sex marriage, and theirs would become a same-sex marriage upon Ikuko-san's transition. She said that she had discussed her transition with the rest of her family, and although they understood and were supportive, she still hoped they would 'be able to forgive [her]' for the breakup of the nuclear family unit that her transition entails. Similar stories abound: Takafumi Fujio, a trans man and trans-rights activist whose oral history is recorded in McLelland et al. (2007), says that he married a man and gave birth to two daughters, more in the hope that it would 'fix' him and make him a 'real' woman than out of any actual desire to be a mother or a wife. On transitioning, he divorced his husband, who now – unusually for Japanese family-court arrangements – has full custody of their children.

This connection between gender identity and (presumed or actual) sexual orientation was a common theme amongst my respondents.

> I had my first *crush*. I was about eleven, and it was a girl, and so... Then, I couldn't conclude that, um, 'Oh, I like women, as a woman', it's more like 'Um... this could be like what's called "same-sex love"', but I didn't necessarily feel like that? It felt more like a man liking women, kind of thing? So that was the point when I realised... that was the beginning of my gender journey, in a way. How you identify is so closely tied with

your language, right? What's available [to you]. So initially the only thing I could feel was 'Oh, maybe I'm a boy in my head and then, like, a girl'... But what does that even mean, right? Identity-wise, I didn't have a word.

And I remember actually writing something similar to one of my closest friends at the time. We had this *kōkan nikki*, an exchange diary thing that was hugely popular back then. But I was exchanging the diary between my best friend, basically. And one day, I wrote 'I think I like this girl, but not as a girl, but I feel like I like this person as a boy.' And I didn't think much of it at the time, but then when I received the reply, or when the diary came back, my best friend had written *sonna koto iu Hotaru wa daikirai*... Uh, yeah, so, 'I hate you for writing that...'

(interview with Hotaru-san, 7 December 2018)

The above quotation from my respondent Hotaru-san throws into relief the ambiguous nature of the relationship between gender identity and sexual orientation. For them, the lack of any language to describe their experiences was the hardest part of growing up trans: the only example available to them at the time of being 'a girl' who liked other girls was that of lesbianism. This presented Hotaru-san with two problems. Firstly, as evidenced by their friend's reaction to a confession of romantic attraction to girls in their shared diary, lesbianism was something to be hidden and shamed. Secondly, it did not sufficiently explain their feelings of masculinity or a masculine identity relative to the girls they were interested in. The feeling that homosexuality was insufficient as an explanation for the way trans boys related to the girls they liked (and trans girls to the boys they liked) is a common one. This was certainly the experience of the trans playwright and film director Wakabayashi Yuma in an interview with the Japanese website *LGBTxER*.[6] In the exchange quoted here, he recalls the first time he was able to talk about trans identity with a fellow trans man (a co-worker at his part-time job in Osaka) and the other man's girlfriend:

We also talked about my high school girlfriend.

'What was it like when you were dating?' they asked me. Although I couldn't really remember what dating her had been like, I replied that I had thought I wanted to become her boyfriend.

---

6 Accessible online at: lgbter.jp/lgbter/yuma-wakabayashi/ Last accessed: 10/05/20 at 11.25 JST

> Then, his girlfriend told me: 'Aw, that's normal. It's simply that you're a man and you liked this girl. That just means you're straight.'
> Really! It's normal that I fell in love with that girl! Straight away, I felt convinced and my heart was relieved.

For both Hotaru-san and Yuma-san, one of the earliest signs of their transmasculine identities was that '[they] liked girls, but as a boy would' – that is, not necessarily with a sense of themselves as lesbian, but with the more nagging sense that it was their gender identity, not the orientation of their sexuality, that was out of kilter. What is also noteworthy in this vignette is the relief Yuma-san felt at being told that his feelings for the girl he liked were 'normal' and 'natural'. Since heterosexuality is held to be the 'natural' state for male–female relationships, Yuma-san's male identity normalised what would have otherwise been an 'aberrant' lesbian desire. What this shows is that neither cisgender identity nor heterosexuality are unmarked natural categories: Yuma-san in particular had to consciously process his emotions to reconcile them with the heterosexual ideal.

One major issue experienced in common by all four individuals quoted above is this enforced association of gender transition with heterosexuality. Both Ikuko-san and Fujio-san – and indeed all married trans people in Japan – were/are forced to divorce their spouses in order to transition legally. The reason for this is that Japan does not recognise same-gender marriages. There have been assorted attempts to challenge the divorce requirement at the municipal or regional level: for example, a case was brought by a trans woman to the Osaka Family Court in March 2019. She had the full support of her family (a wife and adult daughter) in her transition and petitioned the Osaka court to allow her to transition without divorcing her wife.[7] The case was immediately rejected. This is one of the 'crisis moments' where the nature of the state's assumptions about acceptable relationships are made clear through challenge: a transgender person may enter into an opposite-gender marriage on completion of their legal transition, but they may not begin or continue in same-gender relationships if they wish for these relationships to be formally recognised. The reasoning presented for this is that heterosexuality is 'natural' and homosexuality 'unnatural', which falls short of explaining the necessity of using state force to maintain the boundaries of what is blissfully preordained. Dealing with enforced divorce

---

7   Okitsu 2019.

carries not only the affective labour of caretaking the other members of the family unit and processing collective emotions around transition, but also a potentially-steep financial and legal cost, including the loss of financial tax-related rights; the right to make decisions regarding medical and end-of-life care on the spouse's behalf; hospital visitation rights; custody rights; and all the other benefits that marriage entails. Depending on the type of divorce, which can be anything from a 'mutually-agreed divorce' (*kyōgi-rikon*) involving little more than paperwork at the local ward office, to arbitration by a district court (*saiban-rikon*), forced divorce costs married trans people in Japan time, stress and money – to say nothing of the personal, emotional toll taken on couples who wish to stay together as partners or co-parents after one spouse transitions, the trauma of which is often experienced as 'denied grief', given the lack of social awareness and support around this issue.

We can see from both Hotaru-san and Yuma-san's testimonials that the link between sexual/romantic attraction and an 'opposite-gender' social role is not merely something imposed by the Japanese state, but rather something that also wells up from within the community. The overwhelming assumption I heard, read and eavesdropped on amongst LGBTQ people in Japan is that trans people are heterosexual after transition. Although Japan, unlike the US and UK, has never mandated eventual heterosexuality as a requirement for transition, there is little to no room in the public consciousness for trans people who are lesbian, bisexual or gay. Even publications such as *FtM Life Magazine 'Like Boy'* and *Laph*, which are aimed at a trans-masculine audience, assume that the trans men who comprise their readership are interested solely in women. The men who grace their covers are all masculine in presentation, flat-chested (whether post-operative or not) and shown alone or with feminine women, never with other men in poses suggestive of romance or attraction. Admittedly magazine shoots are always within the realm of the aspirational and the fantastic, but Shu Min Yuen (2020), who has done extensive ethnographic work amongst FTM communities in Tokyo, including with the editorial staff and readership of *Laph* Magazine, has corroborated both the predominance of heterosexuality and interest in cis women on the part of trans men, as well as their investment in 'living stealth', i.e. not being outed as trans in the workplace and the broader community.

This assumption of heterosexuality on the part of trans men in particular formed a large part of the dialogue during a discussion panel consisting of the trans playwright and director Endō Mameta, in conversation with

Figure 7.1: Examples of FTM lifestyle magazines, from the 2019 Kansai Queer Film Festival at the Kyoto Seibu Kōdō. Photo: L. Gamberton. **Colour**, p. 223.

Wakabayashi Yuma and the American trans director Jules Rosskam at the 2019 Kansai Queer Film Festival. Endō, who does a great deal of work with transgender youth, talked about the prevalence of casual misogyny and heterosexism amongst the teenage trans boys he mentors and whose youth group he runs. He described them making crude sexist and sexual comments about women and girls; ranking girls they knew based on looks; assuming that a woman's or girlfriend's role is to take care of them and their needs, etc. He elaborated further on the difficulty of interrupting in the moment, in ways familiar to other male allies of women and feminism: when is it appropriate to interject? How can an older mentor figure clearly communicate what is or is not acceptable? The presumption of heterosexuality exists as much within trans communities as it does in the cisgender, heterosexual mainstream, and prevailing sexist attitudes towards women and girls are absorbed as much by trans boys as by their cis counterparts.

We can see Rubin's (1975) observation that the designated-at-birth sex category 'decides' the sexual orientation of the individual (in that people in the 'woman' class are expected to be interested only in men and vice versa) play out in the hegemonic assumption of trans people's heterosexuality. Trans people are expected to be available for social reproduction along normative romantic, sexual and domestic lines. Trans people must do the emotional work of reconciling their 'aberrant' queer desires to the comprehensible framework of heterosexuality, as we saw with Yuma-san.

The Limits of an Ethnomethodology of Gender

My thinking on ethnomethodology and its limitations draws shape and force from this insight from Veena Das: 'One instance of the application of the idea of reason turning demonic is that it blocks us from accepting such things as the humanity of the other on trust [...] The point is not that such doubts might not arise in the weave of life but that they cannot be settled by the production of more and more evidence. (2018: 172) As we have seen from the examples above, gender presentation can be creatively managed only to the degree that it remains in the social sphere. As soon as it rubs against legal and medical systems, much of the agency of trans people evaporates in the strictly binary settings of the gender clinic and the courts.

This is where we must confront the limits of ethnomethodology as a method of understanding gender as lived experience. In putting emphasis on the micro-perspective of individual encounters that are spatially and temporally limited, the intersubjectively crafted nature of gender presentation is revealed, together with the micro-aggressions, misgendering and constant doubt that marks the experience of everyone who falls short of the cisgender ideal. But this focus on the minutiae of everyday life cannot account for the larger societal and economic forces that shape the structural constraints around transgender lives. How can we tell that 'people who do not medically transition are [believed to be] cis' is an element of the natural attitude to gender in Japan? Because there is no legal recognition of trans people who do not medically transition. How can we tell that membership in one of two binary gender categories is believed to be 'natural'? Because the law contains no provisions for non-binary gender transition or legal recognition of non-binary existence. How can we tell that gender confirmation surgery (GCS) is the 'defining' metric of whether transition is completed or not? Because it is only after GCS – after the physical transformation of the body – that the trans person is allowed to change their symbolic, legal gender. How can we tell that being cis is presumed to be superior and preferable to being trans? Because every aspect of the law governing transition is designed to force trans people into being as 'cis' as possible.

For trans people in Japan, the rulebook of 'how to perform gender properly and with appropriate permission from the authorities' is very clear: it can be found in the text of the *Act on Special Cases in Handling Gender for Persons Diagnosed With Gender Identity Disorder* (*Seidōitsusei-Shōgaisha no Seibetsu no Toriatsukai no Tokubetsu ni Kansuru Hōritsu*), hereafter the *Gender Treatment Act* (passed 2003, revised 2008). The full requirements of the law and their implications for individual transitions are analysed in full by Taniguchi (2013);[8] I will not reproduce them here in full, but wish to note two points of particular relevance. The first is that surgical transition, including genital reconstruction, is required to change the name and gender on one's *koseki*. The second is that the 2008 revision permitted people who have already had children to transition, as long as their children had already reached the age of legal adulthood and there were no minors in the home, where the 2003 ordinance forbade parents from transitioning at all.

Examination of my ethnographic vignettes shows these macro-level forces in granular detail. In the case of Makoto-san, the 'crisis' their ambiguous gender presentation evoked manifested itself in think-of-the-children moral panic. Ikuko-san is a 'good wife and wise mother' in the traditional Japanese formulation: she looks after her sons' wellbeing, does their laundry (including buying 'office shirts' for her older son's job interviews) and is considerate of their feelings; she has typically feminine interests like cooking, playing the violin and growing her own vegetables; and she takes on 'motherly' caring responsibility for younger or newly-out people in the local LGBTQ community. Yet she is legally not allowed to fill the role of 'wife and mother' because same-sex marriage is 'unnatural'. The moment of ethnomethodological crisis came for her when the harmony of her supportive family was overridden by the requirement to choose between her true gender or her marriage. For Hotaru-san's student, their interests of knowing how to relate to Hotaru-san's 'proper' gender overrode the breach in civility that being so bold to a social superior would usually entail.

However, as mentioned previously, there is a secondary distinction of crisis in Hotaru-san's own reception and interpretation of these events as they relayed them to me. They were able to laugh at the neighbourhood gender watch because the whole 'crisis' was invisible to them until their neighbour

---

8   Available at: outrightinternational.org/sites/default/files/APLPJ_14.2_Taniguchi.pdf (Last accessed: 12/09/21 10:42 AM GMT)

offered a very flustered apology, which they could then graciously accept. But in the academic sphere, the challenge to their gender was delivered in person and in public, in a way that put them on the spot and threatened both their dignity and their authority. In the former example, the crisis happened behind the scenes; in the latter, they were directly under the spotlight. This second and more confrontational encounter in Hotaru-san's narrative shows us something interesting: that it is not always the trans or gender-nonconforming person who bears the brunt of the crisis. Makoto-san told me that they had experienced many confrontations by cisgender women who had accused them of being 'a man' or told them to 'get out of women-only spaces' in gendered bathrooms, in the 'ladies' cars' of trains and subways, and in gender-segregated hospital bays. Despite this, they were always able to assert their 'female' sex and be understood as the wronged party in the interaction.[9] Hotaru-san, as a professor, is allowed to express grievance and be sympathetically received. Despite the extreme minority status of trans people in Japan, they are still often able to come out on top of any attempt to challenge or humiliate them on the basis of their gender expression. Doing so – managing the microaggressions of being confronted in single-sex spaces or questioned invasively on their gender in professional settings – occupies a great part of gender-work as emotional labour: trans people must remain calm and conciliatory lest we come across to bystanders as aggressive, unreasonable, hysterical, etc.

Conclusion

The demand placed on every trans person by a cissexist society is: 'Prove it!' The 'ideal' way for Japanese trans people to prove it, of course, is through faithful conformation to every article of the *Gender Transition Act*. However, transition to these standards is a process; it takes time, money, medical certification and a great deal of bureaucracy. How else to 'prove it' in the meantime between coming out and finishing transition, than through a stark and radical change in the gendered attributes of one's clothes, shoes and hair? Especially when we consider this material performance in the applied contexts of a specific culture, in this case Japan: one is not only a 'woman', but a *Japanese* woman; and not only a Japanese woman, but a woman performing 'Osakan'

---

[9] As they told me in concluding one of these anecdotes: 'Oh yeah. That lady got really embarrassed.'

versus 'Kyotoite' versus 'Tokyoite' womanhood, etc. Womanhood itself is a fraught concept worthy of problematisation. Giles links it with transition as both being minoritised, constructed categories of gender:

> All women labour to be women, and that work is also the work of transition. This is not to say that there is a natural pre-gendered state from which women labour to be women, nor that the marked difference between 'trans people' and 'women' as intersecting classes is immaterial, but simply that all womanhood is alienated labour for another's purpose, that all gender is always suspect.

This performance for others, or 'alienated labour', frequently encompasses the use of 'women's speech' [*joshi-kotoba*], as magisterially analysed by Inoue (2006), and the *habitus* of bodily politeness. No-one embodied this more than my respondent Hanako-san, an older trans woman who lives and works in Osaka. When I asked her, during the course of our semi-structured interview, to describe her sexual/gender identity in her own words, she gave this reply:

> I'm MtF [male-to-female]...well, as far as my sexual orientation goes, I'm asexual. And on top of that, of course, I do have GID [i.e. a medical diagnosis of Gender Identity Disorder]. As well as that, I'm an Osaka aunty. (laughs) 'Osakan' works as my identity. (laughs) That's number one, the most important thing. Our way of getting along with people is to be very friendly and... nosy, I guess? (laughs)

'There's a nuance to this word 'nosy' (*osekkai*)', my teacher (herself from Kyoto) said. 'She means the kind of person who always has sweets in her bag to distribute to passing children. Someone who's very familiar and inquisitive, but in a kindly way; someone who does what she thinks is best, but out of a sense of generosity.'

Nōmachi (2009) discusses the amount of careful attention required to absorb a feminine *habitus* in the context of pink-collar clerical work:

> Although I'd heard of various methods for stopping hiccups, this was the first time I was consciously able to stop them. I managed to stop my hiccups *twice*. I realised I had a kind of 'fighting spirit' in this regard, and I felt pleased that I'd mastered one more aspect of being an adult woman (if only something as trifling as hiccups!)
>
> (*ibid.*, 2009: 22)

Aside from the 'dainty' management of sneezes and hiccups, other aspects of this feminine *habitus* include putting one's face in one's hands when embarrassed; laughing with a hand over one's mouth; pulling in the elbows while one walks. This 'training' of the body into a feminine deportment has a rich history and practice in Japan: although few of my respondents wore kimono outside of the obligatory cotton *yukata* at hot springs or in midsummer,[10] traditional clothing and its influence on gendered mannerisms remain symbolically powerful today. Dalby (1983), Mitsuhashi (2008) and Vollman (2011) have all discussed the adaptation of deportment required in learning how to move while wearing women's kimono. Even though none of my own respondents were particularly enamoured of *kitsuke* (kimono dressing), it can play an important emotional and cultural role for other trans people in Japan. Some municipalities and city wards, including Tokyo's Setagaya Ward, hold Coming of Age Day events for LGBTQ youth in which trans participants are encouraged to wear whichever form of kimono reflects their gender identity best. The trans writer and researcher Mitsuhashi Junko has written extensively on the role of *kitsuke* study clubs in shaping her female identity and giving her deeply meaningful experiences of sisterhood with other women: '[Many of the cisgender women] kindly accepted me for the way I was and even gave me some friendly advice and comments about how to wear kimono, saying 'Junko, you look really pretty in that kimono'; 'Your way of putting on an *obi* is beautiful, can you tell me how to do mine like yours?' Those moments brought joy and peace to my heart...I always wanted to be a woman amongst women. I feel that I finally made the dream come true.' (quoted in McLelland et al, 2007: 310) Many of Mitsuhashi's anecdotes on kimono dressing are set in Kyoto, although she herself is from Tokyo, which serve to reinforce this association of specifically-Japanese femininity with the cultural capital (in both senses) of Kansai. It is this kind of regionally-specific, culturally-imbued awareness of gender through the media of bodily comportment, feminine discourse and speech markers, and female-coded mannerisms that I suggest forms the lion's share of gendered Japanese interaction in the day-to-day. Mitsuhashi's enthusiasm for *kitsuke* also serves as an example of how trans people can embrace the

---

10 During the semi-structured interview with my respondent Hanako-san, I asked her whether she enjoyed kimono dressing, as her LINE profile picture at the time was her wearing an elegant Oshima silk kimono in the formal plum garden at Kyoto's Kitano Tenmangu shrine. 'No', came the immediate response, 'I hate it actually, it's impossible to do anything while wearing one – I just wanted to look nice in the pictures.'

material aspects of gender presentation for their own personal fulfilment and gender euphoria.[11]

It is this euphoria, and the pleasure that is also a part of doing gender in the everyday, with which I wish to leave the reader. Much of the focus on the work of transition in this chapter has been on the demands made of transgender people that are not intended for their own benefit, but it would be misleading to conclude that all conscious plays and performances of gender are undertaken from dour necessity. Even as I performed femininity for a set purpose, not as true personal expression, I also found ways to have fun with it, including the adoption of some feminine mannerisms like covering my mouth while laughing. During the conversation with which this chapter opens, in which my Japanese language tutor and I were discussing my gender presentation in the field, she said something mildly complimentary that made me laugh and hide my face in my hands out of performative embarrassment – 'You see!' she cried triumphantly, her point having been made. 'You do it too now, automatically!'

References

Dalby, Liza. 1983. *Geisha*. New York: Vintage Publishing.

Dale, S. P. F. 2012. An introduction to *X-jendā*: Examining a new gender identity in Japan. *Intersections: Gender and Sexuality in Asia and the Pacific* (31). Available from: intersections.anu.edu.au/issue31/dale.htm [Accessed 15 September 2021]

Das, Veena. 2018. Of mistakes, errors and superstition: Reading Wittgenstein's remarks on Frazer'. In Giovanni da Col and Stephen Palmié (eds), *The Mythology in Our Language: Remarks on Frazer's 'Golden Bough'*, 153–179. Chicago: HAU Books.

Garfinkel, Harold. 1967. *Studies in Ethnomethodology*. Hoboken: Prentice Hall.

Giles, Harry Josephine. 2019. *Wages for Transition*. Available from: harryjosiegiles.medium.com/wages-for-transition-dce2b246b9b7 [Accessed 1 September 2021]

Hochschild, Arlie. R. 2012 [1983]. *The Managed Heart: Commercialization of Human Feeling*. Berkeley and London: University of California Press.

Inoue, Miyako. 2006. *Vicarious Language: Gender and Linguistic Modernity in Japan*. Berkeley: University of California Press.

Ishii Yukari. 2018. *Toransujendā to Genzai Shakai*. Tokyo: Meiji Shoten.

---

11 The opposite of 'gender dysphoria', gender euphoria refers to the feeling of joy, comfort or fulfilment in transition, whether through surgery, hormones, personal dress, being gendered correctly by strangers, using one's true name etc. For a fuller definition and history of the term, see: www.digitaltransgenderarchive.net/files/3197xm05t [Accessed 20 September 2021]

Israeli-Nevo, Atalia. 2017. Taking (my) time: Temporality in transition, queer delays, and being (in the) present. *Somatechnics* 7 (1): 34–49.

Luvaas, Brent. 2019. Unbecoming: the aftereffects of autoethnography. *Ethnography* 20 (2). Available from: journals.sagepub.com/doi/abs/10.1177/1466138117742674?journalCode=etha [Accessed 11 September 2021]

McLelland, Mark, Katsuhiko Suganuma and James Welker. 2007. *Queer Voices from Japan: First-Person Narratives from Japan's Sexual Minorities.* Washington DC: Lexington Books.

McKenna, Wendy and Suzanne J. Kessler. 1978. *Gender: an Ethnomethodological Approach.* Chicago: University of Chicago Press.

Mitsuhashi Junko. 2008. *Josō to Nihonjin* Tokyo: Kodansha.

Nōmachi Mineko. 2009. *Okama Dakedo OL Yattemasu.* Tokyo: Bungei Shunjū.

Okitsu Hiroki. 2019. Kekkon-go ni seidōitsusei shōgai to shindan, shujutsu seibetsu henkō o shinsei (trans. ,Gender identity disorder diagnosis and surgery after marriage: petition for legal gender change'). *The Asahi Shinbun*, 8 February. Available from: www.asahi.com/articles/ASM284DC6M28PLZB00Y.html [Accessed 20 September 2021]

Rubin, Gayle. 1975. The traffic in women: Notes on the 'political economy' of sex. In Reyna R. Reiter (ed.), *Toward an Anthropology of Women,* 157–210. New York: Monthly Review Press.

Shu Min Yuen. 2020. Unqueer queers – drinking parties and negotiations of cultural citizenship by female-to-male trans people in Japan. *Asian Anthropology* 19 (2): 86–101.

Stokoe, Elizabeth. 2006. On ethnomethodology, feminism, and the analysis of categorical reference to gender in talk-in-interaction. *The Sociological Review* 54 (3): 467–494. Available from: journals.sagepub.com/doi/10.1111/j.1467-954X.2006.00626.x [Accessed 27 March 2021]

Taniguchi Hiroyuki. 2013. *Japan's 2003 Gender Identity Disorder Act: The Sex Reassignment Surgery, No Marriage, and No Child Requirements as Perpetuations of Gender Norms in Japan.* Available from: outrightinternational.org/sites/default/files/APLPJ_14.2_Taniguchi.pdf [Accessed 13 September 2021]

Tsuruta Sachie. 2009. *Seidōitsusei-Shōgaisha no Esunogurafi. Seigenshō no Shakaigaku.* Tokyo: Harvest-sha.

Vollmann, William T. 2011. *Kissing the Mask: Beauty, Femininity, and Understatement in Japanese Noh Theater.* New York: Ecco Press.

Wallace, Jane. 2020. Stepping-up: 'Urban' and 'queer' cultural capital in LGBT and queer communities in Kansai, Japan. *Sexualities*, 23 (4): 666–682. Available from: eprints.whiterose.ac.uk/144775/1/Wallace%202019%20%28Stepping%20 Up%29%20Final%20Submitted%20Version.pdf [Accessed: 15 September 2021]

Ward, Jane. 2010. Gender labor: Transmen, femmes and collective work of transgression. *Sexualities* 13 (2): 236–254.

West, Candace and Sarah Fenstermaker. 1995. Doing difference. *Gender and Society* 9 (4): 8–37. Available from: www.csun.edu/~snk1966/Doing%20Difference.pdf [Accessed 1 April 2021]

West, Candace and Don H. Zimmerman. 1987. Doing gender. *Gender and Society* 1(2): 125–151. Available from: www.gla.ac.uk/0t4/crcees/files/summerschool/readings/WestZimmerman_1987_DoingGender.pdf [Accessed: 9 May 2021]

Yonezawa Hotaru. 2003. *Toransujendārizumu Sengen. Seibetsu no Jiko Kettei-ken to Tayōna Sei no Kōtei* Tokyo: Shakai Hihyōsha.

EPILOGUE

Gender, Substance, Fantasy

Undisciplined Observations on Gender Presentations in Japan

Fabio Gygi

To think about gender in the context of fieldwork, whether one's own or others', is an unsettling experience. No theory of gender is sufficiently attuned to grasp the minute nuances of gender presentations in everyday life and the myriad contexts in which they become relevant. Gender is the ultimate paradox: it is highly malleable, artificial and socially constructed; at the same time it is normative, predetermined and inescapable. Gender is one way in which the researcher is drawn into the field, as their presentation of gender is made sense of, commented on, corrected, interrogated or embraced. Editing the chapters in this volume with Gitte Marianne Hansen has transported me back to many of my own encounters with gender and gender presentation in Japan: how the difference that I experienced helped me make sense of my own difference as a gay man, and how this difference, when brought home, created a sense of alienation from my own milieu, which threw into sharper relief the arbitrary contours of the social world to which I no longer wholly belonged. No one can ever entirely come back from the field. In this spirit I wrote the following kaleidoscopic observations. They are undisciplined because they refuse to form a coherent theory of gender in Japan. Instead, they offer glimpses of scenes, encounters and experiences that speak to the chapters in this volume.

I Under the Sign of Gender

My first exposure to Japanese understandings of gender came at the age of 14, when Ikeda-Sensei, my *aikidō* teacher, chided a bearded, middle-aged man with the words: 'You look like a woman!' Eddy had started the beginners' class only a few months before and was now wearing the white training uniform, the *keiko-gi*. The *keiko-gi* is unisex and the only faux pas that Eddy had committed was to tie his white belt over his belly button. While we, the bystanders, knew that the belt in martial arts is worn around the lower abdomen to support breathing, we were quite surprised that a difference of about ten centimetres should turn somebody who presented so obviously as a man into a woman. It was a powerful illustration of the ways in which gender presentation is based on signs – such as the height of the belt in an otherwise unisex white uniform – and of how these signs are often given more importance than to what we understand to be the biological markers of gender – such as dense facial hair, in this case. Especially in the Japanese performing arts (and I would count the martial arts among them), the semiotic system of gender eclipses any concern with the 'truth' of underlying bodies.

I remembered this incident more than ten years later when I was backstage at the National Theatre in Tokyo to visit the mentor of a close friend of mine before a performance of traditional Japanese dance (*Nihon-buyō*). Over the space of an hour I observed the transformation of this established academic and author in his late 50s into a young *geisha*, with the help of several of his assistants and students. I was interested in the transformative aspect of clothing and wanted to ask him what clothes say about the 'truth' of the body. While the standard kimono is a semiotically rich garment whose colour, decoration, materials, dyeing and weaving techniques speak to the gender, class, occupation and social status of the wearer – even down to their state of mind, when we include the black kimono of mourning – the cut of the fabric itself is unisex. It envelops the body like a tube and mutes differences of shape rather than highlighting them – unlike a codpiece or a bodice, for example. What gives the body its erotic charge is not to be found in the body itself, but in the dialectic relationship between covering and revealing. The kimono is part of a semiotics of gender that creates a distance between the presented gender and the underlying body. While the kimono restricts movement and thus free expression for those who wear it in the way prescribed for female roles (both on stage and in everyday life), it does not accomplish the work of gender by itself. While thick layers of white make-up were being applied to his face, he explained to me how the wearer must master a repertoire of bodily movements that are, in their turn, gendered: one can expose one's neck for added sex appeal (the experienced assistant does this with a single yank), or one can hitch up the bottom seam to allow for the swagger of a masculine role. While wearing a kimono is initially restricting and the possibilities of committing a faux pas are considerable, it also gives the wearer a reassuring sense of the extension of their body in space, a sense of compactness and presence that is heightened by the limitations it places on one's gestures: it feels as if one's body was cut out of the space surrounding it with great precision. When he finally got up, decked in full regalia – the complicated belt tied at the appropriate height – he turned to me and said, 'Don't I look like a fabulous drag queen?'

II Pornographic Encounters

An exchange year at a Japanese all-boys' high school in the 1990s introduced me to pornography. Among the members of the high school sport clubs, VHS tapes were surreptitiously circulated as a kind of underground currency. Lucky the boy who had an older brother at university! Our black school uniforms prevented us from making excursions into the cordoned-off area at the local video rental store. The bulky, unmarked VHS tape that was eventually handed to me after *kendō* practice in the dank clubroom came with instructions: 'Make sure you watch it alone. *This* is Japanese culture!'

I did eventually take a furtive look under the cover of night on my host family's VHS deck. I remember to this day what I saw: a scene in which a female police officer was raped by two masked men. This was so shocking and discordant with my everyday experience of the polite Japanese way of life that it was difficult to process at first. Much sexual innuendo and bravado were on display among my classmates, but at the much-anticipated school festival, the only occasion when it was possible to meet students from the all-girls' school, the loudest boys turned bright-red and could hardly stammer a word. Furthermore, in stark contrast to the hardcore content, genital areas were pixelated (see also Kodaka in this volume). When I asked the classmate who had given the tape to me why it was pixelated when everything else was so explicit, he grinned and said: 'So there is some mystery left when you see the real thing!'

As I learned to read Japanese, I noticed that this mystery is also reproduced in print. Even in pornographic publications the slang term for 'vagina' is written with a 'double hole' ◎ in the middle, reproducing, typographically, the miniature shock of encountering an unspeakable word, of reading something you should not read. This illegibility reproduced the unspeakability of the word: both a means of censoring and of heightening the erotic frisson of imagining what the word gestures towards. Even now, this term for 'vagina' is one of the few words that cannot be broadcast. Unsurprisingly, the same does not apply to the penis, a bodily appendage that even has its own popular festival, the Kanamara *matsuri* in Kawasaki.

The pixelation of obscene material, specifically of pubic hair, the vagina and the penis (but excluding the anus) is an artefact of modern censorship and stands in strong contrast to the explicit depictions of sex scenes in erotic woodblock prints in early modern Japan (*shunga*, literally 'spring pictures'). Here penetration is highlighted and even magnified: almost three-dimensional, engorged penises and pink vulvas are the focal point, in contradistinction to the featureless, white void of the bodies, leading some to conclude that '*shunga* dismiss the erotic possibility of skin' (Screech 2009: 109). Even in these depictions, the kimono is rarely taken off completely; apart from the social and gendered semiotics, its pattern is used to structure the picture and to fragment the body into different zones of engagement: the faces exquisitely inward-looking, the bodies unmarked and placid, the genitals exhibiting their own liveliness as if belonging to an independent and impersonal reality of desire. While there is little doubt that the 'spring pictures' were consumed as masturbatory aids, they were also often included as part of a bride's trousseau – as if to say 'here, this is what you can expect to happen, this is the reality of conjugal relations'.

The digital censorship of pornography has the opposite effect of mystification. The 'mosaic', as it is called in Japanese, hides and entices at the same time: the viewers know there is something worth watching because they cannot see it. The mystery of the real is thus perpetuated rather than addressed. The architect Rem Koolhaas argues that the mosaic signifies the rapprochement of virtual and real worlds. The effect is almost poetic:

> Emerging from the pure abstraction
> of the censored zone:
> jets of sperm –
> white squares that turn into small blobs
> and land on real flesh. (Koolhaas and Mau 1995: 103)

III The Great Reveal

For many upwardly-mobile Japanese men of my generation, the quintessential experience of a 'genital reveal' happened in a DX strip theatre, where the female performers, usually on a slowly revolving stage, spread their legs for the male audience to take a close-up look, finally without pixelation. The atmosphere in such moments is marked by a tense curiosity and even a sense of reverence; the act itself is called *go-kaichō* (lit. 'the honourable opening of the curtain'), a term that is otherwise reserved for the rare display of a hidden Buddha statue. But what kind of 'truth' is revealed in such a moment? As the vagina, garishly illuminated by the stage lights, becomes the focus of the gaze of the rapt spectators crowding around, the woman herself retreats into the background and the organ that is displayed assumes a life, a meaning, a reality all of its own, curiously separate from the person.

How to describe a pornographic scene, something meant to arouse people, in a way that does not become pornographic itself? The Swiss author Adolf Muschg has tried to grasp the atmosphere in such a venue and what happens when the salarymen start to join the performers on stage one by one, egged on by their peers. His writing reproduces the sense of disorientation, the attempt to create some kind of distance from which this scene – at once erotic, burlesque and surreal – makes sense. The comparative frame constantly shifts, inducing a cognitive vertigo in the reader: he is reminded of a gymnastic event, a school class in front of a particularly mesmerizing exhibit, a medical procedure, a fun fair, eager but inept students in a dance class, mothers who tenderly look after their overgrown children, a factory floor 'where robots, camouflaged as naked women, sheathe, defuse and unclamp male parts in a fully automated process' (Muschg 1995: 61). Here too, as in many of the earlier chapters in this volume, it is the monetary transaction that delimits and contains the emotions and affects aroused by the body: 'Respectable people come here to palpitate the body with their eyes, to penetrate it with their desires. They paid at the entrance to not feel any shame about it' (1995: 48–49).

Donald Richie, who acted for many years as a kind of concierge for the Western intelligentsia in Tokyo, delighted in taking visitors to the local DX theatre, where patrons could voyeuristically enjoy others having sex and indulge in intercourse themselves. In a diary entry from 1989, he describes the reaction of the photographer Richard Avedon and his agent, Norma Stevens:

Dick and Norma were astonished by this, as most foreigners are. The experience offers no handles; it is so smooth and featureless, so practiced, so benign – it is the last thing that the Christians and the Jews expect from sex. When I took Susan [Sontag] she said it all: 'Well, I guess it is sexy but it is about as erotic as a cake bake-off.' Richard thought of Kindergarten; Norma thought of a day-care centre. They also thought it very 'sad' – which is a common reaction from liberal Americans. This tells more, however, about their assumptions than it does about the Japanese DX theatre. They found it sad. I found it matter-of-fact. But then I think that Americans believe that being matter-of-fact about sex is sad. One must make it special: either celestial or infernal.

(Richie 2004: 234)

IV Hoarding as Gender Failure

My PhD fieldwork on hoarding in Tokyo was initially focused on notions of mental health rather than on gender (Gygi 2019). I quickly noticed, however, that hoarding was understood in two different registers, depending on whether the hoarder was described as male or female. In short, men were considered to be naturally 'untidy' and in need of female help; women who displayed tendencies towards untidiness were, on the other hand, considered to be pathological. They were labelled *katazukerarenai onna* ('women who cannot tidy up') and became the object of a moral panic. Were they unable to tidy up, too lazy, or even unwilling to do so? What fascinated me about this was how the materiality of gender went beyond the body and how material environments – cluttered and disordered rooms – could become gendered themselves. The excess of material accumulation and disorder was often understood to be a lack on the part of the female hoarder, a failure to perform gender properly.

Two kinds of gender work are pitched against each other here: the mundane act of tidying up and caring for one's own and other people's things; and the process of meaning-making that links the mundane disorder back to the women – wives, mothers, office lady colleagues, self-identified career women – from whom it is said to emanate. The former is driven by the fear of the latter: linking domestic spaces to feminised labour carries with it a particular notion of national femininity. Failing to be disciplined, caring and selfless is failing both at being a woman and at being properly Japanese: disorder is cast as an unpatriotic sin of omission.

This particular construction of gender is not unconscious or hidden; on the contrary, it takes place in the public sphere, where women who refuse to care for other people's disorders are chided and disciplined. A well-established psychiatrist, fairly advanced in age, laughed when I asked him about why women were singled out for hoarding behaviour, and said: 'Look at me, I can't tidy up, all my personal affairs are in disorder. But I have [female] staff who do this work for me, and therefore you cannot tell that I am the source of the chaos.' Self-important voices like these drowned out the voices of my interlocutors, who often felt they had nothing interesting to say; for how can you articulate your resistance to the monolithic edifice of gender in the mundane language of housework? This work of articulation was made even more difficult by the re-enchantment of housework that took off at the same time: Kondō Marie and the endless flow of magazines and books and TV programmes that exhort us to magically transform our environment by eliminating everything that does not 'spark joy'.

V Sex Work

At a well-heeled private university in Western Japan, where I took up my first academic position, I occasionally overheard male students talking about visits to brothels. 'I cannot but think of the girls at the brothel as gentleness personified (*yasashisa no katamari*)', a member of one of the university sport clubs said after a seminar, offhandedly. There was something about the phrasing that stuck in my mind. *Katamari* literally means a lump or a clod, something that by way of crystallisation attains a fixed form; metaphorically, it can mean personification or embodiment.[1] There was an odd tension between the objectification of female sex workers – equating them to a 'lump of gentleness' – and the deferential awe with which the phrase was uttered. I was not sure what particular service was provided by the women described in these terms, but as the soliciting of vaginal intercourse is technically illegal in Japan, I assumed that the topic of discussion must have been some kind of sexual service short of penetration. I was wise enough by then not to ask any questions, knowing well that such a conversation would quickly derail into inappropriate territory and probably end with a jocular invitation for me to

---

1   Two different characters are used to mark the semantic difference: 固まり is used for the concrete, material sense of the word, while 塊, combining the radical for 'earth' with the character for 'soul', is more abstract.

join them. The topic had come up before at an after-seminar drinking party, and when I innocently asked why young, athletic men would pay for sexual services, the answer was unanimous: '*Sensei*, these girls are *professionals*!'

Later I learned that the service provided consisted of the man lying passively on his back, while the female sex worker with the aid of liberal lubrication put power to her elbow; a precise reversal of the standard image of heterosexual penetrative sex, during which the active male partner arouses, manipulates, and generally manhandles the reactive female partner (the mainstay of straight pornography). The fact that this is a service offered for pay justifies the active–passive role reversal: while procreative penetrative sex is implicitly understood by men to be 'work', this kind of sexual relief is construed as *iyashi*, as 'healing', because the active work is undertaken by the female sex worker. Providing sexual relief, in other words, is providing relief from having to be active and dominating in all areas of life; but such a reversal has to be isolated from the everyday domestic sphere lest it should undermine the patriarchal conception of the head of the household. By turning sexual relief into a paid-for service, and thus cutting off any relationship that such intimate contact is bound to create, male sexual desire[2] is contained, compartmentalised and kept from contaminating and destabilising present and future domestic arrangements. This is part of a long and venerable tradition in Japan of keeping sexuality as procreation and sexuality as play in separate spheres. Because the service is paid-for and impersonal, the female workers reveal themselves to the customers as gendered substance, literally: professional gentleness personified, without the need for care, consideration or reciprocity.

VI Ari no mama

The pervasive nature of the sex/gender system becomes visible in the most mundane of contexts: a master maker of Japanese dolls tells me that he receives many requests to perform 'sex changes' on antique dolls. Most of the requests are about transforming male Ichimatsu dolls into female ones. This involves a change of hair (boy dolls have shaved heads), but also changing the rudimentary genitals that most dolls have. Despite the fact that boys were traditionally more cherished because they continued the family household,

---

[2] That all men have voracious sexual appetites is taken for granted in the world of water business, where examples to the contrary are hard to come by for obvious reasons.

in the current climate of cutification female dolls are considered to be more desirable and thus more valuable.

However, when I ask the doll maker how he carries out such requests he replies: 'Oh no, I don't. The dolls were made as male and female and I am not authorized to change that.' He refuses to interfere in another doll maker's work for monetary gain; but he uses an expression that is strangely familiar: *ari no mama*, meaning 'the way things are, what is given, what is there', here perhaps also 'the way things were made'. This was the phrase I used to come out to my Japanese host parents, years after my homestay with them: with a plea to be accepted the way that I am. *Ari no mama* was a crucial part of the Japanese rhetoric of gay and lesbian coming-out in the 90s. While there are semantic parallels with the idea of 'nature' (the Japanese translation of the English word 'nature', *shizen*, is a Sino-Japanese way of expressing a similar notion of given-ness: *onozukarashikaru*), *ari no mama* is an appeal to one's given, ontological state, but not therefore to something that is fixed. 'Nature' is always malleable, but to form it requires constant work. In that context, the plea to be accepted *ari no mama* is a plea to be relieved of this work of presenting as straight, of conforming to the expectations of having a family, of creating and maintaining a straight persona. This is not to say, however, that presenting as gay is less of an acquired style of gender, as Francioni shows in his chapter in this volume.

VII The Limits of Gender Presentation

Queer or not, there is pleasure to be had in doing the work of gender with relish and in enjoying the performance as performance rather than as referencing some kind of underlying 'nature'. Gay friends would sometimes share anecdotes, gleefully recounting the giving of Valentine's Day chocolates and their return on 'White Day' (March 12), and the intricate manipulation of heterosexual office politics that this entailed. A lesbian friend who worked at a maid café took pride and pleasure in performing as an object of male desire, precisely because for her the stakes were so low and she was an excellent performer. 'Passing' in this context is not a kind of deception, but part of the work of gender, in that the performance is both artificially natural and deeply superficial. It is sincere, but not authentic, and it is precisely because it lacks authenticity that it entails a degree of freedom.

Experimenting with gender presentation, however, has its socially upheld limits. I used the first-person pronoun *boku*, used by boys and younger males in a social hierarchy, throughout my high school and university days. A few years ago, my *aikidō* teacher jokingly referred to me as *boku*, as if it were my first name. I took this to mean that maybe my time as a *boku* had come to an end and shifted to the more neutral and formal *watashi* from then onwards. I even experimented with the more informal masculine *ore* at a drinking party, but this created so much cognitive dissonance that at the end of the night a female senior took me aside and said: '*Ore* does not sound like you at all.' I don't think I have used it since then.

In this sense, gender is presented – linguistically, sartorially, habitually – but it is also given by those to whom it is presented. This gives the 'audience' of one's gender presentation the power to normalise it – although of course this audience can change from one context to another. This work of normalisation to which the foreign body is subjected can take a number of forms: being physically corrected or shouted at, being excluded from proceedings, being shunned or joked about, or being rendered the material of countless anecdotes. But it can also be expressed as fantasy: an acquaintance of mine, a rather highly-strung lawyer, still tells others that I have a hidden zip at my back that would open up and reveal a Japanese person hidden inside: his creative way of reducing the cognitive dissonance of interacting with a foreign body in a familiar idiom.

VIII   Futures

Gender presentation is, as we have argued in the introduction with reference to Judith Butler, a practice of improvisation within a context of constraint. What counts as improvisation and what as constraint can, however, change radically, sometimes in a short period of time. We are witnessing many of these changes first-hand and it is sometimes tempting to describe this development as emancipation and progress. Goalposts have been moved, but normative ideas about what is permitted and what is not have not moved with them. The reader might think that we live in slightly more tolerant times in 2022, but you only need to walk down an ordinary London street in broad daylight in a mildly androgynous outfit to see what colourful invective members of the public will feel entitled, nay compelled, to hurl at you.

References

Gygi, Fabio. 2019. Hôtes et Otages: Entasser des objets chez soi dans le Japon contemporain. *L'Homme* 231–232: 151–71.

Koolhaas, Rem and Bruce Mau. 1995. *Small, Medium, Large, Extra-Large*. 2nd edition. New York: Monacelli Press.

Muschg, Adolf. 1995. *Nur ausziehen wollte sie sich nicht: Ein erster Satz und seine Fortsetzung*. Frankfurt am Main: Suhrkamp.

Richie, Donald. 2004. *The Japanese Journals: 1947 – 2004*. Edited by Leza Lowitz. Berkeley, CA: Stone Bridge Press.

Screech, Timon. 2009. *Sex and the Floating World: Erotic Images in Japan 1700–1820*. London: Reaktion Books.

COLOUR FIGURES

Figure 3.1 One of crossdressers' shared wardrobe. Text, p. 72.

THE WORK OF GENDER

Figure 3.2 Two dansō waiting for customers in the office near the lockers. Text, p. 73.

COLOUR FIGURES

Figure 3.3 Marta Fanasca posing as André in a promotional flyer for Dreamland. Text, p. 75.

Figure 4.1: A screenshot of Deadball's homepage for the Uguisudani branch, 23 August 2019. It displays deals for sessions and links through to information about available women, rules, terminology and even a careers page. The top right tagline reads... 'To you who want to quit [using] the sex industry... if you play, your relationship [with your wife] will be harmonious! Her gratitude will double!' The word 'play' here is a euphemism for using sexual services. Visible just beneath this is a link to the Sakura Research and Screening Facility, which is used by Deadball for routine sexual health screening. Text, p. 91.

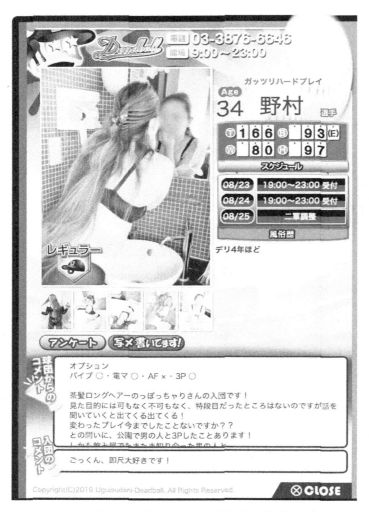

Figure 4.2: A worker's profile in the style of a baseball card, 23rd August 2019. She is a 'regular' level player, which denotes her price. The profile contains basic information such as height and weight, how long she has been in the delivery health industry, as well as detailed descriptions of what kind of 'play' she offers. Her tagline reads: 'I love to give head and swallow!'. Text, p. 92.

COLOUR FIGURES

Figure 5.1: Oikawa, Mukai, Uehara and Azuma (from left to right) at SILK Fes November 2018. Photo: Maiko Kodaka. Text, p. 128.

Figure 6.1: On the south side of the station, a passerby mistakes Fuji for a popular musician. Photo: R. J. Simpkins. Text, p. 155

THE WORK OF GENDER

Figure 6.2: Reina's mask was effective in drawing attention. Photo: R. J. Simpkins. Text, p. 164

Figure 7.1: Examples of FTM lifestyle magazines, from the 2019 Kansai Queer Film Festival at the Kyoto Seibu Kōdō. Photo: L. Gamberton. Text, p. 197.

Index

f=figure; **bold**=extended discussion or key reference

Adler and Adler 68
advertising 65, 105, 159, 174, 185
affective attachment 153
affective elements 157
affective ethnography: definition 21
affective industry 81
affective labour 2–4, 64, 65, 78, 181, 192, 196
affective relationships 150, 155, 160, 166, 168, 171
age 110, 113
agency 5, 13, 18, 21, 125
Agustín, Laura M. 96–97, 98
aikidō 206, 215
aiko (patronage) 172
aikyō (charm, attractiveness) **169–173**, 176
Akagawa Manabu 128
Akihabara xiii, xvii, 61n; *dansō* escort company **63–66**
alcohol 35, 36, 158
Alexy, Allison 156
alienation 18, **167–168**, 206
Allison, Anne 2–3, 52, **100**, 109; *Nightwork* xi
amae: 'dependency' 110; 'indulgence' 42
amayakasu (needs) 111
An An (women's magazine) 122
Anderson, Ben 176
anime xiii, xiv, xvii, 61n, **63–64**, 76
anonymity **17–18**, 156
anthropologists xix, 8, 98, 99, 168, 180
anthropology xviii, 19, 21, 26, 62, 67, 138, 150, 155, 182, 188
Aoyama Kaoru 94n8

aragoto (tempestuous young man) 9–10
ari no mama (the way things are) **213–214**
Arinomama Dakishimete (Embrace Me As I Am, 2019) 125
Asagaya 154, **160–162**, 166
Asai Michiko 42
atashi (feminine pronoun) 23, **48–49**, 181
atmospheres 147, 148, 149, 151, 157–173 *passim*, **175–177**
authenticity **19–21**, 176; commodification **15–19**; sex work in 'delivery health' shop 1, **24, 88–117**
autoethnography **186–188**
Avedon, Richard 210–211
Azuma Sōsuke (*eroman*) 127, **128f**, 129, **136–138, 221f**

bar staff 1, 12, 23, 54, 56
Beauvoir, Simone de xii
becoming: non-linear ~ **186–188**
Bernstein, Elizabeth 105, 106, 135; 'bounded authenticity' concept **16–17**; *Temporarily Yours* (2007) 16
biology 4, 6, 15, 26, 38, 40, 79–80, 193, 207
bodily capital 74, 103–104
bodily presentation 33, 42–47, 55
boku (first-person masculine pronoun) 23, 48, 49, 181, 214–215
Borovoy, Amy 35
boundaries xv, 16, 17, 69, 78, 101, 102, 106–107, 149, 150, 155, 162–163, 169, 174, 191, 192, 195

bounded authenticity 24, 25, 105, 109–110, 113, 121, 136, 140; definition (Bernstein) 135
Bourdieu, Pierre 103
boy bands 61, 124, 128, 141
boyfriend experience 82–83, **130–132**
Brazil **3–4**
brothels 1, 93, 131, 212
Bukowski, Charles 156
Burghoorn, Wil xix
Burrell, Jenna 69
busu (plain) women 24, 91, 102, 113
busu shirōto (plain amateurs) 105
Butler, Judith xii 9n7, 39, 57, 134, 151, 156, 159, 176, 215; *Bodies that Matter* (1993) **13, 14**; *Undoing Gender* (2004) 14
butler cafés xiii, xiv–xviii, 61, 64

capitalism 2, 64, 65, 167; late ~ 3, 17, 18, 105
Casey, Edward S. 174
catch-phrases 49–50
censorship 100, 209
chi-mama (assistant manager) 31
children 14, 18, 41, 42, 63, 129, 142, 190–191, 192, 193, 199, 201, 210
chitsu-tore (vaginal exercises) 123
cisgender people 181, 183, 187, 188, 190, 192, 195, 197, 198, 200, 202; definition 184
citationality of gender **9, 9n7**
class 113, 207; middle ~ 16, 56, 95, 96, 156; upper ~ 47
coercion 19, 96
coffee shops 60, 147, 159, 169, 183
cognitive: ~ dissonance 215; ~ effort 6; ~ skills 2; ~ understanding 8; ~ vertigo 210
Coin-Operated Boy (Dresden Dolls, 2003) 142
coin-operated boyfriend fantasy **141–143**

collective life 151, 167
colour code 6
Coming of Age Day (LGBTQ) 202
coming out: as homosexual **214**; as transgender 188, 200
commissioned performance 4
commodification 1–4, 21, 26, 35; authenticity **15–19**; emotions 65; explicit versus implicit ~ 106; identity **79–81**; interactions with *eromen* and *lovemen* 142; intimacy 24, 62, 64, 66, 131, 135, 139, 143; merriment 38, 57; recognition 120
compact discs 157, 159, 163
consent forms 71, 94
contact shock 188
context 4–5, 20, 156
Cook, Emma 37, 151, 156, 169
coronavirus pandemic 114, 183
countryside 173, 174
cover charge 35, 36f, 38
COYOTE (Call Off Your Old Tired Ethics) 135
cross-dressed ethnography **23–24**, 60–87; 'inside' or 'outside' **66–70**
cross-dressers: wardrobe 72f, **217f**
cross-gender: ~ performance 8; ~ clothing 44
cultural capital 103
cultural genitals 6
customer (culturally incompetent) **xi–xviii**

Daibutsu ('Big Buddha') 43
Dalby, Liza 202
dansō (female-to-male crossdresser escort) 1, 12, 61; commodification of identity **79–81**; rules of game **81–84**; training 68; waiting for customers 73f, **218f**
dansō escort company 23–24, 60–87; 'inside' or 'outside' **66–70**; research site **63–66**; use of pseudonyms 63n2

danyū (male actors) 128
Das, Veena 198
Dasgupta, Romit 41
Deadball 24, **88–117**; fieldwork methodology **93–96**, 112; homepage (screenshot) **91f, 219f**; interviews in Japanese context **98–100**; 'low rates' **99–100**; order of play **90–93**; pricelist **105–106**; professional amateurs **102–105**, 113; reflections on process **96–98**; reputation for safety at work 94, 94n8; rules of game 89, 90; sex work and authenticity **105–107**; sex work as healing **107–112**, 113; sex worker's profile **92f, 220f**; vaginal sex **100–102**, 113; website 94
deep hanging out 78
deictics 47–48
'delivery health' 1, 17–18, 24, **88–117**
depth ontology of the person 19
Derrida, Jacques 9n7, 171, 175
dialogue and dialogical communication 128, **133–134**, 141, 196
diet 23, 75
Digital Daijisen Dictionary 34–35
discourse xviii, 5, 7, 19, 46, 56, 112, 139, 141, 174, 202; social ~ 134
disrespect (Honneth) 133
divorce **195–196**
Doi Takeo 110
doing gender 38; phenomenology and ethnomethodology **5–7**
double self **135**
Dreamland (*dansō* escort company) 62, **63–66**, 68, **70–76**; creating *kei* (creating André) **76–79**; pseudonym 63n2; website 65
DX theatre **210–211**
dynamic ensemble 151, 167, 168

economic capital 103
economic miracle 41, 55, 56
economic stagnation era (from mid-2000s) 55, 57
embodiment **21–22**
emic perspective 184
emotional labour 2–3, 46, 50, 55–56, 65, 104, 110, 113, 119, 120, 132, 135, 181, 192, 200; definition 2
endless availability **34–37**
Endō Mameta 196–197
end-phrase particles **47–48**, 49, 50, 55
enryo (nonverbal empathic orientation) 110
Entertainment Law (1948) 93, 100
eroi (sex-appeal) 54
eromen 25, 141, 142; background **127–133**; fan events 1, 4, 12, **118–123**, 125, 130–**133**; marketing system **129–133**; private fan meetings 130, **134–135**; simulation ritual **136–140**; telephone dates **130–131**; 'three musketeers' **128–129**; vicious circle (performing and consuming recognition) **133–136**
erotic capital 120, 132
ethnicity 110, 110n12, 113
ethnographic research 21, 69; personal cost of knowledge acquisition **21–22**
ethnography xviii, 14, 98; advantages 18
ethnomethodology **5–7**, **184**; experiments 182–183; ~ of gender (limits) **198–200**
Eurocentrism 15
everyday life 4–5, 8, 9n8, 10, 13, 25, 39, 48, 52, 131, 154, 156, 165, 180, 183–184, 189n3, 198, 203, 206, 213
exercise 23, 103
exposure 176; and threshold of intimacy **163–167** (**164f**), **222f**

Facebook 183, 185
Faindā no Mukou ni Kimi ga Ita ('It was You Behind Viewfinder', AV, 2009) 123

Falk, Monica Lindberg xix
family relationships 154–155
Fanasca, Marta vii, 23–24, 25, 60–87; accessing Dreamland 70–76; creating *kei* (creating André) 76–79; posing as *dansō* 75f, 219f; rules of game 81–84
fandom 12n, 25, 120, 140, 153, 154
fantasy 17–18, 21, 23–24, 26, 33, 40–57 *passim*, 105, 131, 135–142 *passim*, 215; definition (Purcell) 120
fashion health clubs (erotic massage parlours) 93
female fantasies 124–127
female gaze 24
female to male (FtM) 69; magazines 196, 197f, 223f
female performers: banned from stage (1629) 8
femininity 22–23, 26, 120, 131, 139, 142, 173, 176; forms performed for other women 6; as *kata* 7–12
feminism 3, 5, 65, 126, 156, 197
Fenstermaker, Sarah 189
fieldwork 21–22; insider versus outsider status 68–69
Fine, Cordelia: *Delusions of Gender* (2010) 6
Fisch, Michael 167
fitness training 74–75
Foucault, Michel 13
Francioni, Marcello vii, xix, 22–23, 31–59
freedom 18, 20
Freud, Sigmund: *Uncanny* (1919) 166
frightening person 147, 153, 155, 157, 158, 169, 172, 173, 175, 176
Fudanjuku (*dansō* boybands) 61
Fūeihō (1948) 35n4
Fujii, James A. 167
Fujimoto Yukari 126
fujoshi 61n, 65, 66
fun 109
Fushimi Noriaki 47

fūzokujō (woman in sex industry) 91

gachimuchi (burly) and non-*gachimuchi* body types 42–47, 48
Galbraith, Patrick W. xvii
Gamberton, Lyman R.T. viii, 25–26, 180–205
Garfinkel, Harold 5, 189, 189n4
gay bar: serving gender 22–23, 31–59
geisha 207
gender xi–xix, 110, 120; 'biological fact' 4; co-construction 20; intersubjective artefact 4, 21; 'psychic reality' 4, 19; relational and situational 20; role in service at gay bars 31–59; social construction 5; in and as theatre 7–12
Gender: Ethnomethodological Approach (Kessler and McKenna 1978) 5–6
gender binary 12, 23, 25–26, 79
gender confirmation surgery (GCS) 187, 198
gender dysphoria 203n
gender euphoria 203, 203n
gender identity 6, 7, 15, 21, 69, 193
Gender Identity Disorder (GID) 201
gender labour 78; definition 181–182
gender limits 20–21
gender presentation 5–7, 8n, 10, 12, 14, 21, 23, 39; versus 'gender expression' 4; limits 214–215; master identity 13; situational 13; 'undisciplined observations' 206–216
Gender Treatment Act (2003, revised 2008) 25; full title 199
gender as work 1–30; authenticity, Japanese self, limits of gender 19–21; chapter by chapter 22–26; fieldwork and embodiment 21–22; gender in and as theatre 7–12; literature survey 2–20; masculinity and femininity as *kata* 7–12; performance versus performativity 12–14; phenom-

enology and ethnomethodology 5–7; sincerity and authenticity commodified **15–19**
gender at work: *dansō* escort company 23–24, **60–87**
gendered division of labour 47, 167
gendered language 33, 47, 49, 51, 55
gendered performances 12, 19, **146–179**
gendered power 34, 151, 168
gendered space 25, 151, 168, 172, 174
gendered subject 4, 13
genital pixelation 124, 208, 209, 210
genpuku ceremony 8n
Getreuer-Kargl, Ingrid 168
Geschiere, Peter **166**
Gide, André 15
gijiren'ai (performed love stories) 82n
Giles, Harry Josephine 192, 201; *Wages for Transition* (2019) 181, 182
Girl's Pleasure (*josei-muke*, 2009) 123
girlfriend experience 105
GIRLS' CH (2012–) 121, **124, 126,** 128, 130–131; office in Shin-Nakano 130
giving gender 20, 25, 78
go-kaichō (lit. 'honourable opening of curtain') 210
Goffman, Erving 15
good life 134
Gygi, Fabio **vii–viii, xviii, xix, 1–30, 206–216**; *ari no mama* (way things are) 213–214; great reveal 210–211; hoarding as gender failure **211–212**; pornographic encounters **208–209**; under sign of gender **206–208**

habitus **201–202**
hadaka no otsukiai (raw, honest relationship) 111n, 111–112
Hambleton, Alexandra 125
Hansen, Gitte Marianne viii, xi–xix, 1–30, 206
Hanyū Yuzuru 7
Hardt, Michael 2, 3, 3n

hegemonic discourses 41, 122, 134, 141
Hendry, Joy 67
hentai reputation 52, 53
hermeneutic phenomenological approach 21–22
heteronormativity 26, 56, 119
heterosexual matrix (Butler) 39, 57
heterosexuality 122, 122n1; assumptions of ~ **193–198**
hima-sō da na (idle) 45
hiroba (public squares) 157
Ho, Michelle 79
Hoang, Kimberly K. 103
hoarding as gender failure **211–212**
Hochschild, Arlie R. 2, 46, 119
homosexuality 65, 90n, 195
honban (vaginal sex) 24, 90, 93, 93n6, 100–102, 113, 212
Honneth, Axel 119, **133–134**
honorifics **47–48, 50–51**
hontō no jibun (real self) 76
hooks, bell 57
Hoopers (*dansō* boybands) 61
hormone replacement therapy (HRT) 187
hospitality 148, **171, 174–175,** 176
host clubs **17,** 65, **132**
hostess clubs 3, 32, 41, 109; Osaka (1995) xi–xii, xiii, xiv, xvii
housewives 3n, 41, 57

iaidō (sword-work) 181
Ichikawa, Kumehachi 9
Ichimatsu dolls **213–214**
ideal man 41, 42, 79–80, 142
ideal woman 41
identity 134; commodification **79–81**; *dansō* escort company 23–24, **60–87**
Iijima Tomoko 123
ikanimo-kei (lit. 'He's-clearly-[gay]-style') 43
Ikebukuro xiv, xvii
Ikeda Riyoko: *manga Versailles no Bara* 77

Ikeda-Sensei 206–207
imagined community (Anderson) 56
immaterial paradigm (Hardt and Negri) 2, 3
'in-store' relationship 132
incest 126n
indebtedness 24, 25, 95
indīzu (indie) scene 152
inemuri (napping) behaviour **168**
'inner truth' vs. 'outward performance' 20
instax photographs 119, 127, 130
interviews 94, 94n7, **96–98**; Japanese context **98–100**
intimacies of exposure 149–150
intimacy xvii, 4, 15, 54, 105, 113, 121, 132, 175, 176–177; commodification 24, 62, 64, 66, 131, 135, 139, 143; emergence **154–159**; marketisation 139, 143; space for ~ **159–163**; threshold **163–167** (**164f**), **222f**
intimate alienation **167–168**
intimate strategies (Layder) 151, 169
iraira oyaji (comedy skit) 45
Isaka Maki 9n8
Ishida Hitoshi 40
Israeli-Nevo, Atalia **187**
Italy 77
Ivy, Marilyn: *Discourse of Vanishing* (1995) 174
iyashi (healing) **107–112**, 113, 213

Japan xi–xii, xvii; gay bars ('how' versus 'what' roles) **39–42**
Japan Rail 174
Japanese language ideology 56
Japanese Men's Language **47–48**
Japanese self **19–21**
jirai no omise ('landmine' shop) 92, 102–103
jōge-kankei (superior-inferior rules) 50
Johnson, James Weldon 5n
josei (woman; feminine) 40

josei-muke (adult videos for women) **121–124**; female fantasies of belonging to men **124–127**; female protagonists 'always centre of male attention' 126
josei-muke fan community **24–25**, **118–145**; simulation ritual **136–140**
josei-muke fūzoku industry **131**
joseigo (Japanese Women's Language) **47–48**
joshi-kotoba (women's speech) 201
jōshiki (common knowledge) 46
joshiryoku danshi ('boy with girl power') 7

Kabuki theatre **8–10**, 11, 12
Kabukichō (Tokyo) 88
kado o ireru (shaving off forelocks) 8n
kakkoi (cool) 70
kakkoii (physical appearance) 54
Kano Ayano: *Acting like Woman in Modern Japan* (2001) 10
Kansai 182, 191, 202
Kansai Queer Film Festival (2019) **197f**, 197, **223f**
Kansai University Queer Film Festival (annual) 183
kao ('face') **133–134**
Kapferer, Bruce **138**
karaoke 7, 32, 35, 37, 45, 47, 75, 119
kata (form) **7–12**
katei-sābisu ('devotion to one's family', or 'family-servicing') 35
Kato Estuko 96
Katsu (bar help) 31, **43–46** (**44f**), 49, 53, 54; dismissal 50; rare use of end-phrase particles 49
kawaii (cute) 48, 54, 79, 91
kei (type) 76, **80**
keigo (honorific register) 37
keiko-gi (white training uniform) 207
kendō (fencing) 181, 208
Kessler, Suzanne J. 189, 189n4

kimono **202**, 202n, **207–208**, 209
kissing **106**
kitsuke (kimono dressing) **202–203**
knowledge creation: role of failures **22**
Koch, Gabriele 95, 104, 109n11, 114
Kodaka Maiko **viii**, **24–25**, **118–145**, **221f**
Kōenji (Tokyo) 25
Kōenji Station, Tokyo (music performance) 1, **25**, **146–179**; emergence of intimacy **154–159**; exposure and threshold of intimacy **163–167** (**164f**), **222f**; female intimate strategies **169–175**; female musicians **146–148**, 150, 151, 152, 154, **158–176**; intimate alienation **167–168**; male musicians 148, 149, 150, 154, 155, 156–167 *passim*, 176; masked female performer **163–165** (**164f**), **222f**; negotiating rail space as stage for male intimacies **169–175**; reasons for musicians to perform at ~ 153; 'space for intimacy' **159–163**; stakes involved **151–154**
kōkan nikki (exchange diary) 194
komyunikēshon (companionship) 109
kon-katsu (marriage hunting) parties 125
Kondo, Dorinne K. **7–8**
Koolhaas, Rem 209
koseki (family registry) 184, 193, 199
koshi sapōto (waist support) 70
kōsu ('courses') 89
Kumada Yōko **17–18**
'*kun*' versus '*san*' **129**, 129n5
kyaba-jo (hostess) **51–52**
kyōgi-rikon (mutually-agreed divorce) 196
Kyoto 182, 183, 185, 188, 191, 201, 202

language 45, **133–134**, 141; talking the talk 42, **47–51**
language ideology 47
Laph magazine 196
Larsen, Nella 5n

Layder, Derek 151, 169
lesbianism 82, 194, 195, 214
LGBTQ 53n, 61, 65, 66, 79, 181, 182n, 188, 191, 196, 199, 202
LGBTxER website 183, 194
liminality (Turner) **138–139**
'liminoid' moment 139
limits of gender **19–21**
listening 1, 23, 32, 37, 46, 47, 60, 99, 108, 111, 149, 157, 172, 173
London xviii, 188, 215
love 16, 42, 60, 64, 76, 79, **81–83**, 121, 133, 139, 143, 155, 193, 195
love for free 135, 140, 142
love hotels 88, 89
lovemen 141, 142; background **127–133**; fan events 1, 4, 12, **118–123**, 125, **130—133**; marketing system **129–133**; private fan meetings **130**; simulation ritual **136–140**; telephone dates **130–131**; vicious circle (performing and consuming recognition) **133–136**
Lunsing, Wim **20**
Luvaas, Brent 187

Mac, Juno 97
Magnanti, Brooke 111
Mai:lish (maid café) xiii–xvii *passim*
maid cafés 63, 63n3, 64, 65, 143, 214
make-up 44, 78, 103
makegumi (loser) 157
Makino Eri **122–123**
male to female (MtF) 201
male gaze 25, 168
mama (mother) 31
manga xiii, xiv, xvii, 61n, 63, 64, 76, 126
marriage **125**, 126, 139, 140
Maruta Kōji 18
masculine versus non-masculine binary **39–40**, 47, 50–55 *passim*
masculinity 4, **22–23**, 24, 26; beautified ~ 74, 74n; forms produced for other men 6; as *kata* **7–12**

masutā (master) 31
Matsuo Hisako 12n
McKenna, Wendy 189, 189n4
McLelland, Mark J. 90n, 193, 202
media 7, 40, 63, 65, 96, 100, 118, 120, 121, 122, 126, 129, 134, 141, 188
medical transition 186, 188, 198
megane kei (studious type) 76
mi ni tsukerareta ('attached to body') 7
mi ni tsukeru (wearability, embodiment) 74
miseko (bar help) **23**, 31
misogyny 127, 197
Mitchell, Gregory 3–4
Mitsuhashi Junko 90n, **202–203**
Miyazaki Rieko 123
Miyazaki Tsutomu 63
mizu shōbai (nightlife) 34
monetary transaction 16, 26, **80–81**, 105, 109, 113, 210, 213
moral panic 184, 190, 199, 211
Morinaga Maki 9
motenasu (make customer welcome) 34, 35
Mukai Riku (*eroman*) 127, **128f**, 129, 132, 134, 137, **221f**
Murakami Takanori 40
Muschg, Adolf 210
Mūtan (1983–) 128–129, 129n6

Nagai Taimizu (newspaper) 101
Nakamura Atsuhiko 130
Nakamura, Karen 12n
Nakamura Miri 3
nation-state 41, 47, 56
natsukashī (nostalgic) 173
natural attitude **6**, 13, 14, 21, 184, 189, **189n3**
nature 11, 12, 15, 19
Negri, Antonio 2, 3, 3n
neko ('bottom'; receptive sexual role; lit. 'cat') 39, **52–55**
nenja (adult male lover) 8n

neoliberalism 18, 132
Newcastle University xiii; workshop (2018) xviii, xix
Nietzsche, Friedrich W. 19
Nihon-buyō (Japanese dance) 207
nihon-shiki bā (Japanese-style bars) 32
nikumaki asupara (asparagus rolled in bacon) 7n
Nōmachi Mineko **201**
nomikai (drinking parties) 78
nomiya (drinking venues) 35
noren curtain 181
nostalgia 173, 174

o-make (free items) **35**
objectification 126, 129, 142, 212
observer effect 188
ōen-suru ('to support') 138
Oikawa Daichi **128f**, 129, **221f**
ōji kei (Prince Charming type) 76
ojō-sama (customers) xvii
'*Okaerinasaimase, goshujin-sama*' ('Welcome back, my lord') xiii, xiv
'*Okaerinasaimase, ojō-sama*' ('Welcome back, my princess') xiii, xiv
okama ('fag') 40
Okayama 183
omu-raisu (omelette with fried rice) xiii
ōmukō (audience interaction) 9
onē ('fairy', 'nelly') 40
onē-kotoba (fairy speech, older sister speech) 42, **47–51**, 55
onna (woman) 40
Onna Shibaraku (play) **9–10**
onnagata **9–12**
onozukarashikaru (given-ness) 214
ore (first-person masculine pronoun) 23, 48, 75, 215
orgasm 123, 126
Osaka xi, 89, 154, 182, 185, 188, 194, 201
Osaka Family Court 195
Osaka University Queer Film Festival 183

INDEX

osekkai (nosy) 201
osu (male) 43
otaku 61n, 65, 66; image **63–64**
otoko (man) 40
otokorashii (manly, masculine) 40, 43
otokoyaku (stars embodying male roles) **10–12**
otome xvi
Otome (Maiden) Road xiv
oyaji-gyaru or *ossan-joji* ('geezer girl') **6–7**
Ōzuka Ryōji 47

participant observation 34, 62, 150, 181, 182, 183, **184–185**, 186, 188
passers-by 25, 149
passing **5**, **5n**, 9n8, 214
pathological mentality (lack of love) 133
patriarchy 126, 174, 176, 213
Penal Code: 'obscene objects' 100
performance 214; versus performativity 2, **12–14**
performative labour (Mitchell) **3–4**
performativity (Butler) 2, 9n7, 38, 134, 141; versus performance 2, **12–14**
performer-audience relationships 158, 169, 171, 175
performers xi–xviii
personhood 21; American notions **20**
Pflugfelder, Gregory M. 40, 53n
phenomenology **5–7**
Phillips, Nicola viii–ix, **24**, **88–117**
police 25, 63, 93, 95, 152, 157, 208
politeness 47–48, **50–51**
popular culture 63, 126
Porn 2.0 **129–130**
pornography 2, 24–25, 52–53, 118, 124, **208–209**
poverty 93, 96
power 21, 24
power differentials 23, 134
power dynamics 37, 38, 112
power relations 151, 168

privacy 155, 177, 186
professional amateurs **102–105**, 113; sex work in 'delivery health' shop 1, **24**, **88–117**
pronouns 23, 47, **48–49**, 75, 79, 181, 214–215
prostitution: definition 93, 93n6, 100
Prostitution Prevention Law 93, 93n4, 100, 101
public space **146–179**
Purcell, Natalie J. 120, 131
pyramid of desirability 37–**42**, 47, 51, 55, 57

Queen, Carol 16
Queer Eye for Straight Guy (television programme) 19

race 5n, 110n12, 120
raibu hausu (live houses) 152
real world 118, 209
reality 17, 100, 105, 110, 136–143 *passim*, 153, 160, 176, 189n3, 209, 210; ethnographic ~ 14; inner ~ 15, 182; psychic ~ 4, 19; social ~ 5, 139, 140
recognition **133–135**, 141, 142, 143; commodification 120; guaranteed ~ 140; Honneth **119–120**; 'vital human need' (Taylor) 133
recognition and intimacy as commodities **24–25**, **118–145**
regular customers xii, xv, xvi, 24, 37, 48, 50, 54, 62, 65, 89, 90, 92f
representation: definition **10**
researching identities **23–24**, **60–87**
Richie, Donald **210–211**
Rihabiri no Sensei (Physiotherapist, 2018) 125
risōtekina otoko (ideal man) **79–80**
Robertson, Jennifer 12n
rojō raibu (street lives) 148
romantic relationships xiv, 82, 121, 123, 126, 139, 140, 141, 143, 155

rōrukyabetsu danshi ('cabbage roll' boys) 7; definition **7n**
Rosskam, Jules 197
Rubin, Gayle 6, 197

sābisu gyōkai (service industry) 34
sābisu keigo (honorific language) 50
sābisu or *sekkyaku* (service, lit. 'dealing with customers face-to-face') **34–35**
sābisu-seishin (lit. 'spirit for service', or 'attentiveness') 35
sabu-karuchā (sub-culture) 32
safe space 25, 66, 139
saiban-rikon (divorce via arbitration by district court) 196
Sakura Research and Screening Facility **91f**
salaryman doxa **41–42**, 56
salvage ideology **141**
Sasakawa Foundation viii, ix, xviii, xix
sasshi (empathy) 110
saunas 4n, 52
Schieffelin, Bambi B. 47
searching for identities **23–24, 60–87**
Sedgwick, Eve 126–127
sei (Chinese character for 'sex' and 'gender') 40
seikō (sexual intercourse) 93n4
self **135–136**, 141
self-confidence 127, 133
self-esteem 25, 126, 141, 142
self-help literature 19
self-realisation **133–134**, 135, 140
semi-structured interviews 34, 62, 182, 183, 201
senpai (veteran colleagues) 75
sentō (bathhouse) 181
service: as endless availability **34–37**; limits 35
serving gender: performing gender roles at gay bar **22–23, 31–59**
Setagaya Ward (Tokyo) 202
setto ryōkin: cover charge 35, **36f**; set price 32

sex: biological understanding 26
sex work 8, 35, 35n4; authenticity **105–107**, 113; 'delivery health' shop 1, 24, **88–117**; as healing **107–112**, 113; legal versus illegal ~ **92–93**
sex worker-client balance or imbalance **103–105**
sex workers 12, **16–18**, 135; male ~ 3–4
sexism 78, 197, 200
sexual innuendo 33, 38, 42, 45, 55, 208; as availability **51–54**
sexual labour 55–56; price and value 114
sexual orientation 6, 7, 8n, 12, 193
sexual services: definition 93
sexuality 143, 213
shain bar (corporate member bar) 130
shasei sangyō (ejaculation business) 93
Shaver, Frances M. 112–113
Shinzen no Kai (Friendship Society) 183, **184–185**
shirōto (amateurs) 104
shizen (nature) 214
shōbai (sales) 34
shōchū (barley vodka) 32, 36
shōjo manga (mainstream *manga*) 126
shōta kei (mischievous little brother) 76
shotto bā (cocktail bar) 32
Shu, Min Yuen 196
shunga (erotic woodblock prints; lit. 'spring pictures') 209
SILK Fest (2018) **128f, 221f**
SILK LABO (2009–) 118, **121–126**, 128, 130, 145; typical film **125–126**
Simpkins, R.J. ix, 25, **146–179**
simulation ritual **136–140**
sincerity: commodification **15–19**
sing the body contingent **25–26, 180–205**
singing 11, 146; *see also* karaoke
Smith, Molly 97
soaplands (Turkish baths as brothels) 93, 93n6, 101, 104
social contract 191, 192

socialisation 8, 190
socio-economic status 37
Soft On Demand (SOD) **121–125**, 128, 129–130, 137, 138, 139, 141–142
soi-ne (cuddling) services 143
Sontag, Susan 211
sōpurando ('massage parlour') 41
sōshokukei danshi ('herbivore boys') 7
sotsugyō (retirement from nightlife) 43
staged seduction (Takeyama) 12, 17, 54
Steger, Brigitte 168
stereotypes xiii, 23, 25, 45, 47, 77, 79
sterilisation mandates 190n5
Stevens, Norma 210–211
Stickland, Leonie **11**, 12n
stigma 17, 65, 95, 98, 102, 113, 138
Stokoe, Elizabeth 189
street musicians 12, 22, 25, **146–179** (155f, 164f), **221–222f**; backstories 153
stress 119, 140, 196
subjectivity 5, 14, 98, 133; female ~ versus male ~ **126–127**
sugoi (cool) 70
sukauto sareru ('scouted') 153
Supreme Court of Japan 190n5
surgical transition 74, 187, 188, 199
Suzuki Ittetsu (1979–) **128–129**
Swallowtail (butler café) xiv, xvi, xvii

tachi ('top'; penetrative role during intercourse) 39, 42, 44, 52–55
Taguchi Momoko 124
Takafumi Fujio 193
Takarazuka theatre **10–11**, 12, 12n, 138
Takeyama Akiko 21, 24, 81, **132**; *Staged Seduction* (2016) 12, 17, 54
Taniguchi Hiroyuki 199
tanoshimu (to have good time) 37
tanoshimaseru: 'actively passive stance' 46, 47; 'to make someone have good time' 37
Tatsuki **44–46**, **52–53**; assistant bar manager 31; use of end-phrase particles 49; use of gender language 49
Taylor, Charles **133–134**
Tazu **31–55**; use of end-phrase particles 49
teishu kanpaku (dominant husband) 42
theory of recognition **133–136**
Thorne, Barrie: *Gender Play* (1993) 14
tobi (construction worker) 43
Tokyo 17, 60–61, **88–89**, 104, 182, 183, 202
Tokyo: National Theatre 207
Tokyo: Shinjuku Ni-chōme (gay district) 22–23, **31–59**
transgender ethnomethodology **188–190**
transgender people 1, **25–26**, 90n, **180–205**; definition 184
transition as gender-work **25–26**, **180–205**; assumptions of heterosexuality **193–198**; autoethnography and non-linear becoming **186–188**; central research question **183–184**; ethnomethodology of gender (limits) **198–200**; at home and in world **190–193**; methodology **182–186**; transgender ethnomethodology **188–190**
trauma 96, 142, 165, 196
Treanor, Brian 174–175
trust xix, 16, 18, 22, 68, 70, 94n7, 99, 111, 155, 156, 166, 186, 198
Tsukino Taito (1979–) **128–129**
Tsunoda Maiko 123
Turner, Victor **138–139**

uchi (inside), *soto* (outside) **66–70**
uchi-ness: layers 69
Uehara Chiaki (*eroman*) 127, **128f**, 129, 134, 137, **221f**
Ueno Chizuko 126–127
Uguisudani (Tokyo) 88, **91f**, 94, 113
underwear 119, 136–137, 191

United Kingdom xviii, 97, 99, 196
United States 2, 97, 196
Usui Takakito 190n5

Velcro 70–71
vicious circle (performing and consuming recognition) 133–136
violence 13, 35
virtuality (Kapferer) 138
voice register 23, 75–76
Vollmann, William T. 202
vulnerability 22, 25, 96, 156, 158, 165

Wakabayashi Yuma 194, 197
wakashū (boy) 8–9, 40, 53n
Ward, Jane 20, 78, 181
Washida Kiyokazu 133–134
watashi (first-person pronoun) 49, 181, 215
West, Candace 5, 12–13, 189
Wissinger, Elizabeth 2
Woman is Woman (2018, dir. Maisy Goosey Suen) 185
womanhood 40, 188, 201
women xi–xii, xvii, 35, 45, 55, 78, 139–140; gender roles 41–42; objectification 142; personal safety 152–153; white-collar workforce (1980s) 41
Wong, Heung-Wah 125, 126, 141
Woolard, Kathryn A. 47
Words of Ayame (1776) 9n8
work of gender 151, 214; 'collective intersubjective construction' 13–14; at home and in world 190–193; never done 26; transition as ~ 25–26, 180–205
Work of Gender (this book): advantages over existing literature 1–2; purpose 1; chapter by chapter 22–26
workforce statistics 34

Yagi 31, 43–45, 49, 53, 54
yaoi (boys' love) xiv
yaoi manga xiv, xvi
yarashii (dirty-looking) 40
yasashisa no katamari (gentleness personified) 212, 212n
Yau, Hoi-yan 125, 126, 141
yukata (summer kimono) 72

Zenith bar (Tokyo) 31–59 (33f, 36f, 44f)
Zimmerman, Don H. 12–13, 18